Them Dukes! Them Dukes!

A guide to TV's The Dukes of Hazzard

Book 3 in the BRBTV fact book series

Billie Rae Bates

BRBglobal

Copyright © 2014 by Billie Rae Bates. All rights reserved.

ISBN: 1-4196-2320-6 (print edition)
First electronic edition: April 2003
Second electronic edition: January 2006 (first print edition: January 2006)
Third electronic edition: August 2006 (second print edition: August 2006)
First Kindle / mobile edition: May 2014 (third print edition: August 2014)

Part of the World Wide Web since 1998, BRBTV is an outgrowth of a love for, and many years of research into, several classic television shows of the late '70s and early '80s. The information contained here is compiled and / or written by Billie Rae Bates and the complete volume is copyrighted as such.

No part of this work may be reproduced or transmitted in any form or by any means, electronic or mechanical, including photocopying, recording or by any information storage or retrieval system without written permission from the author, except for inclusion of brief quotations in a review.

This work has not been approved, licensed or sponsored by any entity involved in creating or producing "The Dukes of Hazzard" TV series.

"The Dukes of Hazzard" is a Lou Step production, in association with Warner Bros. Television (see the detailed Credits chapter for complete credits). "The Dukes of Hazzard" is a registered trademark of Warner Bros. Inc. of Burbank, Calif. The theme song, "Good Ol' Boys," is a copyright of Warner-Tamerlane Publishing Corp. and Rich Way Music Inc., words and music by Waylon Jennings. All rights reserved.

BRBTV makes no claims, expressed or otherwise, on the trademark properties of "The Dukes of Hazzard" or any other registered trademarks listed in this book.

Cover art by Dale Cuthbertson.

Where not otherwise noted, photography / scanning / screenshots by Billie Rae Bates.

Dedicated to my "Dukes" buddy, my own cousin James Harold, whose sweetness and kindness I greatly value in my fondest childhood memories, and whose peace and happiness I desire more than the success of any book.

And dedicated to the memory of Jo McLaney, Christopher Mayer, Glenn Call and Don Schisler, each of which were kind enough to assist with the material in this book.

To see other books and reports available from BRBTV,
check out the home page at
BRBTV.com

To contact Billie Rae Bates, email
BillieRaeBates@yahoo.com
or visit
BillieRae.com

THEM DUKES! THEM DUKES! A GUIDE TO TV'S THE DUKES OF HAZZARD

CONTENTS

Foreword
Introduction

Cast 15
Characters 33
Episodes 83
    Beyond the Series 163
Credits 175
Up for Debate 181
Fun & Useless Information 183
    Exploring the Show's Roots in Georgia 210
    The Etheredges: Contributing to the "Dukes" Culture 220
    Where it all Began: Jerry Rushing 222
    Keeping the Love Alive: Jo McLaney 224
    20 Minutes of Fame: "Dukes" Fans and the 2005 Movie 226
    Good Old-Fashioned Faith and Values 235
    Raise the Flag — and Forget the Flack! 237
    The Hazzard County Business Directory 239
    The 2005 Search for a "Dukes" VP 242
    DukesFest 243
    Other "Dukes" Events 258
    Meet Some Lees 318
    Art Imitates Life 337
    "Dukes" History Also Inspires the Art of this Avid Fan 344
And Now a Word From 347
    John Schneider: *The end — and return — of Jonathan Kent* 347
    Ben Jones: *He ain't crazy OR dumb* 350
    Christopher Mayer: *Below the radar just wasn't as fun* 353
    Byron Cherry: *The show must go on!* 361
    Don Pedro Colley: *Sheriff Little speaks* 366
    Felix Silla: *Reminiscing about his "Strange Visit"* 370
    Don Schisler: *It all started with a phone call* 371
    Tom Sarmento: *Keeping the motor running* 374
    Tony Kelley: *Keeping the motor running, too!* ... 377
    Anthony De Longis: *Dealing up action and adventure* 380
Birthdays 385
Websites 389
Merchandise 391
Acknowledgments 411

THEM DUKES! THEM DUKES! A GUIDE TO TV'S THE DUKES OF HAZZARD

FOREWORD: JUST THE GOOD OL' BOYS

Nearly every Sunday of my childhood, in the 1970s and 1980s, my little cousin Jimmy (one year younger!) and I were rather captive to the regular weekly trips to Grandma and Grandpa's house just north of Saginaw, Michigan. And every Sunday afternoon, while all of the adults were in the nearby dining room hoopin' and hollerin' over the "tricks" and partners and whatnot of the regular weekly euchre or pinochle games (very heated and high volume — trust me), Jimmy and I were huddled in the kitchen ... mixin' moonshine.

Our "moonshine" was Mountain Dew from the classic bright-green two-liter bottle, and our inspiration was "The Dukes of Hazzard." Every Sunday afternoon was our chance to pour our makeshift "moonshine" from Grandma's fridge into Dixie cups and compare notes from the past Friday night's episode of our favorite show. I think Jimmy probably most enjoyed the car chases, being a boy and all (he did go on to love "Knight Rider," after all). Maybe I just wanted to be like Daisy Duke. Whatever the fascination, these two little kids were positively enthralled.

Yea, in your dreams, girl! What chick didn't want to wear those famous "Dazzey Duks," as Duice called them?

Later, in high school, my freshman-year boyfriend Will joked about my dad's 1978 white Ford pickup truck — the "Uncle Jesse truck." Yes, quite frankly, it was exactly like Jesse's pickup. Was it a sign? Then, many lifetimes later, downtown in the big city of Detroit, I found myself talking "Dukes" with my buddy Big Dee at my newspaper job, more than a decade after the show went off the air.

The following of the "Dukes" really is legion. It was amazing to rewatch the "Dukes" episodes in my adulthood, to see the scenes I hadn't seen since they first aired between 1979 and 1985. I was watching through adult eyes, this time. Perhaps what really struck me was that there really wasn't much to the episodes — same general storylines, same elements, same character motivations, often the exact same dialogue. Yet this was a show that became wildly popular round-about 1980, leaving studio executives shocked and amazed. No one woulda thunk it.

I have to admit, there are parts of me that would really love to live in Hazzard County, right now, in my adulthood, no matter where I've lived in the past or what I've done for a living. There's something so wonderfully sweet about Hazzard, with its beautiful, dusty back roads, perpetually dry and sunny weather, quaint downtown with the general store and police department and jail and newspaper office and whatever else. Everything is so simple there — the living really is easy. Does Hazzard County exist, somewhere in Georgia, right now? Did it, in the late 1970s?

Well, ironically, for the first edition of this book, I was living in Metro Atlanta, not far from where the series was originally filmed. And sometimes, as I got to know the people there, I didn't for a minute doubt that Hazzard County did exist — and maybe still does, in some ways.

Here's a little slice of Hazzard: The high-heeled shoes our gal Daisy wore looked suspiciously like Candie's shoes, Candie's that were much like this vintage 1980s pair of mine.

BRB

Introduction

Gy Waldron is certainly no dummy.

Blessed by talent and perhaps just-plain circumstances, he created a phenomenon that he probably didn't dream would live on and on, across generations.

It all began with a real-life North Carolina moonshiner named Jerry Rushing and a cute little film called "Moonrunners" (which, ironically, was a bit edgy, truth be told). It was the mid-1970s, and the Kentucky-born Waldron was a writer by trade. This was his feature-film debut. Mix in there a little "Smokey and the Bandit" and a love for fast cars, CBs and that Southern country thing, and you had the perfect pop-cultural timing for the "Dukes." So Waldron parlayed his "Moonrunners" concept into a TV series and made it fly. And boy, did it fly!

"The Dukes of Hazzard" filmed its first five episodes in the region where the story took place, rural Georgia, in areas around Covington and Conyers not too far from the big city of Atlanta. There at a Holiday Inn off I-20, the cast gathered for the first time around the swimming pool to do a read-through of the first episode. That was 1978, and the show premiered in January 1979. When it looked like this whole thing was going to work after all, the crew relocated to California and laid the pedal to the metal. But that road to fame was a little bumpy. No one expected just how much fame that would be, for one.

"I was anticipating horrible reviews," Waldron said in TNN's special "The Life and Times of the Dukes of Hazzard," "and I think of the 200 reviews that we got, I think we got four that were good. In fact, we frequently have a lot of jokes about it, because Southerners know the reality of what we are. We have a very Gothic tradition in the South. That's how we learn to laugh. We learn to laugh at ourselves and each other. But we also have some very, very strong family traditions there. And we played those up. The critics never picked up on it."

Tom Wopat said of the bad reviews, during his interview in Country Music Television's 2005 "Inside Fame" special on the show, "It was disappointing that they took it to task so much. Took it seriously, I guess." But, he said, laughing, "Our show was silly enough and had enough crazy crap in it that people got interested in it."

James Best surmised, in the same CMT special, that Hollywood was embarrassed because it was a Southern show. "But boy, they took the money fast enough," he quipped.

In his autobiography, "Best in Hollywood," Best writes: "When beginning work on a new series, the last thing an actor thinks about is that it might become such a success that it will become an albatross around his neck. He dreams for success and recognition. As actors, we do not perform in hopes of toiling unnoticed for years. … We grab that ring and hope that we are prepared to deal with the good, the bad, and the ugly of any success that might follow. When we went down to Georgia to film the first episodes, the whole cast believed that 'The Dukes of Hazzard' was supposed to be a write-off for Warner Bros. At that time, the studio was in trouble. They agreed to buy just five episodes. They really did not know what they had at the time."

As Ben Jones says in his autobiography, "Redneck Boy in the Promised Land," "The show's success perplexed the critics, annoyed the snobs, and infuriated the manners police. The national PTA condemned the show's recklessness. Prudes decried the shortness of Daisy Duke's shorts. But the show kept soaring in the ratings."

"The base of 'Dukes of Hazzard' was the family unit," John Schneider said, "and the relationships that Uncle Jesse had with everybody." Even with the less savory characters. "Boss Hogg was greedy, but he would never have anybody hurt," Schneider said.

And that approach resonated with viewers, once the show hit its stride after experimentation or two with other elements. Wopat, who is sometimes called "the thinking man's Duke," said in the CMT special, "The first five episodes that we shot in Georgia, it had a little more grit to it."

The fandom of the "The Dukes of Hazzard" takes on many forms. Here, a female fan expresses her love with a little careful airbrushing, on the weekend of DukesFest 2008 in downtown Covington, Georgia. She told BRBTV that she wanted to alternate every other nail with the Confederate flag but was told at the salon that they wouldn't do that design. Yikes.

"When the show started, we were on at 9 o'clock," Catherine Bach said, "so when you're on at 9 o'clock, you're a little more risqué." The producers realized kids were loving the show, so it was moved to the 8 p.m. timeslot in December 1981.

The show ran for seven seasons, from January 26, 1979 to August 16, 1985, Friday nights on CBS. Across 147 episodes, the antics of cousins Bo, Luke and Daisy Duke, shepherded by their Uncle Jesse, came alive. (So did the toy-store shelves, incidentally; see our Merchandise chapter to learn more!)

It was seven years of comings and goings, a contract dispute or two, a controversy over "replacement Dukes," ratings that went up, ratings that

BEHIND THE SCENES

> "It boggles the mind. I forget about it on occasion, and it's brought back to me pretty quickly, usually. It was like high school. I had great deal of fun doing it; we had lots of laughs and formed great relationships."
>
> — Tom Wopat, on "The Dukes of Hazzard," on PopEntertainment.com

went down. Storylines that included an alien and a Mean Green Machine. A whole lotta dips in the Hazzard pond. "It was not all sunglasses and autographs," Best said in the 2005 CMT special.

"We did the wrong thing for the right reasons," Schneider said of his and Wopat's famous walkout in 1982. "Shame on me." Wopat said, "We lost a ton of money, John and I did. And they lost a ton of money. It probably contributed to the show's demise, in the long run."

Bo and Luke were back within a year of the walkout, but it was never quite the same. The show went off the air in 1985, after all that drama. "It was time to quit," Ben Jones said. "We all wanted to go and do other things."

Things in Hazzard County were a little quiet for a few years, though the fan base was still immense. Then the show re-emerged in 1996 on TNN (when it was The Nashville Network), airing five nights a week.

After the cast members reunited for the funeral of Sorrell Booke, the idea was hatched to do a movie special. "It's like we never left," Tom Wopat said on the set of 1997's "Dukes of Hazzard: Reunion!" for John Schneider's behind-the-scenes video coverage. Denver Pyle died just a few months after the movie aired. Another reunion movie followed in 2000, this time with a Hollywood theme.

Then, much to the delight of fans, the show returned once again, to CMT. Also in 2005, we got that-thar remake movie, not well-received by fans, then a prequel movie in 2007 (everything old is new again, in Hollywood!). Heck, we don't mind, even if the prequel wasn't that well-received, either! All of this has kept the love alive.

For sure, "Dukes" fan events have been in great abundance in the years since the show went off the air, especially post-2000, in locales all over the country, not just the South. And the toys have continued to pop up on store shelves. In fact, there was major attention paid when, in 2012, the rumor circulated that Warner Bros. planned to remove the Confederate flag from the roof of the General on new licensed "Dukes" toys. What? Fans raised a ruckus. Ben Jones raised a ruckus. And then ... WB released a statement basically denying it had ever even considered such a heinous thing. Wow. If that situation showed anything, it was the power of the "Dukes," still, 27 years after the show was canceled.

What BRBTV offers you here is a fun reference guide to the show — a place where you can look up who played what's-his-face in that one episode, what that other particular episode you might have missed was about, just when that fabulous Abraham Lincoln Hogg came to town, what the name of Cooter's daughter was, and just about anything else you can think of. The BRBTV book series follows a formula — cast list, character guide, episode guide, and so on, in an easy-to-page-through format that you can have at your side while you're watching the show. So enjoy.

And, as Waylon Jennings said ... *Welcome* ... to Hazzard County.

From the collection of Andrea Melchiori of Portage, Michigan: A "Dukes"-covered TV Guide signed by John Schneider's mom, Shirley.

CAST

**Who was who?
Let's find out.**

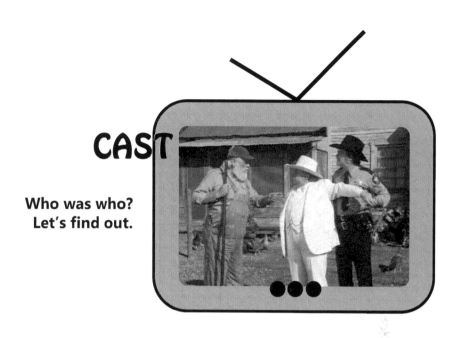

Here's your guide to who played who (or is that "whom"?) on "The Dukes of Hazzard," arranged by the first names of the characters. Note that some characters had no last name, or only a last name, as far as the show was concerned. Also note that sometimes the same first name was used for different characters in different episodes! Refer to the Characters chapter for a little bit more about these folks (the characters, anyways!), and refer to the Fun & Useless Information chapter for a little bit more about the folks who played 'em.

Abel ... **Ancel Cook**
Abraham Lincoln Hogg ... **Sorrell Booke**
A.C. Tate Jr. ... **Gailard Sartain**
Ace Parker ... **Jerry Rushing**
Adam Venable (Josiah Benson) ... **John Larch**
Adams ... **Frederic George**
Agent Buchanon ... **John Crawford**
Agent Caldwell ... **Frank Marth**
Agent Callas ... **Bill Cort**
Agent Swan ... **Bob Shaw**

Alabama Jones ... **Melinda Naud**
Alan Fairchild ... **Greg Michaels**
Alice ... **Mary Jo Catlett**
Alien visitor ... **Felix Silla**
Amos Petersdorf ... **Harvey Vernon**
Amos Stigger ... **Ray Guth**
Amy Creavy ... **Roz Kelly**
Androvich ... **Lee Delano**
Andy Slocum ... **P.R. Paul**
Anita Blackwood ... **Anita Cochran**
Anna Lisa ... **Shanna Reed**
Anna Louise ... **Stepfanie Kramer**
Arnie ... **Jeffrey Josephson**
Artie Rathburn ... **Sammy Jackson**
Artie Bender ... **James Cavan**
Arvey Stillwell ... **John H. Fields**
Augie Dettweiler ... **John Quade**
Avery ... **Ernie Hudson**
Bad Barney ... **William Edward Phipps**
Baldwin ... **Floyd Levine**
Baldwyn ... **John Lawrence**
Banyon ... **Andy Wood**
Barnes ... **Bob Hastings**
Bart Barton ... **Michael J. Cutt**
Baxter ... **Joel Bailey**
B.B. ... **Billy Ray Sharkey**
B.B. Bascomb ... **Jay Acovone**
B.B. Davenport ... **Mickey Jones**
Beauregard Mason ... **Kenneth O'Brien**
Beckman ... **Byron Webster**
Becky Mae ... **Debra Feuer**
Ben ... **Greg Finley**
Ben Jordan ... **Hari Rhodes**
Ben Wilkenson ... **Redmond Gleeson**
Bender ... **Michael Ensign**
Benny the Quill ... **Boyd Bodwell**
Benswanger ... **Warren Berlinger**
Benteen ... **Del Monroe**
Bertha Jo Barlow ... **Cynthia Rothrock**
Bessie Lou Perkins ... **Dianne Anthony**

A Duke and a gentleman: John Schneider often kept up with "Dukes" collector Jo McLaney; he sent her this signed shot from his role on the WB's "Smallville." (Learn more about Jo's collection in the Fun & Useless Information chapter.)

Bessie Lou ... **Ella Mae Brown**
Betty Jo Page ... **Shannon Tweed**
Bib Tucker ... **Dan Priest**
Big Billie Tucker ... **Joy Garrett**
Big Daddy Hogg ... **Les Tremayne**
Big Dan Hogg ... **Marty Zagon**
Big Jim Downey ... **George Murdock**
Big Jim Mathers ... **Joe Higgins**
Big John ... **Claude Humphrey**
Billie Ann Baxley ... **Shawn Weatherly**
Billie Jean ... **Audrey Landers**
Billy ... **Joel Brooks**
Billy Boy Harper ... **Johnnie Collins III**
Billy Gene Harper ... **Richard Fullerton**
Billy Joe Billings ... **Andrew Robinson**
Billy Joe Coogan ... **Michael Alldredge**
Billy Joe Fong ... **James Hong**
Billy Ray ... **Chris Mulkey**
Billy Ray ... **Richard Schaal**
Black Jack Bender ... **Paul Lambert**
Blaine ... **Jack Garner**
Blake ... **Frank Annese**
Bo Duke ... **John Schneider**
Bob Dexter ... **Richard Jensen**
Bobbie Lee Jordan ... **Michele Greene**
Bobby Joe the robot ... **Robert Shields**
Bonnie ... **Holly Roberts**
Bonnie Lane ... **Colleen Camp**

Borov ... **Hank Garrett**
Boss Bowman ... **William Bramley**
Boss Hopkins ... **F. William Parker**
Boss Sharkey ... **Earl Montgomery**
Brock Curtis ... **Barry Van Dyke**
Brodie ... **Champ Laidler**
Bubba ... **Dennis Burkley**
Bubba ... **Travis McKenna**
Bubba Malone ... **Ji-Tu Cumbuka**
Buck ... **Bruce M. Fischer**
Buck Owens ... **Buck Owens**
Buck Simmons ... **Britt Leach**
Buddy ... **Stephen Lee**
Budge ... **Chip Heller**
Bull ... **Bruce M. Fischer**
Bumper ... **Charles Cyphers**
Burke ... **Anthony Eisley**
Burke ... **Wayne Grace**
Burl Tolliver ... **Mel Tillis**
Burnett ... **Al White**
Burt Robey ... **James Crittenden**
Buzz Kilroy ... **Daniel Anderson**
Cale Yarborough ... **Cale Yarborough**
Candy Dix ... **Roberta Leighton**
Captain Slater ... **Brion James**
Carl ... **Don Stroud**
Carla ... **Lois Areno**
Carney ... **Steve James**
Carrie Morton ... **Phyllis Hall**
Carson ... **Bill Gribble**
Carter ... **Brett Halsey**
Carter Stewart ... **Lyle Talbot**
Cash Calloway ... **Ben Thomas**
Catfish Lee ... **Sonny Shields**
Charlie ... **James Avery**
Charlie Burns ... **Phillip Clark**
Charlie Cooper Jr. ... **Randal Patrick**
Chet Garvey ... **Harrison Page**
Chickasaw Thins ... **Robert V. Barron**
Chief Lacey ... **Norman Alden**

Cindy ... **Rebecca Reynolds**
Cindy Bilou ... **Randi Brough**
Cindy Lou ... **Tara Preston**
C.J. Holmes ... **Robert Alda**
Clara Coltrane ... **Mary Treen**
Clarence Stovall ... **Bill Erwin**
Clark ... **Billy Ray Sharkey**
Claude Billings ... **Charles Tyner**
Clayton ... **James Reynolds**
Cleary ... **Michael Prokopuk**
Clooney ... **George McDaniel**
Clyde ... **Ernie Lively**
Clyde Amos ... **Richard Paul**
Clyde Berney ... **Robert Aaron**
Col. Cassius B. Claibourne ... **Morgan Woodward**
Collins ... **David Gale**
Cooter Davenport ... **Ben Jones**
Corey ... **Alex Kubik**
Cosgroves ... **Jerry Summers**
Cowan ... **Michael MacRae**
Coy Duke ... **Byron Cherry**
Coy Randolph ... **Buck Flower**
Crystal ... **Hugh Gillin**
Culpepper ... **Eddie Ryder**
C.V. Gumble ... **Anne Haney**
D. Jasper Fenwick ... **Jim B. Baker**
Daisy Duke ... **Catherine Bach**
Darcy Kincaid ... **Steve Hanks**
Dawson ... **Carlos Brown**
Deke ... **Earl Colbert**
Dell Webber ... **Ray Young**
Dempsey ... **Morgan Woodward**
Dennis ... **Mark Withers**
Denny Logan ... **Gary Graham**
Deputy Cletus Hogg ... **Rick Hurst**
Deputy Enos Strate ... **Sonny Shroyer**
Devere ... **Leo Gordon**
Dewey Hogg ... **Robert Morse**
Dewey Stovall ... **Paul Brinegar**
Diane Benson ... **Robin Mattson**

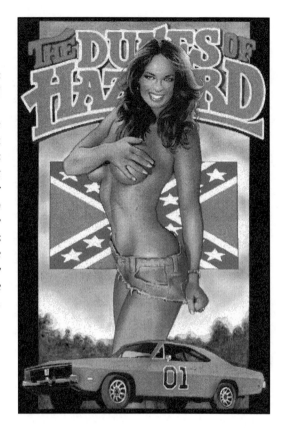

Not for the faint of heart: She's inspired not only rap songs and copycats in faded cutoffs ... Catherine Bach as Daisy Duke also inspired talented Detroit artist Matt Busch, who has illustrated "Star Wars" book covers, comics, the box art for the "Reservoir Dogs" action figures and more. You can buy this poster from Matt at his website, MattBusch.com. The original of this art is owned by pop star Uncle Kracker! Image courtesy of Matt Busch.

Dickens ... **David Hayward**
Digger Jackson ... **Charles Napier**
Dixon ... **Grant Owens**
Dobro Doolan ... **Ernie Brown**
Doc Appleby ... **Parley Baer / Elmore Vincent**
Doc Homer Willis ... **Adam Wade**
Doc Henry Petticord ... **Pat Cranshaw**
Doc (Ronald) Carney ... **Warren Munson**
Dodie ... **Candy Bleick**
Don Purcell ... **Jesse D. Goins**
Donna Fargo ... **Donna Fargo**
Dooley ... **Mayf Nutter**
Dottie West ... **Dottie West**
Dr. Debbie Davis ... **Lori Hallier**

Dr. Floyd ... **Ken Hixon**
Dr. Talmadge ... **Ken Hixon**
Dugan ... **Taylor Lacher**
Dunlap ... **Brett Halsey**
Dusty ... **Hunter Von Leer**
Earl Becket ... **Philip Brown**
Ed Monroe ... **Ralph Pace**
Eddie ... **Lewis Van Bergen**
Eddie Hollis ... **Joseph Whipp**
Eddie Lee Mennis ... **Jeffrey Osterhage**
Eddie Scarlins ... **Al White**
Eli ... **Jim Boeke**
Elmo Smith ... **Dennis Haskins**
Elton Loggin ... **Ritchie Montgomery**
Emerson P. Craig ... **Peter Hobbs**
Emery Potter ... **Charlie Dell**
Emma Partridge ... **Elizabeth Kerr**
Ernie ... **Caskey Swain**
Ernie Ashburn ... **Chris Hendrie**
Ernie Ledbetter ... **Darryl McCullough**
Esther Venable ... **Cynthia Leake**
Eustice Hastings ... **Earl Boen**
Ezra Bushmaster ... **Nicolas Coster**
Farmer Perkins ... **Kevin Hagen**
Fielding ... **Stafford Morgan**
First workman ... **Gerald McRaney**
Flint ... **Ted Markland**
Floralee ... **Candi Brough**
Flossie ... **Rhonda Shear**
Floyd Herky ... **Doug Hume**
Floyd Baker ... **Peter Brown**
Floyd Barclay ... **Pat Studstill**
Floyd Calloway ... **R.G. Armstrong**
Floyd Jones ... **Doug Heyes Jr.**
Floyd Malone ... **Kevin Peter Hall**
Francee ... **Randi Brough**
Frank ... **Robert Phillips**
Frank Baldwin ... **John Lawrence**
Frank James ... **Nick Benedict**
Frank Scanlon ... **Don Gordon**

Frank Scanlon (disguised) ... **David Haney**
Frankie (Francis) Lee Olmstead ... **Marya Small**
Fred Andrews ... **Edward Edwards**
Freddy Fender ... **Freddy Fender**
Gabriela ... **Patricia Manterola**
Gail Flatt ... **Audrey Landers**
Garrett ... **James Horan**
Gaylord Duke ... **Simon MacCorkindale**
George ... **Jason Bernard**
George Henry ... **John F. Goff**
Gerry McCobb ... **Sandy Acker**
Ginny ... **Janie Fricke**
Gorman ... **Roger Hampton**
Granny Annie Coggin ... **Lurene Tuttle**
Gregory ... **John Laughlin**
Grogan ... **Charles Bartlett**
G.S. Baldwin ... **Floyd Levince**
Gumbs ... **Tom Oberhaus**
Gussie Peabody ... **Annie O'Donnell**
Hadley ... **Bill McLaughlin**
Hammer ... **Bill Fletcher**
Hank ... **Roger Pancake**
Hanson ... **Noble Willingham**
Hard Luck Jones ... **Fred Stuthman**
Harley ... **John Dewey-Carter**
Harry Bobo ... **Frank Birney**
Harry Joe ... **Dennis Holahan**
Harry Ray ... **Royce D. Applegate**
Harvey ... **Ralph Pace**
Harvey Dunsmore ... **Jay Garner**
Harvey Essex ... **Stu Nisbet**
Hatfield ... **Mitch Carter**
Hazel ... **Sandra Dorsey**
Hector ... **Nick Benedict**
Hector Farley ... **Henry Jones**
Heep ... **Burton Gilliam**
Helen Hogan ... **Joann Pflug**
Henry Flatt ... **Hal Smith**
Henstep ... **J. Pat O'Malley**
Herky ... **Bob Hoy**

H.H. Harkness ... **Curtis Credel**
Hickey Burns ... **William Mims**
Hixx ... **Robert Gray**
Hobie Harkens ... **A.P. Smith**
Hoby Willis ... **Ned Bellamy**
Hodges ... **Paul Kent**
Holly Comfurt ... **Miriam Byrd Nethery**
Holly Mae ... **Pamela Bryant**
Homer ... **Barry Gremillion**
Homer ... **Shug Fisher**
Homer Griggs ... **Harry Caesar**
Homer Sneak ... **Daniel Currie**
"Honest" John Ledbetter ... **Jack Gordon**
Hortense Coltrane ... **Frances Bay**
Hoyt Axton ... **Hoyt Axton**
Hudson ... **Joseph Burke**
Hughie Hogg ... **Jeff Altman**
Hurley ... **Alan Autry**
Iggins ... **Bernard Fox**
Igor the Terrible ... **Alexander Kuznetsov**
Ira ... **Wally Taylor**
Irving ... **Arte Johnson**
Jack Morris ... **Duke Stroud**
Jackie ... **Karen Witter**
Jacks ... **Curtis Taylor**
Jake ... **Kaz Garas**
James Fenwick ... **Whit Bissell**
Jamie Lee Hogg ... **Jonathan Frakes**
Janco ... **James Carrington**
Jane ... **Kellee Patterson**
Jason Dillard ... **Brett Halsey**
Jason Steele ... **William Smith**
J.D. Hogg ... **Sorrell Booke**
Jean ... **Sandy Wescott**
Jeb ... **Terrence Evans**
Jeb McCobb ... **Walter Barnes**
Jeb Morton ... **Jay W. Baker**
Jeb Stuart Duke ... **Christopher Hensel**
Jenkins ... **Brion James**
Jenny Duke ... **Doris Dowling**

Jenny Walden ... **Beth Schaffel**
Jerry ... **Scott Lincoln**
Jesse Duke ... **Denver Pyle**
Jesse James ... **Paul Koslo**
Jillie Rae Dodson ... **Tisch Raye**
J.J. Carver ... **Ramon Bieri**
J.J. Sunday ... **Peter Breck**
Jo Jo ... **Mike Moroff**
JoJo ... **Wallace Merck**
Joe Bob Depree ... **Monty Jordan**
Joe Landis ... **Frank Pendle**
Joe Ward ... **Michael Crabtree**
Joey Brian ... **Chuck Wagner**
Joey Sagalo ... **Larry Bishop**
John Harris ... **George McDaniel**
John Henry Comfurt ... **Edward Edwards**
John J. Hooper ... **Joe Dorsey**
John Zimbra ... **Vernon Weddle**
Johnny Paycheck ... **Johnny Paycheck**
Johnny Ryan ... **Larry Watson**
Jonas Jones ... **Hal Williams**
Jordan ... **Charles Guardino**
J.P. Pruitt ... **Hank Underwood**
Jud Kane ... **Randy Hamilton**
Jude Emery ... **John Shearin**
Jude Porter ... **Carl Kraines**
Judge Buford P. Potts ... **Barney Phillips**
Judge Charles Druten ... **Ted Gehring**
Junior Harper ... **Al Wyatt Jr.**
J.W. Hickman ... **Larry D. Mann**
Kate ... **Karen Lamm**
Kate Baxley ... **Bobbie Ferguson**
Kelly ... **Clancy Brown**
Ken Collins ... **Rayford Barnes**
Lacey ... **Craig Littler**
Lacey ... **Roy Jenson**
Larson ... **Jason Evers**
Laura Bardsley ... **Jeannie Wilson**
Laverne ... **Lila Kent**
Lavinia Gray ... **Melanie Vincz**

L.B. (Longstreet B.) Davenport ... **Ernie W. Brown**
Lee Benson ... **Judson Scott**
Leeman ... **Steven Williams**
Lenny ... **Charles H. Hyman**
Lenny ... **Richard Winters**
Leo ... **Colby Chester**
Leona Hayes ... **Janet Meshad**
Leroy ... **G. Yon**
Leroy Little ... **Spencer Milligan**
Les Sloane ... **Lance LeGault**
Lester Starr ... **Ronnie Schell**
Lil ... **Dana House**
Linc McKay ... **James McIntire**
Linda May Barnes ... **Tracy Scoggins**
Lipton ... **Robert Phalen**
Lisa ... **Linda Hart**
Loggins ... **Kaz Garas**
Lois ... **Judith Baldwin**
Lois ... **Sonya Y. Maddox**
Loretta Lynn ... **Loretta Lynn**
Lori Comfurt ... **Lori Lethin**
Lori Mae ... **Victoria Johnson**
Lorna Mallory ... **Barbara Horan**

Before Bo and Luke: The 1975 film "Moonrunners" was the precursor to "The Dukes of Hazzard," featuring a moonshiner named Uncle Jesse, a Cooter and a balladeer named Waylon Jennings! The film was written and directed by "Dukes" creator Gy Waldron and was inspired by the story of real-life 'shiner Jerry Rushing. It starred James Mitchum, Kiel Martin, Arthur Hunnicutt, Chris Forbes and George Ellis, also featuring Ben Jones (but not as Cooter). Image courtesy of Hot Rod Movie Posters and SD455.com.

Lou Ann Moffet ... **Nancy Clay**
L.S. Handley ... **John Hancock**
L.S. Pritchard ... **Randi Brooks**
Lucinda Meadows ... **Jan Clayton**
Luke Duke ... **Tom Wopat**
Lulu Hogg ... **Peggy Rea**
Ma Harper ... **Fran Ryan**
Mabel ... **Ginny Parker**
Mabel (Myrtle) Tillingham ... **Lindsay Bloom**
Mabel Wooster ... **Doris Hess**
Mack Magee ... **Dean Dittman**
Madame Delilah ... **Leslie Easterbrook**
Malone ... **Don Fox Greene**
Mama Coltrane ... **Lucille Benson**
Mama (Jo) Max ... **Stella Stevens**
Mandy (Crash) Jo ... **Jennifer Holmes**
Manny ("Repo Men") ... **Rodney Amateau**
Manny ("Deputy Dukes") ... **Pat Renella**
Marjorie Dane ... **Elinor Donahue**
Marty Garbade ... **Billy Green Bush**
Marv ... **William Allen Young**
Mary Belle Digby ... **Ellen Murray**
Mary Beth Carver ... **Lydia Cornell**
Mary Beth Malone ... **Stella Parton**
Mary Kaye Porter ... **Jeanne Wilson**
Mary Lou Pringle ... **Morgan Brittany**
Mary Lou Tompkins Craig ... **Janeen Best**
Mason ... **Joseph Whipp**
Mason Dixon ... **Dennis Rucker**
Matt Mallory ... **Richard Hill**
Maury ... **David Graf**
Max ... **Clayton Landey**
Maybelle ... **Suzanne Niles**
Mean Joe Hatcher ... **Gregory Walcott**
Mel Tillis ... **Mel Tillis**
Melanie DuBois ... **Danone Simpson**
Merle ... **William O'Connell**
Meznick ... **Bob Yerkes**
Mick ... **Michael Halsey**
Mickey Burns ... **William Mims**

Mickey Gilley ... **Mickey Gilley**
Mickey Larsen ... **Dennis Burkley**
Miller ... **J.J. Johnston**
Milo Beaudry ... **Richard Moll**
Mindy Lou Hale ... **Laurette Spang**
Mitch Henderson ... **Robert Tessier**
Miz (Emma) Tisdale ... **Nedra Volz**
Molly Hargrove ... **Andra Akers**
Molly Harmon ... **Jenny Neumann**
Moody ... **Morgan Stoddard**
Morgan ... **Alex Harvey**
Morgan ... **Jack Yates**
Morgan ... **Theodore Wilson**
Morton ... **L.Q. Jones**
Moss ... **Dennis Haskins**
Moss ... **Patrick Wright**
Mr. Adams ... **Ben Slack**
Mr. Winkle ... **Bill McLean**
Mrs. Hooper ... **Toni Sawyer**
Mrs. Walker ... **Nora Boland**
Murkin ... **Jon Locke**
Myrna Robey ... **Martha Smith**
Nancylou Nelson ... **Kim Richards**
Natasha ... **Dawn Jeffory**
Ned Beemer ... **Bob Aaron**
Neil Bishop ... **Fred McCarren**
Nelson ... **George Whiteman**
"Nervous" Norman Willis ... **Mike Genovese**
Newtie ... **Shug Fisher**
Norman ... **Nick Shields**
Norman Scroggs ... **Terry Wilson**
Norton ... **Anthony DeLongis**
Otis J. ... **Dale Pullum**
Otis Plunkett ... **Ralph Strait**
Pa Beaudry ... **J.S. (Joe) Young**
Parker ... **Judson Scott**
Pastor ... **Joe Mays**
Patch ... **Keith Brunsmann**
Patch Loring ... **Ben Davidson**
Peggy ... **Mallie Jackson**

Percy ... **Steven Williams**
Perry ... **Ted Markland**
Pete ... **Charles Napier**
Peters ... **M.C. Gainey**
Peters ... **Richard Humphreys**
Petey Willis ... **Donald May**
Phil ... **Charles Cyphers**
Phil ... **Russ McCubbin**
Phil Ackley ... **Richard Hill**
Pop Durham ... **Hal Smith**
Potter ... **Robert Gray**
Powers ... **J.N. Roberts**
Professor Crandall ... **Walker Edmiston**
Pruitt ... **Andrew Robinson**
Quirt McQuade ... **Cliff Pellow**
Rafe Logan ... **Terence Knox**
Rance ... **Ray Colbert**
Randall ... **John Crawford**
Rayford Davis ... **Taylor Lacher**
Rayford Flicker ... **Michael Keenan**
Reynolds ... **Regis J. Cordic**
Rhuebottom ... **John Wheeler**
Rick ... **Billy Streater**
Rick ... **Sam Melville**
Riker ... **Gary Hudson**
Robby ... **Chad Sheets**
Rocky Marlowe ... **Leo Gordon**
Rod Moffet ... **Jason Lively**
Rogers ... **Don Fox Green**
Rollo ... **Ken Foree**
Rose Ellen ... **Miriam Byrd Nethery**
Rostosky ... **Marc Lawrence**
Rowby Jethro ... **Tom McFadden**
Roxanne Huntley ... **Carlene Watkins**
Roy ... **Gary Grubbs**
Roy Landry ... **Roger Robinson**
Roy Orbison ... **Roy Orbison**
Roy Winters ... **Ed Peek**
Roz ... **Karen S. Mistal**
R.P. "Droopy" Cathcarte ... **Claude Earl Jones**

Ruby ... **Terry Browning**
Rudy ... **Jason Lively**
Ruel McBride ... **James Carroll Jordan**
Russ ... **Brian Libby**
Russ Collins ... **William Sanderson**
Russ Mitchel ... **Steve Sandor**
Russel "Snake" Harmon ... **Sam Melville**
Ruth ... **Susan Walden**
Sally ... **Kathrine Bauman**
Sally Jo ... **Jo McDonnell**
Sam ... **Pat Buttram**
Sam ... **Sam Edwards**
Sam McCobb ... **Cindy Acker**
Sam Porter ... **Mike Moroff**
Sam (Samantha Rose) ... **Robin G. Eisenmann**
Sandy Bilou ... **Candi Brough**
Sandra ("Kate") Rhodes ... **Simone Griffeth**
Sara Jane ... **Ann Walker**
Sarah-Ann Willis ... **Lori-Nan Engler**
Scroggins ... **William Russ**
Sen. Jason W. Maynard ... **Kirk Scott**
Sharp ... **Chris Mulkey**
Sheriff Buster Moon ... **James Hampton**
Sheriff Ed Little ... **Don Pedro Colley**
Sheriff Emmett Ragsdale ... **Joseph Burke**
Sheriff Emmett "Spike" Loomis ... **Jim Mohlmann**
Sheriff Floyd ... **Sandy Ward**
Sheriff Grady Byrd ... **Dick Sargent**
Sheriff Lester Crabbe ... **Clifton James**
Sheriff Rosco P. Coltrane ... **James Best**
Sheriff Snead ... **Troy Melton**
Sherry Tolliver ... **Dorothy Collier**
Shotgun ... **Gillaaron Houck**
Shoulders ... **Med Flory**
Simon Jethro ... **William Watson**
Simon Jones ... **Chuck Hoyes**
Skip Cook ... **Rick Johnson**
Slade ... **Anthony DeLongis**
Sledge Beaudry ... **John Dennis Johnston**
Slick ... **Bob Hastings**

Slocum ... **Sid Haig**
Spanner ... **Patrick Wright**
Squirt ... **Henry Gibson**
Stacy Williams ... **Doris Dowling**
Starkey ... **Ritch Brinkley**
Steele ... **Lewis Charles**
Stoney ... **John Matuszak**
Sue Ann Hanson ... **Sally Hampton**
Sue-Ann Blake ... **Diane Lander**
Sue Ann Bliss (McGraw) ... **Tori Lysdahl**
Sue Ellen Pettigrew ... **Melanie Vincz**
Sunshine ... **Sunshine Parker**
Suzy Holmes ... **Susan Walden**
Swamp Molly ... **Neva Patterson**
Swifty Barnes ... **Cal Gibson**
Tammy Wynette ... **Tammy Wynette**
Taylor ... **Bob Hastings**
Terry Lee ... **Danny Cooksey**
Tex Tompkins ... **Christopher Stone**
Thackery ... **Tim O'Connor**
Thelma Claire (T.C.) Rogers ... **Pat Klous**
Three Pack ... **Tommy Madden**
Tinker Churchill ... **Mary-Margaret Humes**
Tiny ... **Anthony Brubaker**
Toby ... **James Bradford**
Tom Colt ... **Burton Gilliam**
Tom Pryor ... **R.G. Armstrong**
Tommy ... **Bobby Fite**
Tommy Dunkirk ... **Sam Melville**
Tony ... **Tony Cacciotti**
Trixie ... **Katherine (Kitty) Moffat**
Turk Foley ... **David Hayward**
Turk ... **Robin Strand**
Vance Duke ... **Christopher Mayer**
Vern Cook ... **Glenn Moshower**
Vic ... **Michael Greene**
Vic McGraw ... **Reid Smith**
Virgil / Charlie "Coop the Snoop" Cooper ... **Lou Richards**
Vonnie Fairchild ... **Nancy Hinman**
Wade ... **Gary Grubbs**

BEHIND THE SCENES

"When I was structuring this show for TV, I followed the record industry. I looked at the strength of country music, and I realized that if we could get people who listen to country music to watch 'The Dukes of Hazzard,' we would have the strongest audience in television."

— Gy Waldron, in Country Weekly, April 1997

Wade (Ward) S. Davis ... **Brian Libby**
Walden ... **Herbert Jefferson Jr.**
Warren ... **L.Q. Jones**
Wayne Norris ... **Roger Torrey**
Wendel ... **Avery Schreiber**
Wheeler ... **Michael Alldredge**
Whitney ... **Grant Owens**
Wilbur ... **Bruce Glover**
Wilbur Fudge ... **Jay Ripley**
Willie ... **C. Pete Munro**
Willie ... **Woody Strode**
Willis ... **Kris Marquis**
Woody ... **James Best**
Zack ... **Duke Robbins**
Zack ... **Jan Eddy**

Derrick Perkins of Kentucky and one of his General Lees. Read more about him in the Meet Some Lees section.

CHARACTERS

How can you keep all them Dukes straight?

Ever have a hankerin' to know what was the name of Cooter's daughter, or exactly how the various Hoggs are related? Here's your handy-dandy guide to the many characters of the "Dukes," and believe you-me, they are characters! As in the Cast chapter, they're arranged by first name. For some characters, both parents are not known. When dates are mentioned, they follow the timeframe of when the show originally aired. And note: That whole cousin thing can get a mite-bit complicated! Cousins may share the same uncles and grandparents, or they might not; this guide generally errs on the side of caution.

Abraham Lincoln Hogg
b. April 6, 1926
Great-great-grandmother: Sadie Hogg
Great-grandfather: Thadius B. Hogg
Great-aunt: Emma Lou Hogg
Parent: Big Daddy Hogg
Uncle: Silas Hogg
Sibling: Jefferson Davis Hogg

Cousins: Cletus Hogg, Big Dan Hogg, Mabel Tillingham, Jolene Hunnicutt of the TV show "Alice"
Nephews: Hughie Hogg, Dewey Hogg, Jamie Lee Hogg
Gentle, loving, honest man in a black suit and black Cadillac convertible who is a foil to his scheming twin, J.D. Hogg. Dear old friend of Jesse Duke. Loves to donate to good causes. Overwhelmingly voted Best "Dukes" Character by BRBTV.

A.C. Tate Jr.
Parent: A.C. Tate
Boss Hogg's rival in Chickasaw County.

Ace Parker
Used-car dealer in Hazzard who appears in the episode "Repo Men."

Adam Venable (Josiah Benson)
Child: Esther Venable
Man involved in a criminal case who was relocated to Hazzard in the government's protection program.

Agent Buchanon
Agent with the Bureau of Alcohol, Tobacco and Firearms who pursues Hard Luck Jones in "Follow That Still."

Agent Caldwell
FBI agent who consults with the Dukes on "Diamonds in the Rough."

Agent Callas
FBI agent in "Swamp Molly."

Agent Swan
FBI agent in "Swamp Molly."

Alabama Jones
Siblings: Floyd Jones, Simon Jones
Robber in cahoots with Boss Hogg in "The Law and Jesse Duke."

Alan Fairchild
Uncle: Carter Stewart
Cousin: Vivian Stewart
Spouse: Vonnie Fairchild
Man who schemes to get his uncle's inheritance in "Heiress Daisy Duke."

Alex
Chauffeur for Boss Hogg.

Alice
Cousin: Swamp Molly
Tomboy female ("big-boned," maybe?) with a crush on Bo Duke.

Amos Petersdorf
Grandchild: Sue Ellen Pettigrew
Former Ridge Raider and ex-fire chief who reunites with his pals to take on Boss Hogg in "Return of the Ridge Raiders."

Amos Stigger
Crop duster in Hazzard.

Amy Creavy
Tough, beautiful, red-haired racecar driver of the Placid County Powderpuff Division who steals Luke Duke's heart in "Luke's Love Story."

Androvich
Russian caretaker of gymnast Natasha in "Comrade Duke."

Andy Slocum
Problem teen that the Duke boys take on in "Big Brothers, Duke."

Anna Lisa
Kidnapper in "Lulu's Gone Away."

Anna Louise
Partner to Mary Beth Carver.

Arnie
Crook who conspires to steal federal reserve cash in "Too Many Roscos."

Artie (Arthur) Bender
Artist whom Boss Hogg pays to appear dead so his paintings will be more valuable.

Artie Rathburn
One of Helen Hogan's crooked associates in "Route 7-11."

Augie Dettweiler
Alleged smuggler appearing in "Hazzard Connection."

Avery
Bad guy dealing with Boss Hogg in "Dear Diary."

Bad Barney
Associate of Boss Hogg who appears in "Big Brothers, Duke."

Banyon
Bad guy hired by Boss Hogg in "Goodbye, General Lee."

Barnes
Bad guy pursuing Boss Hogg in "Witness for the Persecution."

Baxter
Bad guy in "The Return of the Mean Green Machine."

B.B.
Dognapper in "A Boy's Best Friend."

B.B. Davenport
Cousin: Cooter Davenport (and possibly Earl the undertaker and L.B. Davenport)
Big lug of a guy who is a mechanic and proprietor of Unit 2 in Hazzard County. Drives a big old beat-up pickup truck.

Beauregard Mason
Infamous fence that negotiates to buy General Stonewall Jackson's sword from Boss Hogg in "Along Came a Duke."

Beckman
Swindler pursuing a priceless Egyptian vase in "The Canterbury Crock."

Becky Mae
Young beauty and friends of Bo and Luke Duke whose house they drop by looking for clothes (!) in "The Ghost of General Lee."

Ben
Bank robber in "Dr. Jekyll and Mr. Duke."

Ben Jordan
Federal Trade Commission agent in "The Sound of Music — Hazzard Style."

Ben Wilkenson
Backwoods hillbilly who doesn't like his privacy disturbed.

Bender
Employee of mobster J.J. Carver.

Benswanger
Man whose car is stripped in "Arrest Jesse Duke."

Bertha Jo Barlow
Friend of Daisy Duke who kick-boxes in the ring in the first reunion movie.

Bessie Lou Perkins
Blond waitress at the Boar's Nest whom Bo Duke takes a shine to, introduced in "Hazzard Connection." (Middle name spelled as "Loo" in the credits of "And in This Corner, Luke Duke.")

Bessie Lou
Polite new switchboard operator in Hazzard featured in "Vance's Lady."

Betty Jo Page
Driver of Waylon Jennings' traveling country-music museum who is rather suspicious of the Dukes in "Welcome, Waylon Jennings."

Bib Tucker
Voluntary fireman and member of the sheriff's reserve in Hazzard.

Big Billie Tucker
Blond, female boss of Rapaho County.

Big Daddy Hogg
Great-grandmother: Sadie Hogg
Grandfather: Thadius B. Hogg
Sibling: Silas Hogg (and possibly Emma Lou Hogg)
Children: Jefferson Davis Hogg, Abraham Lincoln Hogg
Swindler who comes to town in the episode "Big Daddy." Talks about going to church and singing in the choir, of all things.

Big Dan Hogg
(May share aunt, uncle and grandparents with J.D. Hogg)
Cousins: J.D. Hogg, Abraham Lincoln Hogg (and possibly Cletus Hogg, Mabel Tillingham and Jolene Hunnicutt of TV show "Alice")
Nephews: Hughie Hogg, Dewey Hogg, Jamie Lee Hogg
Swindling cousin of Boss Hogg's in Rapaho. Comes to town to wheel and deal with Boss in "Targets: Daisy and Lulu."

Big Jim Downey
Crooked, intimidating associate of Boss Hogg who negotiates to buy counterfeiting plates from him in "Granny Annie."

Big Jim Mathers
Hatchapee County hotshot who comes to town in "Miss Tri-Counties."

Big John
One of the counterfeiters in "Repo Men."

Billie Ann Baxley
Sibling: Kate Baxley
Beautiful blond motorcycle stunt racer who, with her sister, dresses up as a police officer to rob people in "Coy vs. Vance."

Billie Jean
Swindler in cahoots with Boss Hogg in "No More Mr. Nice Guy."

Billy
Film director working with Brock Curtis in "The Dukes in Hollywood."

Billy Joe Billings
Parent: Claude Billings
Silver thief in "The Hazzardville Horror."

Billy Joe Coogan
Crooked guy from Cedar City who becomes sheriff's deputy in Hazzard then blackmails Boss Hogg in "The Ransom of Hazzard County."

Billy Joe Fong
Sibling: Scarlet Fong
Operator of the CB shop in Hazzard, and a member of "Hazzard's only Chinese family."

Billy Ray
Con artist who arranges a boxing match for money between Luke Duke and Catfish Lee in "And in This Corner, Luke Duke."

Billy Ray
Kidnapper in "Lulu's Gone Away."

Black Jack Bender
Old mobster buddy of Boss Hogg who comes to town for "The Meeting."

Blake
Flunky of movie producer Jason Dillard in "The Dukes in Hollywood."

Bo (Beauregard) Duke
b. 1958
Great-grandfather: Joe Duke
Grandfather: Grandpa Henshaw
Uncles: Jesse Duke, Phillip Duke, Albert Duke
Aunts: Lavinia Duke, Katrina Duke, Bessie Duke
Cousins: Luke Duke, Daisy Duke, Coy Duke, Vance Duke, Jud Kane, Gaylord Duke, Jeb Stuart Duke
Blond and boisterous country boy, never minding a bit of trouble in his life. Parents killed in a car crash (according to "Dukes" creator Gy Waldron on the third-season DVD extras). Played linebacker for Hazzard High. Graduated from high school in 1976. Likes the ladies. Competed in the NASCAR circuit. Under probation with U.S. government (with cousin Luke Duke) and because he cannot handle guns as a term of

The prototype of the 12-inch Bo Duke action figure announced by Figures Toy Co. in 2013; see more in the Merchandise chapter. Photo courtesy of Figures Toy Co.

that, has become a good bowman. After the episodes, races cars professionally. CB handle: Lost Sheep.

Bob Dexter
Stunt car driver who gets injured in the "Carnival of Thrills."

Bobbie Lee Jordan
Female orphan runaway who witnesses a crime and attracts Coy Duke's attention in "Coy Meets Girl."

Bonnie
Blond gal who dates Vance Duke and works at WHOGG Radio.

Bonnie Lane
Female swindler with French-braided hair who comes on to Cooter in "Trouble at Cooter's."

Borov
Russian caretaker of gymnast Natasha in "Comrade Duke."

Boss Bowman
Boss of Choctaw County who appears in "The Hazzardgate Tape."

Boss Hopkins
Boss of Hatchapee County who appears in "The Hazzardgate Tape."

Boss Sharkey
Boss of Wiriga County who appears in "The Hazzardgate Tape."

Brock Curtis
Hunky movie star who appears in "The Dukes in Hollywood."

Brodie
Friend of Bo and Luke Duke who helps them keep a lookout for the fertilizer truck carrying slot machines in "One Armed Bandits." Grew up with the Duke boys.

Bubba
Big guy in overalls who helps kidnap Loretta Lynn in "Find Loretta Lynn."

Bubba Malone
Sibling: Floyd Malone
Con who kidnaps Boss Hogg in "Opening Night at the Boar's Nest."

Buck
Texan associate of H.H. Harkness who comes to Hazzard with a gold swindle in "Gold Fever."

Buck Simmons
Scammer who decides to outwit Boss Hogg's plan in "Strange Visitor to Hazzard."

Budge
Armored-truck hijacker in "Sky Bandits Over Hazzard."

Bull
Thug of Big Billie Tucker of Rapaho County.

Burke
Jewel thief pursuing the emeralds in Enos Strate's locker in "Enos in Trouble."

Burl Tolliver
Sibling: Sherry Tolliver
Farmer who's always dreamed of having a prize-winning horse. In "The Rustlers," his prime horse Manassas gets the attention of Boss Hogg, who arranges a horsenapping.

Burnett
Criminal hired by Boss Hogg to rob the jewelry store in "Lawman of the Year."

Burt Robey
Spouse: Myrna Robey
One-half of the jewel thieving husband-and-wife team in "To Catch a Duke."

Cale Yarborough
Famous racecar driver who visits Hazzard.

Candy Dix
Country-music singer who used to date Luke Duke when he was still in the Marines. Comes to Hazzard seven years later in "Play it Again, Luke."

Captain Slater
Mean-spirited leader of the chain gang in Osage County.

Carl
Jealous business associate to Diane Benson and former stunt driver for her in the Carnival of Thrills.

Carla
Car-stripping babe in cahoots with Boss Hogg in "Arrest Jesse Duke."

Carney
Bad guy in "Danger on the Hazzard Express."

Carrie Morton
Spouse: Jeb Morton
Newlywed who unknowingly buys some worthless swampland in Hazzard County in "Dukes Strike it Rich."

Carter
Jewel thief pursuing the emeralds in Enos Strate's locker in "Enos in Trouble."

Carter Stewart
Granddaughter: Vivian Stewart
Nephew: Alan Fairchild
Georgia-based business tycoon appearing in "Heiress Daisy Duke."

Cash Calloway
Criminal that the twins try to fence their stolen jewels to in "Twin Settings."

Catfish Lee
Two-bit boxer and con artist who picks a fight with Luke Duke in "In This Corner, Luke Duke."

Charlie
Man imprisoned on a chain gang for six years by Col. Cassius B. Claibourne — for jaywalking.

Charlie Burns
Bounty-hunter working with Tex Tompkins to find Jud Kane.

Charlie Cooper Jr.
Reporter at the Tri-State Press and friend of Luke Duke.

Chet Garvey
Pit boss for racer Cale Yarborough.

Chickasaw Thins
Owner of a pool hall in Chickasaw County who fills in for Boss Hogg at the pool tournament in "A Little Game of Pool."

Chief Lacey
Lawman in Springville who contacts Rosco P. Coltrane about Rocky Marlowe in "Deputy Dukes." Also shows up as lawman of Sweetwater County in "The Ghost of General Lee."

Cindy
Female accomplice in the kidnapping of Loretta Lynn in "Find Loretta Lynn."

Cindy Bilou
Sibling: Sandy Bilou
One half of the pretty blond jewelry-robbing twins in "Twin Trouble."

Cindy Lou
Pretty brunette femme helping scam Bo and Luke Duke in "Deputy Dukes."

C.J. Holmes
Child: Suzy Holmes
Oil baron from Tulsa, Oklahoma, whose daughter runs away when he forbids her to marry a farmer, seen in "The Runaway."

Clarence Stovall
Retiring worker who robs Boss Hogg's bank when Boss tries to cheat him out of his pension.

Claude Billings
Child: Billy Joe Billings
Silver thief in "The Hazzardville Horror."

Cleary
Armored-truck hijacker in "Sky Bandits Over Hazzard."

Clooney
Bad guy who hijacks the Dukes' rental truck in "Coy Meets Girl."

Clyde
Security guard at the Hazzard Sheriff Impound Yard. Has the hots for Daisy Duke.

Clyde Amos
Editor of the Hazzard County Gazette.

Clyde Berney
Local acquaintance of the Dukes who appears in "Strange Visitor to Hazzard."

Col. Cassius B. Claibourne
Stern and evil lawman of Osage County ("the most feared lawman in the South") who trumps up a charge against the Dukes and puts them on a chain gang in "Cool Hands, Luke and Bo." Sworn enemy of Boss Hogg.

Collins
Swindler in "Cooter's Girl."

Cooter Davenport
b. April (it's his birthday in "The Canterbury Crock")
Cousins: B.B. Davenport, Earl the undertaker (called Tyrone in one episode) and possibly L.B. Davenport
Uncle: Earl
Spouse: Beverly Hills
Child: Nancylou Nelson

Talented mechanic and patient friend to the Dukes. Has helped them out of many a fix. Keeps the General Lee in good working order. Owner of the Hazzard County Garage / Cooter's Garage, which is in Hazzard County Square, right across from the dreaded police department and the bank. Owns a farm on Jessup Road. Meets up with his daughter after many years (and cleans up right nice). After the episodes, goes to Washington as a congressman (like the man who played him!). CB handle: Crazy Cooter.

Corey
Shady criminal who is in cahoots with Boss Hogg in "By-Line, Daisy Duke."

Coy Duke
Uncles: Jesse Duke, Phillip Duke, Albert Duke
Aunts: Lavinia Duke, Katrina Duke, Bessie Duke
Cousins: Luke Duke, Bo Duke, Daisy Duke, Vance Duke, Jud Kane, Gaylord Duke, Jeb Stuart Duke
Fun-loving blond kid and a bit of a womanizer who worked as a test car driver in Detroit before coming to Hazzard while cousins Bo and Luke Duke are driving in the NASCAR circuit.

Coy Randolph
Unsavory type in "Jude Emery."

Crystal
Developer looking to buy the Dukes land and build a Crystal Mountain Brewery on it in "Coltrane vs. Duke."

C.V. Gumble
Seasoned, wealthy, female moonshine dealer in Chickasaw County who appeals to Boss Hogg to make a run for her in "My Son, Bo Hogg."

D. Jasper Fenwick
Associate of Boss Hogg and moonshine distributor who covets Jesse Duke's old moonshine in "Shine on Hazzard Moon."

Daisy Duke
Great-grandmother: Dixie Duke
Grandfather: Grandpa Henshaw
Uncles: Jesse Duke, Phillip Duke, Albert Duke
Aunts: Lavinia Duke, Katrina Duke, Bessie Duke
Cousins: Luke Duke, Bo Duke, Coy Duke, Vance Duke, Jud Kane, Gaylord Duke, Jeb Stuart Duke
Spouse: L.D. *(between the episodes and the first reunion movie)*
Brunette and buxom country girl, a bit of a tomboy, though beautiful and a high-school prom queen. Parents killed in a car crash (according to "Dukes" creator Gy Waldron on the third-season DVD extras). Doesn't shy away from a challenge. "Drives like Richard Petty, shoots like Annie Oakley, knows all the words to Dolly Parton's songs," Waylon Jennings says in the show's pilot episode. Waits tables at the Boar's Nest (since 1976); has worked as a sheriff's deputy, a reporter at the Hazzard County Gazette, even a NASCAR driver. Wins the Miss Tri-Counties title. At first drives a 1971 yellow-and-black Plymouth Road Runner, later drives "Dixie," the cute little white 1980 Jeep CJ-7. Always loved by Enos Strate. Falls in love with Jamie Lee Hogg and Jude Emery. Uses her feminine wiles numerous times to help the Dukes get an edge in a harrowing situation. (While BRBTV does not applaud the use of feminine wiles — so extensively, anyhow — we do appreciate Daisy's choice of bikini color in that famous roadside scene featured in the show's opening.) After the episodes, earns a Ph.D. in ecology from Duke University (ironically!). CB handle: Bo Peep.

Darcy Kincaid
Handsome Hazzard crop duster and flight instructor to Daisy Duke.

Dell Webber
Bad guy and car thief in "The Late J.D. Hogg."

Dempsey
Criminal involved in marijuana smuggling in "Mason Dixon's Girls." Works with associates Rayford Davis and Johnny Ryan.

Denny Logan
Slimy bad guy in "New Deputy in Town."

Deputy Cletus Hogg
(May share aunt, uncle and grandparents with J.D. Hogg)
Cousins: J.D. Hogg, Abraham Lincoln Hogg (and possibly Big Dan Hogg, Mabel Tillingham, Jolene Hunnicutt of the TV show "Alice")
Inept Hazzard County sheriff's deputy who fills in while Enos Strate is working in California. Briefly falls in love with Daisy Duke. Grew up with the Dukes, and is often sympathetic when Boss Hogg is trying to swindle them. Fired from his job at the junkyard right before coming on as a deputy. Debut episode: "Enos Strate to the Top." Just one question, though: If Cletus is only "one-eighth Hogg," how is his last name Hogg?

Deputy Enos Strate
Bumbling, virginal Hazzard County sheriff's deputy. Likes to drink buttermilk. Lives on Spring Lake Drive. His daddy used to run moonshine. Grew up with the Duke boys and has always loved Daisy Duke. Leaves Hazzard for the Los Angeles Police Department in 1980; returns shortly thereafter. Almost marries Daisy as protection against her testimony in a criminal charge in the episodes, then almost marries her again after many years in the reunion movie. After the episodes, returns to L.A. law enforcement.

Devere
Mobster who comes to town for "The Meeting."

Dewey Hogg
Uncles: J.D. Hogg, Abraham Lincoln Hogg
Sibling: Hughie Hogg
Cousin: Jamie Lee Hogg
Another fast-talking chip off the evil Hogg block, only with a black suit and hat instead of white. Tries to fleece the town with a terminal illness act. Schoolmate of Daisy Duke who always pursued her.

Dewey Stovall
Spouse: Lucy Stovall
Choctaw County friend of the Dukes who loses his money gambling in "Route 7-11."

Diane Benson
Lovely boss of the "Carnival of Thrills" traveling stunt show who has felled many a stunt driver, and almost inadvertently costs Bo Duke his life in "Carnival of Thrills."

Dickens
Bad guy in "Share and Share Alike."

Digger Jackson
Escaped convict who comes after Boss Hogg in "Bye, Bye Boss." Boss ran him up years ago for running 'shine.

Dixon
Government agent assisting Josiah Benson in "Good Neighbors, Duke."

Dobro Doolan
Pal of the Dukes featured in the pilot episode.

Doc Appleby
Hazzard County physician.

Doc Homer Willis
Dentist who practices out of an camper RV.

Doc Henry Petticord
Physician in Hazzard County. Doctors up Cooter Davenport when he gets injured in "Duke vs. Duke," and is called into service in "Double Sting."

Doc (Ronald) Carney
Physician to Boss Hogg who mistakes a lab result and tells Boss he's dying in "The Late J.D. Hogg."

Don Purcell
Man who schemes to steal the General Lee in "A Little Game of Pool."

Dr. Debbie Davis
Genetic researcher in Atlanta who appears in "Dr. Jekyll and Mr. Duke."

Dr. Floyd
Physician who treats Bo Duke after his hit on the head in "My Son, Bo Hogg."

Dr. Talmadge
Physician in Capitol City who treats Jesse Duke after the altercation at the jewelry store robbery in "Witness: Jesse Duke."

Dugan
Deputy assistant to state Sen. Jason W. Maynard who comes to town in "Vance's Lady."

Dunlap
Shady associate of Boss Hogg in his horsenapping scheme in "The Rustlers."

Dusty
Texan associate of H.H. Harkness who comes to Hazzard with a gold swindle in "Gold Fever."

Earl Becket
Young, blond, handsome stranger from Texas who intrigues Daisy Duke in "State of the County."

Eddie
Kidnapper in "Lulu's Gone Away."

Eddie Lee Mennis
Cousin: Hoby Willis
Manager of Candy Dix who wants to kill her for a life insurance payout in "Play it Again, Luke."

Eddie Scarlins
Bank robber in "Cale Yarborough Comes to Hazzard."

Eli
Thug of D. Jasper Fenwick.

Elmo Smith
Bank robber in "Cale Yarborough Comes to Hazzard."

Elton Loggin
Radio host on WHOGG in Hazzard.

Emerson P. Craig
Child: Roger Craig
Grandchild: Jamie Craig
Powerful, wealthy, old city slicker who hunts down his grandchild in "A Baby for the Dukes."

Emery Potter
Spouse: Mabel Wooster
Wormy Hazzard County registrar and chief clerk at Boss Hogg's bank. Engaged to Mabel Wooster for 12 years. Deputized when Rosco P. Coltrane is out of commission in "Coltrane vs. Duke."

Emma Partridge
Spouse: Simon Partridge
Friend of the Dukes whose husband leaves her a valuable vase from ancient Egypt in "The Canterbury Crock."

Ernie
Bad guy in "The Ghost of the General Lee."

Ernie Ashburn
Ex-con and driver for Big Daddy Hogg.

Ernie Ledbetter
"Turnip-brain" (according to Luke Duke) male acquaintance of the Dukes in Hazzard.

Esther Venable
Parent: Adam Venable
Attractive, brunette, slightly secretive young woman.

Eustice Hastings
Curator of the Atlanta Museum who loans General Stonewall Jackson's sword to Boss Hogg for his bank display in "Along Came a Duke."

Farmer Perkins
Hazzard County farmer who gets his tractor stolen in "By-Line, Daisy Duke."

Fielding
Thug under the employ of Emerson P. Craig in "A Baby for the Dukes."

Flash
(*Flash P. Coltrane*, according to the "10 Million Dollar Sheriff" two-parter) Sheriff Rosco P. Coltrane's wonderfully ugly Bassett hound, which has a pointed distaste for Boss Hogg and a fondness for Abe Hogg. *Rowf!!!* Debut episode: "Enos Strate to the Top."

Floralee
Twin: Francee
Blond bombshell in a semitruck who with her twin sister makes out with the Duke boys in "Arrest Jesse Duke."

Flossie
Cute brunette who works in truck sales and has a crush on Bo Duke.

Floyd Baker
Wanted fugitive in "Officer Daisy Duke."

Floyd Barclay
Thug of Hughie Hogg.

Floyd Calloway
Old moonshine partner of Boss Hogg whom Boss turned state's evidence on; appears in "Ding, Dong, the Boss is Dead."

Floyd Malone
Sibling: Bubba Malone
Criminal hijacker who comes to Hazzard seeking revenge against Boss Hogg, who put him away three years earlier, in "Opening Night at the Boar's Nest."

Francee
Twin: Floralee
Blond bombshell in a semitruck who with her twin sister makes out with the Duke boys in "Arrest Jesse Duke."

Frank
Swindler after a fortune in diamonds in "Diamonds in the Rough."

Frankie (Francis) Lee Olmstead
Tomboyish female mechanic to Amy Creavy in "Luke's Love Story."

Frank Scanlon
Hitman whom Enos Strate helped incarcerate. Escapes from prison and comes after Enos in "Enos' Last Chance."

Fred Andrews
Spouse: Suzy Holmes
Young farmer who goes to great lengths to marry his college sweetheart in "The Runaway."

Gail Flatt
Parent: Henry Flatt
Beautiful, blond, aspiring gymnast appearing in "R.I.P. Henry Flatt."

Garrett
Bad guy in "Farewell, Hazzard."

Gary Butler
The new lawyer in Hazzard whom the Dukes consult in "A Baby for the Dukes."

A character in its own right: The mighty General Lee (or a car exactly like it!) at the display of the Canadian Dukes of Hazzard Fan Club at the Motor City Comic Con in Novi, Michigan, in May 1999.

General Lee
b. September 1976
Powerful, bright-orange, 1969 Dodge Charger, driven by the Dukes over many a ravine and generating fan mail in its own right. License plate: CNH 320.

George
Chief security guard on the movie set featured in "The Dukes in Hollywood."

George Henry
Associate of Mason Dixon.

Ginny
Female robber of gold dust and one of the previous owners of the General Lee in "Happy Birthday, General Lee."

Granny Annie Coggin
Spouse: Ezra Coggin (though they didn't really marry, Jesse says)
Feisty elderly lady living in Hazzard who's an old friend of Jesse Duke. Carries on her husband's knack for counterfeiting money in the episode "Granny Annie."

Gregory
Con who dives for a bank robber's buried treasure in "The Treasure of Soggy Marsh."

G.S. Baldwin
Big-time moviemaker in "The Dukes in Hollywood."

Gussie Peabody
Switchboard operator in Hazzard.

Hadley
Bad guy dealing with Boss Hogg in "Dear Diary."

Hanson
Crooked associate of Boss Hogg who brokers some short-changing gas pumps with him in "Witness: Jesse Duke."

Hard Luck Jones
Former moonshiner and pal of Jesse Duke, featured in "Follow That Still."

Harley
Ambulance driver featured in "Brotherly Love."

Harry Bobo
Man representing Carter Stewart who comes to town seeking Daisy Duke in "Heiress Daisy Duke."

Harry Joe
Hired thug of Boss Hogg in "Along Came a Duke."

Harry Ray
Thief of a gold bank certificate who appears in Hazzard in "The Hack of Hazzard."

Harvey Dunsmore
Atlanta businessman who is like a "Boss Hogg with class."

Harvey Essex
Government agent who busts Boss Hogg in "The Big Heist."

Hatfield
Boss Hogg's bad guy associate in "The New Dukes" and "The Return of the Mean Green Machine."

Hazel
Guard / deputy at the Hazzard County Jail in the pilot episode.

Hector
Crook who deals with Boss Hogg in "High Flyin' Dukes."

Hector Farley
Friend of Jesse Duke who returns to Hazzard after serving 10 years in prison.

Heep
Recording-industry pirate in "The Sound of Music — Hazzard Style."

Helen Hogan
Owner of the casino in an 18-wheeler in "Route 7-11." Her shuck-'n'-jive is that she's the owner of a company that makes shock absorbers.

Henry Flatt
b. Dec. 1, 1929
Child: Gail Flatt
Man who swindles Boss Hogg out of $20,000 to build a youth center and fakes his own death on July 12, 1979. The Duke boys spot him alive and well in "R.I.P. Henry Flatt."

Henstep
Former Ridge Raider who reunites with his pals to take on Boss Hogg in "Return of the Ridge Raiders."

H.H. Harkness
Dapper young Houston businessman who's a good shot, whom the Dukes encounter amid a gold swindle in "Gold Fever."

Hickey Burns
Bounty hunter chasing Josiah Benson in "Good Neighbors, Duke."

Hixx
Prison buddy of Benson.

Hobie Harkens
Drunken junk dealer in Hazzard who buys the General Lee from the boys in "Goodbye, General Lee" and gives them a lift to town in "Bye, Bye Boss."

Holly Comfurt
Children: John Henry Comfurt, Lori Comfurt
Redheaded second cousin of Jesse Duke, twice removed, who sells her family property for a huge sum of cash in "Southern Comfurts."

Holly Mae
Pretty blond kin of Granny Annie who attracts the eye of the Duke boys in "Granny Annie."

Homer
Clerk at the Hazzard County property deed registry.

Homer Griggs
Owner of a general store in Hazzard.

Homer Sneak
Voluntary fireman and member of the sheriff's reserve in Hazzard.

"Honest" John Ledbetter
Hazzard resident who runs against Rosco P. Coltrane for sheriff in the pilot episode.

Hortense Coltrane
Great-grandfather: Rufus Z. Coltrane
Great-uncle: Hosiah P. Coltrane
Aunt: Clara Coltrane
Uncle: Jasper Coltrane
Parent: Mama Coltrane
Siblings: Lulu Hogg, Rosco P. Coltrane
Skinny sister to the Coltranes who appears in the episode "The Return of Hughie Hogg."

Hughie Hogg
Uncles: J.D. Hogg, Abraham Lincoln Hogg
Sibling: Dewey Hogg
Cousin: Jamie Lee Hogg
Evil, conniving nephew of Boss Hogg who comes to town several times to swindle him and others: Pretends a "genie's" lamp has magic properties, blackmails Boss into making him sheriff, other stuff like that. Attracted to Daisy Duke. Majored in criminal law in college (to be a criminal, not a lawyer) and minored in theater arts. Drives a white convertible Volkswagen Bug. License plate: HUGHIE-1.

Hurley
Bank robber in "Dr. Jekyll and Mr. Duke."

Iggins
Driver for the Comfurts in "Southern Comfurts."

Irving
Bank robber whose partner keeps calling him Stanley in "Double Sting."

Jack Morris
Criminal hired by Boss Hogg to rob the jewelry store in "Lawman of the Year."

Jackie
Pretty blond production assistant on the movie set featured in "The Dukes in Hollywood."

Jake
Goon to "Nervous" Norman Willis.

James Fenwick
Dastardly man in pursuit of the buried Yankee strongbox in "Treasure of Hazzard."

Jamie Lee Hogg
Uncles: J.D. Hogg, Abraham Lincoln Hogg
Cousins: Hughie Hogg, Dewey Hogg
Strong, sensitive, handsome member of the Hogg line, from Atlanta, who dares to love Daisy Duke *(sob!)*. Also happens to be a criminal.

Janco
Bad guy hired by Boss Hogg's rival bosses in "The Hazzardgate Tape."

Jane
Car-stripping babe in cahoots with Boss Hogg in "Arrest Jesse Duke."

Jason Dillard
Hollywood producer with money troubles who appears in "The Dukes in Hollywood."

Jason Steele
Tough, muscle-bound private investigator and bounty hunter based in Atlanta.

J.D. (Jefferson Davis, or "Boss") Hogg
b. April 6, 1926
Great-great-grandmother: Sadie Hogg
Great-grandfather: Thadius B. Hogg
Great-aunt: Emma Lou Hogg
Parent: Big Daddy Hogg
Uncle: Silas Hogg
Sibling: Abraham Lincoln Hogg
Cousins: Cletus Hogg, Big Dan Hogg, Mabel Tillingham, Jolene Hunnicutt of the TV show "Alice"
Spouse: Lulu Coltrane
Nephews: Hughie Hogg, Dewey Hogg, Jamie Lee Hogg
Rotund, highly spirited and endlessly scheming Hazzard County commissioner, bank president and businessman in trademark white flannel suits, driving his trademark white, convertible, 1970 Cadillac Eldorado, who likes to smoke a stogie and eat raw liver and who owns most of Hazzard County. Former moonshiner and lifelong friend (sorta) of Jesse Duke. Used to run 'shine in a car nicknamed the Gray Ghost. Even helped Jesse out at still site No. 22 in 1938 when Jesse was in trouble with the Revenuers. Has tried to cheat the Duke family numerous times, as well as his own family. Ventures to Phoenix to buy Mel's Diner on an episode of TV's "Alice."

Jean
Nurse who works at Doc Petticord's office.

Jeb McCobb
Grandchildren: Sam McCobb, Gerry McCobb
Grisly old moonshiner the Dukes drop in on in "Treasure of Hazzard." His perky blond twin granddaughters are very sheltered but quite fond of Bo Duke.

Jeb Morton
Spouse: Carrie Morton
Newlywed who unknowingly buys some worthless swampland in Hazzard County in "Dukes Strike it Rich."

Jeb Stuart Duke
Uncles: Jesse Duke, Phillip Duke
Aunts: Lavinia Duke, Katrina Duke
Cousins: Luke Duke, Daisy Duke, Coy Duke, Vance Duke, Jud Kane, Gaylord Duke, Bo Duke
Adventurous dirt-bike rider who is on probation in his home of Placid County. Drops in on his cousins in "Along Came a Duke."

Jenny Walden
Former girlfriend of Vance Duke and secretary in a senator's office who discovers her boss' embezzlement and seeks help from Vance in "Vance's Lady."

Jerry
Bank robber in "Enos and Daisy's Wedding."

Jesse L. Duke
Great-grandparents: Jeremiah and Jenny Duke
Spouse: Lavinia / Martha Duke *(two different names were used during the show's run, and a third in the "Dukes" cartoon!)*
Nephews: Luke Duke, Bo Duke, Coy Duke, Vance Duke, Jud Kane, Gaylord Duke, Jeb Stuart Duke
Niece: Daisy Duke
Levelheaded, tough old geezer who watches over the Duke farm on Old Mill Road and the family that lives on it. Moonshined with J.D. Hogg in his younger years. Drove a 'shine-runnin' car he nicknamed Sweet Tilly. Was in trouble with the Revenuers at still site No. 22 in 1938. Lent money to Waylon Jennings and thus became good friends with him. Signed a treaty with the U.S. government to stop making moonshine when Bo and Luke were

caught on a whisky run and put on probation. Drives a white, mid-1970s, Ford longbed pickup truck. Loved and admired by Miz Tisdale. Plays pool like a pro. CB handle: Shepherd.

Jill (Jillie Rae) Dodson
Female friend of the Duke cousins who used to have a crush on Bo Duke.

J.J. Carver
Child: Mary Beth Carver
Mobster in the NASCAR racing circuit.

J.J. Sunday
Thief of a gold bank certificate who appears in Hazzard in "The Hack of Hazzard."

Jo Jo
Manager for Mary Beth Carver.

JoJo
Henchman of Lester Starr.

Joe Landis
Man who schemes to steal the General Lee in "A Little Game of Pool."

Joe Ward
Crop duster who buys out Darcy's business. Friend to the Dukes.

Joey Brian
Backup driver to Petey Willis who appears in "Welcome Back, Bo 'n' Luke."

Joey Sagalo
Counterfeiter and owner of the Rolls Royce in question in "Repo Men."

John Harris
Truck-shipment hijacker in "Cooter's Confession."

John Henry Comfurt
Parent: Holly Comfurt
Sibling: Lori Comfurt
Tall, sturdy young man who's a cousin of the Dukes in "Southern Comfurts."

John J. Hooper
Chickasaw showdog owner who also owns the Hooper Kennels. Appears in "A Boy's Best Friend."

John Zimbra
Investigator for an insurance company in "Carnival of Thrills."

Johnny Ryan
Marijuana smuggler in "Mason Dixon's Girls."

Jonas Jones
Friend of Cooter Davenport who saved his life once in Oklahoma, and whom Cooter tries to protect from the law in "Cooter's Confession." Served time for an armed robbery.

J.P. Pruitt
Owner of the printing company whom Bo and Luke Duke consult in "Mrs. Daisy Hogg."

Jud Kane
Sibling: Luke Duke
Uncles: Jesse Duke, Phillip Duke, Albert Duke
Aunts: Lavinia Duke, Katrina Duke, Bessie Duke
Cousins: Bo Duke, Daisy Duke, Coy Duke, Vance Duke, Gaylord Duke, Jeb Stuart Duke
Little-known handsome brunette Duke sibling who was thought to be killed as an infant in a hospital fire. Was raised by a Mrs. Nelson, who rescued him from the fire. Former Army man who took up boxing and went professional under the name "Killer Kane."

Jude Emery
Texas Ranger who comes to Hazzard looking for a fugitive. Has an attraction to Daisy Duke (don't they all?). Likes to play the guitar. Occasionally rides a horse.

Judge Buford P. Potts
Judge who decides the case of Rosco's lawsuit against the Dukes in "Coltrane vs. Duke" and who hears the case of bank robbery against Boss Hogg in "Dukescam Scam."

Judge Charles Druten
Judge and former fishing buddy of Jesse Duke whose life Jesse once saved when Druten got caught in a bear trap. Reads the will of Boss Hogg's great aunt Emma Lou Hogg in "Baa, Baa White Sheep."

J.W. Hickman
Notorious crime boss of Clarence County and rival to Boss Hogg.

Kate
Temperamental, blond, helicopter-flying ringleader of armored-truck hijackers in "Sky Bandits Over Hazzard."

Kate Baxley
Sibling: Billie Ann Baxley
Beautiful blond motorcycle stunt racer who, with her sister, dresses up as a police officer to rob people in "Coy vs. Vance."

Kelly
Crook who conspires to steal federal reserve cash in "Too Many Roscos."

Lacey
Gambling heavy who cuts a deal with Boss Hogg in "Nothin' But the Truth."

Lacey
One of the Christmas tree thieves in "The Great Santa Claus Chase."

Larson
Crook lawyer who schemes with Boss Hogg in "The Haunting of J.D. Hogg."

Laura Bardsley
University professor searching for a buried Yankee payroll strongbox in "Treasure of Hazzard."

Laverne
Clerk at Boss Hogg's bank.

Lavinia Gray
Blond, buxom, beautiful flimflammer in "The Great Insurance Fraud."

L.B. (Longstreet B.) Davenport
Happy-go-lucky friend of the Dukes who works as a mechanic, blacksmith and general fix-it-upper. Possibly related to B.B. Davenport and Cooter Davenport.

Lee Benson
Nemesis of Luke Duke from their Marines days. Luke helped put him in the brig after Benson robbed and shot his own best friend.

Lenny
Swindler after a fortune in diamonds in "Diamonds in the Rough."

Leo
Henchman to Quirt McQuade in "Mary Kaye's Baby."

Leona Hayes
Road manager for Loretta Lynn who visits Hazzard with her boss in "Find Loretta Lynn."

Leroy
Boss Hogg's criminal contact for his motorcycle theft ring in "The Fugitive."

Leroy Little
Bounty hunter chasing Josiah Benson in "Good Neighbors, Duke."

Les Sloane
Private investigator hired to watch Suzy Holmes in "The Runaway."

Lester Starr
Grimy recording industry publisher in "Daisy's Song."

Lil
Car-stripping babe in cahoots with Boss Hogg in "Arrest Jesse Duke."

Linc McKay
Bad guy and car thief in "The Late J.D. Hogg."

Linda May Barnes
Beautiful blond female who poses as a sheriff's deputy to spring a man in custody, driving all the men in town crazy in the process, in "New Deputy in Town."

Lipton
Wealthy ringleader of a diamond theft in "Targets: Daisy and Lulu."

Lisa
Lovely brunette swindler after a fortune in diamonds in "Diamonds in the Rough." Poses as "Della Dawn."

Lois
One of the counterfeiters in "Repo Men."

Lori Comfurt
Parent: Holly Comfurt
Sibling: John Henry Comfurt
Pretty young lady who's a cousin of the Dukes in "Southern Comfurts."

Lori Mae
Pretty blond waitress at the Boar's Nest.

Lorna Mallory
Scammer who pours on the charm with Vance Duke in "Ding, Dong, the Boss is Dead."

Loretta Lynn
Country music superstar visiting Hazzard County in "Find Loretta Lynn."

Lou Ann Moffet
Child: Rod Moffet
Young widow who appears in "The Boar's Nest Bears."

L.S. Handley
State bank examiner who visits Hazzard in "Sadie Hogg Day."

L.S. (Lisa Sue) Pritchard
Ruthless, beautiful female developer based in Dallas who wants to steamroll Hazzard so she can cash in on its rich coal deposits.

Lucinda Meadows
Spouse: Cyrus Meadows
Former girlfriend to both Jesse Duke and J.D. Hogg.

Luke (Lucas K.) Duke
b. 1955 or 1956
Great-grandfather: Joe Duke
Grandfather: Grandpa Henshaw
Sibling: Jud Kane
Uncles: Jesse Duke, Phillip Duke, Albert Duke
Aunts: Lavinia Duke, Katrina Duke, Bessie Duke
Cousins: Bo Duke, Daisy Duke, Coy Duke, Vance Duke, Gaylord Duke, Jeb Stuart Duke

Responsible, handsome, brown-haired, country boy and former Marine. Parents killed in a car crash (according to "Dukes" creator Gy Waldron on the third-season DVD extras). Under probation with U.S. government (with cousin Bo Duke) and because he cannot handle guns as a term of that, has become a good bowman. Competes in the boxing ring to save the Duke farm, and once boxed in the Marines. Competes in the NASCAR circuit. After the episodes, works for the forestry service. CB handle: Lost Sheep.

Lulu Coltrane Hogg
Great-grandfather: Rufus Z. Coltrane
Great-uncle: Hosiah P. Coltrane
Aunt: Clara Coltrane
Uncle: Jasper Coltrane
Parent: Mama Coltrane
Siblings: Rosco P. Coltrane, Hortense Coltrane
Spouse: J.D. Hogg

Sweet, high-strung, emotional, roly-poly, long-suffering wife of Hazzard's principal businessman. Recording secretary of Hazzard's Flower Club. Shows great compassion for the Dukes when J.D. tries to swindle them. Drives the General Lee like an old pro in one episode. Often threatens to leave or no longer feed J.D. to convince him to give up whatever evil scheme he is pulling. Strong believer in women's rights. Debut episode: "Repo Men."

Ma Harper
Children: Billy Gene Harper, Junior Harper, Billy Boy Harper
Wizened old hag of a bookie in Chickasaw County who keeps her three boys on a tight leash. Visits Hazzard in "Duke vs. Duke."

Mabel
"Hazzard's mobile madam," who helps Bo and Luke out in "Daisy's Song."

Mabel (Myrtle) Tillingham
Cousins: Boss Hogg, Abraham Lincoln Hogg (and possibly Big Dan Hogg, Cletus Hogg and Jolene Hunnicutt of the TV show "Alice")
Talkative switchboard operator in Hazzard who has a crush on Bo and Luke Duke and doesn't shy away from a bribe. Object of Rosco P. Coltrane's crush ("Tell her hey from Rosco!").

Mabel Wooster
Spouse: Emery Potter
Woman patiently engaged to Emery Potter for 12 years before finally marrying him in "People's Choice."

Madame Delilah
Fortunetelling swindler who comes to Hazzard in "The Fortune Tellers."

Mama (Jo) Max
Shrewd, beautiful developer who comes to Hazzard to build a theme park in the first reunion movie.

Mandy Jo
Dognapper in "A Boy's Best Friend."

Manny
One of the counterfeiters in "Repo Men."

Marjorie Dane
Federal Trade Commission agent in "The Sound of Music — Hazzard Style."

Marv
Robot rustler in "Robot P. Coltrane."

Mary Belle Digby
Friend of Daisy Duke who's getting married in "Uncle Boss."

Mary Beth Carver
Parent: J.J. Carver
Pretty blond NASCAR owner whom Bo and Luke Duke investigate for the feds in "Undercover Dukes."

Mary Beth Malone ("Officer Price")
Parent: Nipsy Malone
Pretty blond posing as the officer transporting Rocky Marlowe in "Deputy Dukes" in order to execute some unfinished business for her mobster father.

Mary Kaye Porter
Parent: Henry Porter
Old friend of the Dukes ("5-foot-5 and 115 pounds," as Luke says — and with the Farrah hairstyle!) who comes to town in trouble — in more ways than one — in "Mary Kaye's Baby."

Mary Lou Pringle
Uncle: Hezekiah Pringle
Childhood friend of the Dukes who investigates the "haunted" house of her uncle in "The Hazzardville Horror."

Mary Lou Tompkins Craig
Parents: Bill and Bonnie Tompkins
Spouse: Roger Craig
Child: Jamie Craig
Lovely blond former Hazzard resident and friend of the Dukes who leaves her baby son in the General Lee in "A Baby for the Dukes."

Mason Dixon
Private investigator who drives around in an RV ("his office, his lab, his home," our balladeer says) with two beautiful female associates, Sam and Tinker.

Matt Mallory
Criminal hired to do in Boss Hogg in "Ding, Dong, the Boss is Dead."

Maury
Swindler pursuing a priceless Egyptian vase in "The Canterbury Crock."

Maybelle
Pretty blond femme helping scam Bo and Luke Duke in "Deputy Dukes."

Mean Joe Hatcher
Surly sippin' 'shine buyer for Boss Hogg in "The Legacy."

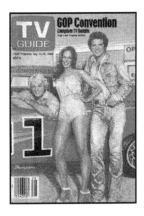

TV Guide "Dukes" covers, from left: July 12, 1980, March 13, 1981, and May 1, 1982.

Melanie DuBois
Lovely blond who goes after the Miss Tri-Counties title, with Big Jim Mathers at her side.

Mickey Larsen
Scammer who decides to outwit Boss Hogg's plan in "Strange Visitor to Hazzard."

Milo Beaudry
Parent: Pa Beaudry
Sibling: Sledge Beaudry
Big, dopey one of the troublesome Beaudry brothers, and the one who has a major thing for Daisy Duke.

Mindy Lou Hale
Pretty young blond working her way through school who comes to Hazzard to sell T-shirts in the annual motocross in "The Fugitive."

Mitch Henderson
Private investigator hired to watch Suzy Holmes in "The Runaway."

Miz (Emma) Tisdale
Sibling: Beulah May
By-the-book, diminutive, Hazzard County postmistress with a sometimes-stern demeanor and a bun on the top of her gray hair. Pines away for Jesse Duke, and will do darn-near anything for the Duke family because of that. Splits time between the post office and the Hazzard County Gazette. Runs the Tisdale Cab Co., even though there's never really a call for a cab in Hazzard. Debut episode: "Enos Strate to the Top."

Molly Hargrove
Famous female former NASCAR driver who woos Daisy Duke into joining the NASCAR circuit — and who has some loan business going on with J.D. Hogg.

Molly Harmon
Wanted fugitive in "Officer Daisy Duke."

Moody
Bad guy who's hired by Boss Hogg to impersonate a Duke boy and rob an armored truck in "Double Dukes."

Morgan
Swindler in "Cooter's Girl."

Morgan
One of Helen Hogan's crooked associates in "Route 7-11."

Morton
Recording-industry pirate in "The Sound of Music — Hazzard Style."

Mr. Winkle
Ventriloquist and impersonator who used to be in show business. Owner / manager of the Hazzard Dog Pound.

Myrna Robey
Spouse: Burt Robey
One-half of the jewel thieving husband-and-wife team in "To Catch a Duke."

Nancylou Nelson
Parents: Cooter and Beverly Davenport

Impressionable young woman who comes to Hazzard to meet her daddy in "Cooter's Girl."

Natasha
Russian gymnast who defects in Hazzard in "Comrade Duke."

Neil Bishop
Reluctant, awkward, polite, handsome, young chicken farmer and robber whom Daisy Duke takes a shine to in "The Big Heist."

"Nervous" Norman Willis
Gangster known as the "Boss of Bosses" who loses his little black book in Hazzard in "Close Call for Daisy."

Newtie
Former Ridge Raider who reunites with his pals to take on Boss Hogg in "Return of the Ridge Raiders."

Norman Scroggs
Assistant editor of the Atlanta newspaper and pal of the Dukes. Nicknamed Scoop.

Norton
Bad guy hired by Boss Hogg's rival bosses in "The Hazzardgate Tape."

Otis J.
Young Boy Scout in "The Great Santa Claus Chase."

Parker
Jewelry-store thief who hits Jesse Duke in "Witness: Jesse Duke."

Pastor
Clergyman appearing in "Close Call for Daisy."

Patch Loring
Grimy, eyepatch-wearing thug of Russel "Snake" Harmon.

Peggy
Feisty, athletic, brunette girl who flips Bo Duke after she teases him to kiss her in "R.I.P. Henry Flatt."

Percy
Crook who deals with Boss Hogg in "High Flyin' Dukes."

Peters
Bad guy in "Bad Day in Hazzard."

Petey Willis
Child: Sarah-Ann Willis
Retired racecar driver who appears in "Welcome Back, Bo 'n' Luke."

Phil Ackley
Sibling: Kate Ackley / Sandra Rhodes (assumed)
Marine buddy of Luke Duke who once saved Luke's life.

Potter
Bad guy who hijacks the Dukes' rental truck in "Coy Meets Girl."

Professor Crandall
Scientist whom Boss Hogg asks to hypnotize Luke Duke in one episode ("Goodbye, General Lee") and Daisy Duke in another ("Heiress Daisy Duke").

Pruitt
Con who dives for a bank robber's buried treasure in "The Treasure of Soggy Marsh."

Quirt McQuade
Atlanta mobster who comes to Hazzard to retrieve the cash Mary Kaye Porter stole from him in "Mary Kaye's Baby."

Rafe Logan
Sibling: Denny Logan
The "second most wanted man in the South" who has a date with the grand jury in "New Deputy in Town." Boyfriend to Linda May Barnes.

Rance
Inventor who brings a stolen robot to town in "Robot P. Coltrane."

Rayford Davis
Marijuana smuggler in "Mason Dixon's Girls."

Rayford Flicker
Con artist who poses as a charity man for Boss Hogg in "Shine on Hazzard Moon."

Reynolds
Lawyer from Atlanta who tells Rosco P. Coltrane he's inherited millions in "10 Million Dollar Sheriff."

Rhuebottom
Owner of a general store in Hazzard.

Rick
Jewelry-thieving partner of Parker in "Witness: Jesse Duke."

Rick
Robber of gold dust and one of the previous owners of the General Lee in "Happy Birthday, General Lee."

Riker
Right-hand man of Mama Max in the first reunion movie.

Robby
Hospitalized boy who idolizes Cale Yarborough.

Rocky Marlowe
Public Enemy No. 1 who's being transported in "Deputy Dukes."

Rod Moffet
b. 1971
Parent: Lou Ann Moffet
Basketball standout who recently lost his father. Vaults the Hazzard team to a big win in "The Boar's Nest Bears."

Rollo
Thug of J.W. Hickman.

Rose Ellen
Clerk at Hazzard bank who has a secret fling with Rosco P. Coltrane.

Rostosky
Mobster who comes to town for "The Meeting."

Rowby Jethro
Sibling: Simon Jethro
Racecar driver who schemes with his brother to steal Cale Yarborough's turbocharger in "Dukes Meet Cale Yarborough."

Roxanne Huntley
Undercover agent with the Bureau of Alcohol, Tobacco and Firearms in "High Octane."

Roy Landry
Counterfeiter who works with Jamie Lee Hogg in "Mrs. Daisy Hogg."

Roy Winters
Internal Revenue Service agent lured to town to nab Jesse Duke in "Hughie Hogg Strikes Again."

Ruby
Ex-girlfriend of Luke Duke now working for Mabel, "Hazzard's mobile madam."

Rudy
Little boy who talks to Bo Duke at the orphanage in the pilot episode.

Ruel McBride
Associate of A.C. Tate Jr. of Chickasaw County.

Russ
One of the Christmas tree thieves in "The Great Santa Claus Chase."

Russ Collins
Swindler working with Sue Ann Bliss in "Mrs. Rosco P. Coltrane."

Russ Mitchel
Swindler who deals furs with Boss Hogg in "Trouble at Cooter's."

Russel "Snake" Harmon
Dangerous, sly figure eluding Jude Emery in the episode "Jude Emery." Has

a snake named Elmer.

Sally
Car-stripping babe in cahoots with Boss Hogg in "Arrest Jesse Duke."

Sally Jo
Blond friend of Daisy Duke who lives in town.

Sam
Hazzard County official in charge of the race in "The Rustlers."

Sam (Samantha Rose)
Beautiful associate of private investigator Mason Dixon in "Mason Dixon's Girls."

Sandy Bilou
Sibling: Cindy Bilou
One half of the pretty blond jewelry-robbing twins in "Twin Trouble."

Scroggins
Boss Hogg's bad guy associate in "The New Dukes."

Sen. Jason W. Maynard
State lawmaker who tries to accuse his secretary Jenny Walden of embezzlement in "Vance's Lady."

Sharp
Flunky of Larson in "The Haunting of J.D. Hogg."

Sheriff Buster Moon
Lawman who fills in for Rosco P. Coltrane in "Return of the Ridge Raiders."

Sheriff Ed Little
Spouse: Rachel Little
Child: Daughter (unnamed)
Brutally big and tall, serious and strict, trigger-happy lawman from nearby Chickasaw County who often chases down the Dukes — or even Boss Hogg. Hates moonshinin'. Doesn't much like litter, either. Debut episode: "My Son, Bo Hogg."

Sheriff Emmett Ragsdale
Young, handsome, blondish sheriff of Choctaw County who thinks Daisy Duke is pretty cute.

Sheriff Emmett "Spike" Loomis
Staunch, stern sheriff of Hatchapee County who relentlessly pursues moonshiners. Infamous for driving a railroad spike through moonshiners' cars since way back in the old days when J.D. Hogg and Jesse Duke were runnin' 'shine.

Sheriff Floyd
Lawman in Hatchapee County, which includes Capitol City.

Sheriff Grady Byrd
Night-watchman at a prison for 20 years who fills in for Rosco P. Coltrane as Hazzard sheriff.

Sheriff Lester Crabbe
Traveling sheriff filling in for Rosco P. Coltrane in "Treasure of Hazzard."

Sheriff Rosco P. (Pervis) Coltrane
b. 1932 or 1940, depending on what episode you believe
Great-grandfather: Rufus Z. Coltrane
Great-uncle: Hosiah P. Coltrane
Aunts: Clara Coltrane, Emma
Uncles: Jasper Coltrane, Wilbur
Parent: Mama Coltrane
Siblings: Lulu Coltrane, Hortense Coltrane
Spouse: Sue Ann Bliss (McGraw)
Nervous, opportunistic sheriff of Hazzard County who likes to call people "dipstick" and treasures his lovable hound, Flash. Was a straight lawman for 20 or 30 years (depending on which episode you believe!) until his pension was defeated in a bond election. Constantly seeking approval and validation from his boss, J.D. Hogg. Constantly cutting down his inferior officers, Enos Strate and Cletus Hogg, and implicating the Dukes in wrongdoings so as to further himself. Loves saying "Shame, shame, everybody knows your name!" Meets fiancée Sue Ann Bliss through a computer dating service. Has a fling with Rose Ellen.

Framed art from the wall of avid "Dukes" fan Don Covell Jr. that certainly honors the pilot episode! And signed by Rosco, to boot!

Sheriff R.P. "Droopy" Cathcarte
Evil, slimy sheriff in Osage County.

Sheriff Snead
Lawman in Capitol City.

Sherry Tolliver
Sibling: Burl Tolliver
Blond, pigtailed divorcee in "The Rustlers."

Shoulders
Right-hand-man to Augie Dettweiler in "Hazzard Connection."

Simon Jethro
Sibling: Rowby Jethro
Racecar driver who schemes with his brother to steal Cale Yarborough's turbocharger in "Dukes Meet Cale Yarborough."

Simon Jones
Siblings: Alabama Jones, Floyd Jones
Criminal who, with his siblings, forms the notorious Jones trio, appearing in "The Law and Jesse Duke."

Skip Cook
Sibling: Vern Cook
Redheaded ultralight flier and friend of Bo and Luke Duke.

Slade
Bank robber in "Enos and Daisy's Wedding."

Sledge Beaudry
Parent: Pa Beaudry
Sibling: Milo Beaudry
Dim-witted backwoods guy who terrorizes the Dukes on occasion, along with his kin.

Slick
Fast-talking, conniving associate of Boss Hogg, shown in "Coltrane vs. Duke."

Slocum
Shyster who's in cahoots with Boss Hogg in "Miz Tisdale on the Lam."

Squirt
Short-statured man who helps kidnap Loretta Lynn in "Find Loretta Lynn."

Spanner
Bad guy hired by Boss Hogg in "Goodbye, General Lee."

Stacy Williams
Dastardly female in pursuit of the buried Yankee strongbox in "Treasure in Hazzard."

Steele
Mobster who comes to town for "The Meeting."

Stoney
Swindler in cahoots with Boss Hogg in "No More Mr. Nice Guy."

Sue-Ann Blake
Postal inspector tracking a mail fraud scheme in "Miz Tisdale on the Lam."

Sue Ann Bliss (McGraw)
Spouses: Vic McGraw, Rosco P. Coltrane
Charming woman whom Rosco P. Coltrane meets through a computer dating service in "Mrs. Rosco P. Coltrane."

Sue Ellen Pettigrew
Grandparent: Amos Petersdorf
Beautiful blond granddaughter of a former Ridge Raider and auditioner to be one of Boss Hogg's "Pretty Piggies" in "Return of the Ridge Raiders."

Suzy Holmes Andrews
Parent: C.J. Holmes
Spouse: Fred Andrews
Blond daughter of a Tulsa, Oklahoma, oil magnate who runs away from her father's control to marry a farmer in "The Runaway."

Swamp Molly
Cousin: Alice
Crooked backwoods gal who's always had a thing for Jesse Duke and once even helped him escape the feds (in '36).

Swifty Barnes
Boss Hogg's right-hand man in the horse-betting operation in "Hazzard Hustle."

Taylor
Armored-truck hijacker in "Sky Bandits Over Hazzard."

Terry Lee
Sad little boy the Dukes try to help in "A Boy's Best Friend."

Tex Tompkins
Wheelin', dealin' gambler who lost money on a boxing match that Jud Kane refused to throw.

Thackery
Mean-old armored-car robber appearing in "Bad Day in Hazzard."

Thelma Claire (T.C.) Rogers
Parent: Jim Rogers
Beautiful, blond, female pal of the Dukes who challenges Boss Hogg for the job of supervisory administrator in "People's Choice."

Three Pack
Little-person sidekick to Madame Delilah.

Tinker Churchill
Beautiful associate of private investigator Mason Dixon in "Mason Dixon's Girls."

Tiny
Hired thug of Boss Hogg in "Along Came a Duke."

Tom Colt
Bad guy who fakes the plague and helps bank robbers in "Double Sting."

Tom Pryor
Honest lawman and friend of Jesse Duke who visits in "Witness for the Persecution."

Tommy Dunkirk
One of a trio of armored car robbers in "The Great Hazzard Hijack."

Tony
Mobster who comes to town for "The Meeting."

Trixie
Pretty blond cohort of Hughie Hogg who poses as a genie from a lamp to fool Boss Hogg in "When You Wish Upon a Hogg."

Turk
Bad guy who's hired by Boss Hogg to impersonate a Duke boy and rob an armored truck in "Double Dukes."

Turk Foley
Sleazy, unethical mechanic and ex-boyfriend to Amy Creavy.

Vance Duke
Uncles: Jesse Duke, Phillip Duke, Albert Duke
Aunts: Lavinia Duke, Katrina Duke, Bessie Duke
Cousins: Luke Duke, Bo Duke, Daisy Duke, Coy Duke, Jud Kane, Gaylord Duke, Jeb Stuart Duke
Handsome, slightly dopey-seeming brown-haired guy, a bit of a womanizer, who was a Merchant Marine before coming to Hazzard while cousins Bo and Luke Duke are driving in the NASCAR circuit.

Vern Cook
Sibling: Skip Cook
Young ultralight flier and friend of Bo and Luke Duke whose business is in Conyers.

Vic
Tall, tough thug under the employ of Big Jim Downey in "Granny Annie."

Vic McGraw
Spouse: Sue Ann Bliss
Swindler working with Sue Ann Bliss in "Mrs. Rosco P. Coltrane."

Virgil / Charlie "Coop the Snoop" Cooper
Reporter friend of the Duke boys. Works at the Tri-State Press. *(Introduced as Charlie in "Return of the Ridge Raiders" but listed as Virgil in the episode's credits; different variations of a newspaper friend of the Duke boys named "Coop," "Scoop," "Cooper" or "the Snoop" were utilized.)*

Vivian
Wealthy woman whose millions Boss Hogg pursues — by hypnotizing Daisy Duke to believe she is Vivian.

Vonnie Fairchild
Spouse: Alan Fairchild
Woman who schemes with her husband to get his uncle's inheritance in "Heiress Daisy Duke."

Wade (Ward) S. Davis
Flimflammer in "The Great Insurance Fraud."

Walden
Special agent who recruits Bo and Luke Duke to investigate mobster J.J. Carver in "Undercover Dukes."

Waylon Jennings
Country-music star (*and the show's balladeer — but shush; the Dukes don't know that*) who brings his traveling museum to Hazzard in "Welcome, Waylon Jennings." Met Jesse Duke years earlier when Jesse lent him money to buy a new guitar.

Wayne Norris
Thug of Hughie Hogg.

Wendel
Bank robber in "Double Sting."

Wheeler
"State elections board" man hired by Boss Hogg in "People's Choice."

Wilbur
Associate of Lipton in "Targets: Daisy and Lulu."

Wilbur Fudge
County controller who steps in as sheriff's deputy in "The Legacy."

Willie
Tall, lean and mean crook who poses as a reverend, under Boss Hogg's employ, in "The Great Santa Claus Chase."

Willie
Grimy thug of Russel "Snake" Harmon in "Jude Emery."

Willis
Little boy who's happy to help Bo and Luke Duke escape Sheriff Rosco's custody with his squirt gun in "The Big Heist."

Woody
Actor and crook who impersonates Rosco P. Coltrane in "Too Many Roscos."

Zack
Swindler in cahoots with Boss Hogg in "No More Mr. Nice Guy."

BEHIND THE SCENES

> "It would've been easy for somebody to get killed on that show."
>
> — Tom Wopat, discussing "The Dukes of Hazzard" on TVLand's "My First Time" special, July 2006

A die-hard "Dukes" fan: There weren't many other shows out there that had such car-appeal! This fan and historian, Jon Holland of Virginia, runs the Hazzard County Car Club and the DukesofHazzard01 website, owns his own General Lee (of course!), and even put together a March 2006 tour of original "Dukes" filming sites in Georgia, with the proceeds going to charity. Here, Country Music Television interviews Jon for the "Inside Fame" special on the "Dukes." Jon built his General Lee himself, using information he got from mechanics who worked on the General Lees for the show. Photos courtesy of Jon Holland.

EPISODES

Jumpin' through the action, one episode at a time.

From the first bit of dust rising on the Covington, Georgia, countryside to that whole bizarre space-alien thing and the movies beyond, here are the synopses for the "Dukes." The episodes have been arranged in the order they aired (though that's not always the same as the order they were filmed) since the first edition of this book, though for this edition we deferred to the DVD order in most cases; see the note later in the guide.

Season 1

"One Armed Bandits," January 26, 1979
Is that them Duke boys chasing the sheriff's car? Isn't that the wrong way around? Well, it's Cooter Davenport behind the wheel, actually. But what's that peekin' out the back of the sheriff's car? A casino slot machine? The Duke boys — with the help of their buddies Dobro Doolan, Cooter and Brodie — hijack Rosco's shipment of slot machines as he's running for reelection against "Honest John" Ledbetter. (Since Rosco's pension is gone, he has no choice but to be the best sheriff that money can buy!) Jillie Rae Dodson (just Jill now) stops by the Dukes farm to tell her old friends Bo

and Luke about how she's trying to help out the orphanage. Later, Jesse's not fond of those slot machines he finds in the barn. He's no fan of gambling. The Dukes hatch a plot to use the one-armed bandits to help out Jill and her orphans' home by making the rounds to the local civic groups, and soon Bo delivers some bags of cash to Jill at the orphanage. Boss, of course, is wondering where the slot machines went, then Rosco discovers a couple of them at a club. He connects the dots, and tries to apprehend Daisy for assisting. This leads to a car chase, wouldn't ya know. Jesse is none too happy when she gets "throwed in jail." He tells his nephews, "For 200 years the Duke family had the whiskey craft. And the government took that away from us. Then we had the land. And the Depression took that. Now all the Duke family has left is what it started with and that's family, and Daisy is family! Now get her out!" And indeed they do, even convincing Enos later of the logic of their ways. Maybe?

"Welcome to Hazzard County," Waylon says ... and away we go! This pilot hits all the high notes as it introduces the characters: a farmhouse scene with Jesse, a Boar's Nest scene with Daisy moppin'-the-floor with an obnoxious customer, plenty of car-chasin' in the General Lee, Daisy enticin' and divertin' in a bikini, and even Luke shirtless. Their buddies Dobro Doolan and Brodie aren't utilized much after this point, as Cooter settles into the spot of Chief Dukes Buddy. Ernie (Brown) Lively, the actor who plays Dobro here, later plays Duke buddy Longstreet B. Davenport, by the way, and his son, Jason Lively, shows up in this episode and a later episode. We just love how Cooter drives a "Starsky and Hutch" car in this one, and we love watching John Schneider's command of his role at such a young age. Though the jump of Lee 1 at Oxford College was the first one filmed, it's not the first General jump shown in the episode. Check out Dale Etheredge on the tractor as the General goes around the Hazzard Square — see the Etheredge family's story later in this book. There's Dale's mom Anne at the orphanage at the end. We get only a brief glimpse here of Jack Gordon as Rosco's competition, Honest John Ledbetter, as he meets and greets voters. Because of the filming in rural Georgia (see our Fun & Useless Information chapter), this pilot has a slightly different look, feel and sound from the later episodes. Take how dark the Boar's Nest is inside, for instance. And a couple fun facts about that very first scene at the Boar's Nest: longtime actor Dennis Haskins of "Saved by the Bell" was there, credited as "Moss," as the obnoxious patron, and several of Schneider's family members were sitting at tables, too.

Bring it on: June 1, 2004 was an exciting day for "Dukes" fans — Warner Home Video released the very first installment of what would become a successful string of DVDs. This complete first-season DVD, a three-disc set, includes such extras as "The 20th Anniversary Hazzard County Barbecue" documentary (shot at Paramount Ranch, one of the "Dukes" filming locations), "Dukes Driving 101: A High Octane Salute" and "The Dukes of Hazzard: Return of the General Lee" videogame preview.

"Daisy's Song," February 2, 1979

Daisy paid a guy in the recording industry $50 to publish her song, and when she hears it on the radio being sung by Jessi Colter, she's mighty excited. The guy isn't interested in giving her any royalties for the song, though, so the Duke cousins investigate this Mr. Lester Starr in Atlanta. The Law happens to drop by, too. A car chase through downtown Atlanta ensues. The Dukes have done discovered a piracy ring. Guess who's at the heart of it? Yup, that roly-poly guy in white. *(You'll be seeing that song-and-dance quite a bit.)* The Dukes devise a sting involving recording artists Donna Fargo, Loretta Lynn and Jessi Colter *(who happens to be Waylon Jennings' wife; in an ironic statement at the beginning of the episode, Jennings says Colter is one of the world's greatest performers, but that he's "more partial to June Carter Cash"!).* Daisy dupes Lester into "making her a star." Boss is trying to hook up with some syndicate guys, even as the FBI is quizzing Rosco about Lester and his pack, and Daisy's alleged singing prowess is caught in the middle. *This episode includes a rare appearance of Miss Mabel, "Hazzard's mobile madam," who's a bit of a departure from the more-wholesome turn the show would develop. Daisy really pushes the envelope in this one with the satin short-shorts she wears to meet Lester Starr. And Cooter debuts his CB call, "Breaker-one, breaker-one, I may be crazy, but I ain't dumb ... " This second outing has a slightly different look from the pilot, as the series was shaping up to fully establish its tone and feel. Though it was distinctly Southern, Hazzard sure looked a lot like this author's small Northern hometown, too!*

Plus, our fellow author Brian Lombard notes the General's disappearing and reappearing roll bar. Notice that as they're parked out front of Lester Starr's studio, when Daisy says "Gee, I knew it was tough to get into show business, but I never heard of them using guns to keep you out," she is sitting where the bar would normally be, but it's gone. Later, as Daisy is parked out back, and as the Dukes speed away, the bar is back in place. "It's not something easily removed!" Brian says. Another note from Brian: "In Season 7, we learn that Uncle Jesse and Waylon Jennings have a history that precedes this episode, so I'm curious as to why Jesse shows no outrage over his friend Waylon being a victim of the pirates."

"Mary Kaye's Baby," February 9, 1979

Bo and Luke are in danger of breaking probation when they discover some moonshine in the back seat of the car they borrowed from Cooter. They start ditching the evidence out the window (we love that guy at the campfire under the bridge!). Then they meet up with an old friend — a very pregnant old friend — who is mixed up with an Atlanta crime lord. It seems Mary Kaye Porter stole some money from him that she figures rightfully belongs to her unborn child (for his college education and all, you know). $118,254.37, actually. The mobster, Quirt McQuade, is dealin' with Boss Hogg, meanwhile, as he's trying to track the cash that should've been delivered to him when Mary Kaye's boyfriend got arrested. Rosco and Enos are hunting down Bo and Luke for hauling that whiskey, some of which is still in the trunk of Cooter's car. Then Mary Kaye starts to have some pains. And it ain't indigestion. It's off to the Duke farm for the new arrival, and a little duck-and-dodge with McQuade. *The shots inside the cars (very tight profiles of the characters) are quite different in this episode, reflecting the show's early filming in Georgia — and it even looks like there were Christmas* decorations up in Covington during this episode's shooting (see the Fun & Useless Information chapter for more on the area). The General Lee does not appear in this episode, but the boys do jump the Plymouth of Cooter's they're driving! We get some more bow-and-arrow action from Bo and Luke in this one, as in the second episode. In this episode, Rosco and Jesse talk about how he was a honest lawman for 20 years before his pension went south; in the pilot episode that timeframe was given as 30 years.

"Repo Men," February 16, 1979

Boss' sweet Lulu wants a Rolls, so Boss goes to used-car dealer Ace Parker to secure one. Bo and Luke, meanwhile, have their eye on a car with a cool engine (formerly owned by Richard Petty), which they figure can put the General Lee in top racing form. Ace sets them up with the unsavory job of repossessing a Rolls as part of their barterin' for the Petty car. The Rolls' owners bite back, so to speak (they do have Dobermans, after all), and they've got a counterfeiting operation to protect. Boss gets wind of the boys' deal with Ace and decides to frame the Duke boys by saying the Petty car is hot. Right on cue, Rosco pulls the boys over after they pick up the car. The bargaining chip for the new legal troubles is for them to finish that Rolls repo job. Daisy gets wind of the setup from Enos. The boys then have to get a little craftier to pull that job, enlisting the aid of Cooter and a cute female doggie. They still get double-crossed, so Uncle Jesse cooks up some "dirty pool." This episode marks the first appearance of Lulu, as well as the first time Rosco calls Boss his "little fat buddy." Catch the chase scene of Bo disemboweling the crooks' cars with a rigged-up "assault" vehicle (a la the film "Grease"). "Dukes" inspiration and former real-life moonshiner Jerry Rushing plays Ace Parker, while Rodney Amateau, who produced and directed during the series run, plays Manny. Gary Baxley, one of the show's stunt guys, appears as Boss' driver in this and other episodes. And Lee 1, star of the pilot episode? Well, he plays the Petty car with a new battered "71" paint job here. You can sure see the lack of padding in Boss' white suit; he looks downright slender as he's talking to Ace and Lulu at Ace's shop. This episode is one of Ben Jones' favorites, he tells BRBTV.

"High Octane," February 23, 1979

As Bo and Luke are reporting in to their probation agent at the courthouse, they see that the Federal Energy Commission is sponsoring a $20,000 contest to find an environmentally friendly alternative to fossil fuel. The wheels are turnin' for the Dukes, who see possibilities in Jesse's old 'shine. Boss Hogg sees the same possibilities, though, and flashes some dollar

Canadian artist and avid "Dukes" fan Jim Wilson offers his own interpretation of the "High Octane" episode in his painting above, reprinted on metal and hanging at BRBTV headquarters. You'll learn lots more about Jim — and see more of his great art — later in the book.

signs at Jesse. But Jesse's not budgin' for Boss, though the Duke boys do manage to talk him into firing up the still he shut down when he signed that treaty with the U.S. of A., though there's that little matter of the cute female Revenuer. She got the suspicion from Rosco that those Dukes might be back in the 'shine and ventures out into the woods to have a look-see. The Dukes then treat her to some Southern hospitality, heavy on the jukin' and drinkin'. Enos tips off Luke to Boss' scheme on the Dukes. Rosco keeps Agent Roxanne busy behind bars then tries to detain Jesse from scooting his way to the contest with his entry. But ole Boss don't quite have the drop on them Duke boys. *This one opens with the third jump of the General Lee, the first jump since the pilot. We see a good shot of the General's license plate, too, which would go on to have new life on General replicas everywhere! Uncle Jesse's pickup is seen for the first time in this one, though it was referenced* earlier. And his "other" vehicle makes its debut here, too: Sweet Tilly, his 'shine-runnin' car.

It was off to Hollywood for filming, after this point. As John Schneider notes in the Season 1 DVD extras, these first five episodes were filmed with no sound stages — "real rooms" were used for each scene. And we'd miss that genuine Georgia scenery, for sure ...

As the action was relocated to the West Coast and continued on for seven seasons, most of the street scenes were shot on the backlot of Warner Bros., James Best notes in his autobiography, "Best in Hollywood." Disney Ranch was used for early back-road car chases, until the studio put an end to that for all the ground that was being torn up, Best says. Then it was off to a more remote desert location further up north, where the key lights sizzled their makeup right off at times, the actor laments in his book.

Thank goodness for mattresses: These shots from John Schneider's own collection show scenes from early filming of the show, "High Octane," below, and "Mary Kaye's Baby," at right. We can't help but love that brown corduroy suit, which Schneider has referenced in interviews. Photos courtesy of John Schneider, Chad Collins and JDS.

"Swamp Molly," March 9, 1979
Bo and Luke are having a little target practice with their bows and arrows on the old outhouse when an old friend of Jesse's, Swamp Molly, arrives with her kin, Alice. Molly talks Jesse and the boys into helping her out in a special run, which Jesse assumes is moonshine. They get Cooter to dress a truck up like an ice-cream truck so they can make the run during the day, right under the noses of the law. But Rosco has had his eye on Swamp Molly, and he knows she's got the Dukes in on this run, plus Boss wants her moonshine. The Dukes encounter Rosco's roadblock, and they find that Molly's not really into 'shine these days — she's graduated to firearms! And the Dukes get implicated! Daisy comes along with a little diversion (no, not a bikini this time). Boss is perturbed because Rosco has called the FBI, so Rosco sends them off with a tale of hallucination. Bo and Luke have a little talk with Swamp Molly about this arms shipment, while Alice gets Jesse out of the way crawdad-fishing in the swamp. When everyone reunites, the quicksand of the Black Hollow lends a hand in gettin' rid of the evidence. *The Hazzard Garage gets a tune-up, so to speak, as we switch over to the West Coast scenery, and the Boar's Nest sure has a lighter look. We love the huge radios Rosco and Enos use to communicate — half the size of a suitcase.*

"Luke's Love Story," March 16, 1979
It's time for the annual Hazzard Obstacle Derby, and the drivers include Enos, Cooter, and one of the Duke boys (depending on how that arm wrestling turns out), but a cute little redheaded racecar driver, Amy Creavy, sets out to speed to the finish line. And she might just change Luke's stick-in-the-mud ways. She at least gets him in a big brawl at the Boar's Nest with Turk, a mechanic who is very protective of Amy and has some slightly illegal ways of winning races. Bo then has his own encounter with Turk when he sees him fussing with Amy's car at the Hazzard Garage. Plus, Bo's making wagers with Frankie, Amy's tougher female partner, putting the pink slip of the General up in the race. And Boss is just plain worried about winning back the trophy cup — especially since it has his mama's ashes in it! He hires Cooter to be a crasher in the derby. Amy takes Luke for a ride in her car Lucifer, and it's almost their last; somebody tampered with the brake lines. But the greater danger is for Luke's heart. *Is that a big-ole mole on Boss Hogg's chin? We have to wonder. Roz Kelly, who played the daring Pinky Tuscadero in ABC's "Happy Days," stays true to form here as Amy.*

"The Big Heist," March 30, 1979

Bo is excited to pick up his brand new boots at the post office, while over at the courthouse, Boss Hogg is getting held up. The robber's car gets towed for being parked illegally, so he hitches a ride in the General as it blazes by. Boss sees him dive into the car, so he naturally assumes his $30,000 was just stolen by the Dukes. The perpetrator "borrows" the General from the boys, forcing them to walk home, then goes to the Boar's Nest, where he runs into a smitten Daisy. Rosco apprehends Bo and Luke, but they sneak away with the help of a kid and his squirt gun. Rosco, Enos and Boss still catch up with them, though. Jesse sorts out the story, especially since the robber, Neil, has wrangled himself an invite to the Duke farm. He's actually a reluctant, polite guy who was unhappy after buying some bad farm equipment off Boss. When the Dukes hear his story, they hatch a plan to make sure he won't get into trouble for stealing the cash — they divert the "trouble" to Boss, whose money came from illegal liquor dealings. *The General does a ski stunt in this one — and Daisy's driving. We love how Rosco, as he's following the General and thinking it's the boys, comments how they're driving better today.*

"Limo One is Missing," April 6, 1979

The big-ole presidential limo is just too much of a temptation when it's sittin' there parked at the Boar's Nest. Cooter gives in, and it's up to the Dukes to find him, hide the car then give it back to its rightful owner. One of the diversionary tactics they use to hide the limo is Daisy hanging her "unmentionables" out to dry while she's chatting with Enos. Boss, meanwhile, has designs on getting that limo back to the Prez himself so he can take the credit. He makes use of his ole abandoned mining town in Choctaw to plot his scheme. The car winds up at the Duke farm. After a few other mishaps, as the boys are trying to get the car across the county line, it's hijacked by one of Boss' guys. The Dukes see Boss taking the Choctaw turnoff road and follow him, then see the limo there — at Boss' chopshop. When everything is finally all straightened out, Uncle Jesse gets a special phone call from the Oval Office — though he's a bit shy about inviting Mr. President *(which at that point would've been Georgia native Jimmy Carter, by the way)* over for dinner. *You might notice in the General's jump in this one that one brief clip shows the car with "10" on its side instead of "01" — the film for that shot was reversed.*

"Deputy Dukes," April 13, 1979

Bo and Luke get their clothing — and some prize money — bamboozled out of them by a couple sweet-talking femmes at the creek. Boss and Rosco then get a call from Chief Lacey in Springville about Public Enemy No. 1, Rocky Marlowe, who needs transport. They send the Duke boys off to get Marlowe, deputizing them, figuring the boys could take all the risk for them. Bo and Luke have got a pretty female officer assisting, but then they encounter two of Marlowe's goons, tailing them. Uncle Jesse blows a gasket when he learns where Boss and Rosco sent the boys ("... pea-pickin', squirrel-brained ... !!!!"). When they get the word that the pretty female officer is just a poser, they go after the boys. Bo and Luke still have the goons on their tail, so they head out on foot with Marlowe and "Officer Price," but then they stumble upon the car of the two femmes who bamboozled them! Nice. Then "Officer Price" sets Marlowe free — with plans of her own. *The lovely Stella Parton shows up here as Mary Beth Malone. Gary Graham shows up as Marlowe's brother, and BRBTV just loved him in Fox's "Alien Nation"! In these early episodes, Rosco is identifying himself without his middle initial.*

"Money to Burn," April 20, 1979

Enos is in hot pursuit of the Duke boys in the General but finally has to give up. Over at the bank, Boss is cooking up a scheme to do a little cool "exchange" of a million bucks of bank currency he's supposed to send to Atlanta for burning. He decides his cousin Cletus will drive the armored car, which will accidentally "burn" with all the money inside (which is really some old phone books). The boys, meanwhile, are working on winning the Choctaw County Rally. They see the armored car burning, and help put it out! Boss is none too pleased and decides to claim that the Dukes took the cash. The money mysteriously makes its way to the Duke house, then Rosco and Enos promptly arrive on the doorstep. Bo and Luke go on the lam, then discover something fishy going on at the Hazzard County Coffin Works, so they devise a scheme of their own. *Rick Hurst makes his debut as Cletus Hogg, though he's got a different uniform on for this spin. Boss is on at least his third driver. We get a little shirt-free action with the boys in this one. And this is the second episode where we see Daisy touching up her lipstick; we laugh about how we saw history repeat itself years later at the 2006 DukesFest (see our photos later in the book).*

"Route 7-11," May 4, 1979

It's time for the Cherokee County Dirt Road Classic, and the General Lee isn't running that great. The repair costs drive Bo and Luke to get a job behind an 18-wheeler, but what exactly are they hauling? Their new boss, Helen Hogan, has been to Hazzard before — selling some no-good stuff. When the boys take to the road, and take a peek inside the truck, they see a casino on wheels, live and in action! Boss and Rosco have their eye on that 18-wheeler, too, and Rosco sneaks inside to take a peek and almost gets trapped inside along with Luke. The Dukes' buddy Dewey Stovall has lost his cash in the casino, and the boys want to help him get it back, which means goading their Uncle Jesse into taking to the tables, himself. He gets all gussied up, along with a red-sequined-gowned Daisy, and they hit a winning streak, much to the chagrin of Helen and her crooked dealers. *A scene with Boss Hogg shows early experimentation with his character: He's being attended by a babe (any babe-appreciation on his part was largely abandoned later as his wife Lulu got more screen time), and he denies that Rosco is his "good buddy" (their friendship was certainly cemented in ensuing seasons).*

"Double Sting," May 11, 1979

The Duke boys in the General have a bad encounter on the road with an ornery driver, Tom Colt, who then goes to the Boar's Nest and offends Daisy. A fight ensues, and all three boys end up in jail. The obnoxious one, though, is discovered to have "The Hazzard Plague." Jesse suspects he's faking it, but the jail is quarantined. The guy's partners, meanwhile, blow into town to rob the bank, dressed as Laurel and Hardy. Daisy makes a trip to the bank herself, in the midst of the robbery, then sneaks onto the top of their RV as they roll out of town. The news gets to the jailhouse, but Bo, Luke and Jesse can't leave to help Daisy, so the boys have to devise a way to break out of jail and make Colt think they're on the same side. The hunky Sheriff Emmett Ragsdale steps into the case, too, and the robbers have their hands full with Daisy. *Arte Johnson plays Irving, the robber with a thing for Daisy, and comedian Avery Schreiber is his partner, Wendel. It's appropriate that Rosco is quarantined — sounds like James Best had a cold. Did ole Waylon's voice sound different this time, too? Daisy gets to wear a sparkly blue circus act outfit, which she put together for Hazzard's Costume Cotillion.*

A Note on Those Short-Shorts

One final note for this first season ... When folks think of Daisy Duke's wardrobe, they of course think of the famous shorts. When we've seen some cute Daisy impersonators at "Dukes" events over the years, though, we've seen an approach that skews more "Hee-Haw" than Daisy.

Our Dukes girl didn't wear red-and-white-checkered bare-midriff tops all tied up under her breasts, and she didn't wear cutoffs with frayed edges. Her short hems were finished, not frayed, from when she cut the legs off of her own pants — and these weren't just jeans. They were just as often tight pants in varying colors, complemented by tank tops and blouses. Her shoes were high-heeled, thin, strappy sandals. Hosiery completed her look. You could say her style was set by the little camisole top and shorts she wore in the very first Boar's Nest scene, included in the show's opening. Sometimes she was seen in full-length designer jeans and a long-sleeved blouse.

And all of this was a style Catherine Bach very much determined, herself. She said in the CMT "Inside Fame" special on the "Dukes" that the producers at first wanted her to wear a tight white top and a poodle skirt in that aforementioned red-and-white-checkered pattern, same as the tablecloths at the Boar's Nest. She countered with her idea of the short-shorts. And the rest is fashion history!

Now, you will see a promotional photo or two done back in the day with Bach in the bare midriff and cutoffs, but we're talking the actual episodes here. Shown above is a typical outfit for Daisy! Much cooler than those chicks on "Hee-Haw." And yep — this is a chick that's saying it, a chick that despite the foreword of this book would never consider herself as adorable as Daisy!

The second-season DVD set features the screen tests of our two boys, John Schneider and Tom Wopat. Meow!

Season 2

"Days of Shine and Roses," September 21, 1979

A moonshiners' reminiscing reunion at the Boar's Nest accelerates into trash-talkin' between Boss Hogg and Uncle Jesse as to who is the best 'shine-runner. They decide to make one last run right into Hatchapee County, land of the dangerous Sheriff Emmett "Spike" Loomis, who is, of course, tipped off about the race by "anonymous" caller Boss. Jesse insists on hauling jugs of water instead of 'shine, but Rosco and Boss fix that, after their sabotage of Jesse's run car doesn't work as well as they'd hoped. The run begins, and Loomis is perched at a roadblock waiting for Jesse, but Cooter and Daisy get wind of Boss' scheme. They meet up with Bo and Luke and perform their own switcheroo on the go. *We love the black-and-white film of Jesse and J.D. 'shine-runnin' at the beginning. The name of Jesse's original car is Black Tilly here but was given as Sweet Tilly in "High Octane." For some reason he can't drive it in this one, as he did in "High Octane," so Cooter gets him a black Mustang instead. Sorrell Booke is padded out here as Boss, and to match up with that, we see him focusing on food again (something that hasn't really been seen since the pilot) as he's fishing his paws* through a big jar of something pickled. As Bo and Luke are out tailing Rosco on the run, Luke leaves the General then seems to get back in through the door rather than the window.

"Gold Fever," September 28, 1979

Uncle Jesse has a toothache, so Bo and Luke flag down Doc Willis to have a look at it. They then encounter three smooth-talkin' Texans led by one H.H. Harkness. Their car trouble requires them to stay over in Hazzard, and they're concerned about protecting their cargo — gold bars. Harkness works out a sweet payment to Boss for lodging the gold at the bank. Boss tells Rosco it's got to be a setup by them Dukes. When Rosco goes to the farm, Bo and Luke sneak out but have to flee again when they are discovered by Enos over at Cooter's. Wouldn't you know it — the gold comes up missing at the bank. The Dukes have to work to clear their name. It helps that Cooter discovers the Texans' limo is stolen, and they realize that not only did the Texans steal their own gold, but the gold is not really gold at all. The bad guys are putting the heat on Boss, meanwhile, to settle up for the loss. *Hunter Von Leer, who was B.D. Calhoun in CBS' "Dallas," among many other roles, plays Harkness' associate Dusty.*

"The Rustlers," October 5, 1979

Mel Tillis plays the Dukes' kin, Burl Tolliver, who has a prizewinner in his horse Manassas. Bo and Luke even time the horse, using the General Lee to clock it at 40 mph, and they agree to help Burl prepare for the race in the Hazzard fair. Boss wants a winning racehorse for his sweet Lulu, so he takes note of Manassas and tries to cut a deal with Burl, using Burl's mortgage as a bargaining chip. He then arranges for a little horsenapping, calling cousin Cletus into service to distract Bo and Luke as Rosco switches out the horse for another. Bo and Luke are blamed when it's realized Manassas is gone. A horse-trader who's been dealing with Boss, Dunlap, has his eye on Manassas, too. So Boss' plans get foiled when his horsenapped horse gets horsenapped again by someone else! Bo and Luke put that together, but not in enough time to avoid being framed again. They do some dealing with Boss to get out of trouble. *Once more, Cletus is in his civvies, lamenting the fact that he's Boss' cousin. Sherry Tolliver is played by the cute-as-a-button Dorothy Collier, who went on, in August 1986, to marry James Best, and who nowadays assists him in his appearances. This episode, like "Granny Annie," "People's Choice" and a few others of the first two seasons, features Daisy's yellow Plymouth Road Runner as opposed to her Jeep, Dixie, which arrives in "The Runaway." We're amused here that the woman whose clothesline Rosco* runs over is named Widow Baxley — that last name is shared by several people behind the scenes of the "Dukes," of course, and would be employed later in a Coy and Vance episode. And speaking of names, Bronson Canyon is mentioned, which in real life is a well-known filming site in California. For some reason, we've always remembered all these years one particular line of Daisy's in this episode, as the boys are racing to get Manassas registered in the race: "A whole lot can happen in a minute." Yep, it can.

"The Meeting," October 12, 1979

The Duke boys are testing out new shocks on the General while Rosco is testing out his new speed radar gun. Syndicate figure Black Jack Bender drops in on his old buddy, Boss ("Curly"). He says he's in the toy business now and needs a safe place to meet with his "associates." Pretty soon, the limos roll in. But as Cooter is polishing the cars, he finds some big-time heat-in-the-seat. The Duke family decides to do a little pokin' around. Bo and Luke smuggle themselves into this big mobster meeting with the catered catfish and champagne dinners. But they hear a little too much and put themselves in danger. They get ushered out for a little "ride," but it's Cooter and Daisy to the rescue. Soon they're scaling the tops of the buildings in town to flee into Cooter's garage (not the first time they've done that!). Now they've got to get to the FBI before the mob gets them, and they have the help of Cletus. Cletus Hogg dons a police uniform to fill in for Enos, who we learn in the next episode is having his appendix removed. Leo Gordon, who plays Devere here, is also Rocky Marlowe in "Deputy Dukes," and he went on to play Sergeant Theodore Kirk in the spinoff "Enos." This is the first time we see Hazzard's switchboard operator, referred to as Mabel in the scenes but Myrtle in the closing credits. This episode features one of those scenes James Best would lament about later — yup, straight into the scummy pond with Rosco. It films great, but we can see why it would've been pretty uncomfortable. Daisy wardrobe note: We'll cede that she's briefly wearing a red checkered shirt here, but it's tucked into her (long!) jeans and neatly buttoned, not haltered! It's worn like a regular shirt and not like "Hee-Haw," in other words. :)

"Road Pirates," October 19, 1979

"Reserve Deputy Sheriff" Cletus Hogg is hanging with the Dukes, trying out some nitrous oxide in his car, while Boss is dealing with Marty Garbade for a $100,000 shipment of TVs. The TVs are hijacked by a bad guy pretending to be from the Hazzard County Sheriff's Department. The finger points to Cletus, and that implicates Bo and Luke, too. To clear themselves, they sneak into the police department and get the info on the ring of hijackers striking the area. It's off to the United Shipping Terminal in Colonial City, where these hijacked shipments are coming from. Bo and Luke decide to hitch a ride in two of the trucks taking shipments through Hazzard that day, with the help of the standard Daisy diversion. The truck that Luke's in gets 'jacked, then Cooter picks up Bo from the other truck so they can go help him. Luke finds himself in a storage barn, which he then has to flee on a motorbike, chased by the hijackers. And yes, there's bike jumping involved. Cletus, with Daisy in her yellow Road Runner, manages to round up the hijackers one by one.

"The Ghost of General Lee," October 26, 1979
The sheriff of Sweetwater County drops off two grimy thugs at the county line, warning them never to set foot in Sweetwater again. The twosome needs some wheels to move on to greener pastures in Cottondale, then they discover Bo and Luke taking a skinny-dippin' nearby. They take off in the General Lee, then drive it into a pond. Rosco and Enos, right behind the General in "hot pursuit," think the Dukes have been killed. Boss promptly uses the opportunity to claim that the Duke boys have stolen his Jefferson Davis-heirloom solid-gold watch. Bo and Luke, meanwhile, are sneaking around the countryside naked, trying to find clothes and get home. Boss delivers the bad news of the boys' death, along with the other bad news of the accusation, to Jesse at the Boar's Nest. But don't worry — the boys get home in time for their own wake, then Jesse and Daisy hide them away. To clear themselves, the boys stage a good old-fashioned haunting, complete with a glowing, ghostly General. *That whole short-shirt-dress thing really works for Bo! This episode is John Schneider's favorite, according to the second-season DVD extras. We love the somber tone after the General goes into the pond — Enos cries, and Rosco is rather speechless. Such a departure from the tone the show had already set.*

"Dukes Meet Cale Yarborough," November 2, 1979
Rosco is chasin' after them Dukes and moves a sign so he can say they went across the state line. Bo and Luke take an out-of-the-way path and encounter famous racecar driver Cale Yarborough. He and his pit boss Chet Garvey are testing out a new turbo-drive method, and they let Bo and Luke take it around the track. The evil Jethro Brothers are after that gizmo, though, so they can win the Illinois 500. Boss Hogg has the Dukes apprehended, but Chet gets them out on bail. The Jethros bug the General Lee to help them get their hands on the technology, then strike up a

"business arrangement" with Boss. Bo, Luke, and Cale then can't figure out how it is that Boss seems to know their every move. As Cale jokes about "adopting" the Duke boys, Luke concocts a plan to fake out Boss Hogg in his roadblocks, painting Cale's Charger and another one just like the General, then leaping over a barricade in the real General. *Mabel Tillingham shows up again on the Hazzard switchboard, again listed as Myrtle in the credits. In an ironic moment in this one, Daisy jokes about how much she loves that flag atop the General. Fave line, Rosco over the CB when Boss hails him: "You're wall to wall, Boss, so go ahead and squall."*

"Hazzard Connection," November 9, 1979
The slippery demo-derby runner Augie Dettweiler is running a scam to smuggle out stolen racecar engines in old jalopies. He gets the Duke boys to unwittingly participate, hiring them via Cooter to deliver some beaten-up clunkers at $35 apiece. Enos spies Bo and Luke doing what he's thinkin' might be breakin' the law. Boss puts a tail on Dettweiler. Over at the farm, both Uncle Jesse and Daisy can tell that Rosco and Enos have their eyes on them. The Dukes realize there must be something fishy going on and decide to try to sting Augie's operation, convincing the scammer to let them drive in the demo derby for him. They first have to earn Augie's trust through a test with the cargo. Then they locate the base of Augie's operation and do a little snooping — and have to fight their way out. *Gerald McRaney of CBS' "Simon & Simon" shows up as a goon who's in on the scam — out-acting the other goons around him, for sure. He was in the running to play Luke Duke.*

"Witness for the Persecution," November 16, 1979
Jesse's old lawman friend Tom Pryor convinces him to let Boss, who's a witness in an important government case, hide out at the Duke farm. The Duke boys, meanwhile, get shot at out near Ned Benson's place by two "city dudes." The dudes turn out to be pursuing our favorite fugitive witness. Rosco, covering for Boss at the office, has no interest in Bo and Luke's tale of getting shot at, and when the boys get home, they see what they're dealing with there! It's not long before they're fleeing the farm with Boss in the back, getting shot at by those city dudes again. Rosco gets full of himself and starts dressing up in white suits — sure to be mistaken for Boss Hogg by those city dudes! Bo, Luke and Cooter realize it and divert the bad guys. Back to getting shot at again. Again. *Love how Jesse's reading the Hazzard County Gazette in this one. Bob Hastings guests as bad guy Barnes. This episode includes BRBTV's favorite "Dukes" scene, when sweet little Daisy*

comes home after a long day at the Boar's Nest, changes into her nightie and unwittingly crawls into bed next to Boss!

"Granny Annie," November 23, 1979

The Dukes do a little work for Granny Annie, and she unknowingly slips 'em some counterfeit cash. She tells them it was left over from her late husband, and they offer to get rid of it for her, but they later discover her with wet ink on her hands, so to speak. Bo and Luke have a talk with her about her new "art" business. Boss has designs on her counterfeiting plates and cuts a deal with Big Jim Downey for them before he even has them in hand, then has Granny Annie thrown in jail, where she enjoys checkers and square dancing with Enos. But just after Boss makes the $50,000 sale to Big Jim, the Duke boys, with the help of B.B. Davenport, do a shuck-'n'-jive to lift the plates. Big Jim then returns to Boss to retrieve his cash, tying up Rosco, who makes a somber CB plea to the Duke boys for help for poor Boss. The Oak Ridge Boys play at the Boar's Nest at the beginning, getting caught in Boss' very first "celebrity speed trap." This is the sole appearance of B.B. Davenport. Frankly, he's adorable. There's a ski car stunt for both the General and Rosco's sheriff's vehicle in this one. In this episode, Al Wyatt Jr. set a jump record in that big one over the train. By the way, our fellow author Brian Lombard notes that the 30-second trailer shown before this episode had a clip not featured in the actual episode. Granny Annie looks at the camera and says "counterfeit!"

"People's Choice," November 30, 1979

Former Hazzard gal T.C. (Thelma Claire) Rogers steps off the bus back in her home county and announces to Bo and Luke that she's going to challenge Boss for the job of supervisory administrator. Boss tries to prevent her official filing by scooting registrar Emery Potter out of town with the means to finally marry Mabel Wooster in Lake Chickamahoney after 12 years of their engagement. The Duke boys intervene, hustling T.C. over to Chickamahoney to get Emery's sig, then hustling Emery back to Hazzard for the official seal. Boss finds a new way to cause trouble — Bo and Luke were supposed to be reporting to their Hazzard probation officer all this time, which is him! Boss also denies T.C. equal airtime for her campaign, so Bo, Luke and Cooter rig it up so Thelma can broadcast over Boss' speech in the town square, then right over his speech on his WHOGG radio station. Boss has the polls closed early and the "election board" men bought and paid for. Poor Emery's wedding to Mabel gets interrupted for the second time when he's called to cast the deciding vote in the election.

"Uncle Boss," December 7, 1980

Get to know Hughie Hogg — that's Nephew Boss to you. He's in town to help Uncle Boss swindle, falsely arrest, jail and otherwise terrorize the Dukes. (So what's new?) Hughie is like a slightly leaner version of Boss, though no less mean, if you know what we mean. He releases the brake on the parked General Lee so it rolls into Boss' convertible outside the Boar's Nest, but that doesn't help his cause. He then decides to set up the boys for charges of grand theft auto. When Rosco comes by the Dukes' barn to uncover the planted auto, Maudine the mule gives him a good swift kick and he doesn't get the car. The one who got the car was Cooter, actually. Daisy, planning to stand up in the wedding of her friends Jeb and Mary Belle, gets caught in the crossfire of Hughie's shenanigans, landing herself in jail. Bo manages to bust her out, but their troubles aren't over. *This episode, and the other appearances that would follow of Hughie and his brother, Dewey, really show the writers' love for pulling kin into the plotlines. This episode is included in the Season 3 DVD set rather than Season 2, though it only aired in Season 3 as a rerun and was originally a Season 2 episode. Elsewhere in this episode guide, we've deferred to the order given in the DVD sets, which varies from the original airdate sources we checked, but with this episode we had to make an exception. As our fellow author Brian Lombard has mentioned (himself an avid "Dukes" fan), DVDs tend to release episodes in production order instead of airdate order, and the episodes often originally air in a different order than they were produced, as noted elsewhere in this guide.*

"Arrest Jesse Duke," December 14, 1979

Jesse gets framed and jailed by Boss and his car-stripping babes, after he was just stopping to see what happened after one of their strippings. Hughie Hogg fills in as acting sheriff for Rosco *(who, we're told, is getting a refresher course at the police academy in Atlanta)*. As Boss decides he better arrest the rest of that vicious car-strippin' "Duke gang," the babes set up the boys so that the General Lee gets stripped, too! The three cousins decide to investigate that fishy new auto-parts store in town, and the women catch them in the act. The car-stripping foursome is breathing fire back at Boss' office. Meanwhile, Hughie catches on that his Uncle Boss is holding out on him in his partnership with the gals, who, of course, get the upper hand on Boss, anyway. But not before the Dukes set out a little bait to zip up the strippers, so to speak, and outfit the General for off-roading. *Hughie Hogg is quite bumbling in this one; he gets considerably more suave and cunning later. Bo and Luke drive the Dixie Jeep in this one, though it won't be given to Daisy until "The Runaway." Further testament that this ep was shot after the next couple: The opening of this episode features some new shots over the music, such as Daisy shoving Boss out of her bed from "Witness for the Persecution," and it also features a new tagline at the very end of Boss saying, "Them Dukes! Them Dukes!"*

"Duke of Duke," January 4, 1980
Gaylord Duke of London, England, third cousin to the Dukes, blows into town in a fast and fancy car that even bests the General Lee. Seems he's inherited property that goes back in the Hazzard family, the old Henshaw place. Trouble is, Boss has already planned to foreclose on the property for back taxes so he can sell it for a purty price to the Dixie King supermarket chain. He arranges for Rosco and Enos to keep Bo, Luke and Gaylord busy (painting road signs) until the taxes are due. The three cousins slip away, of course. While Daisy takes a shine to the Brit (in-between tempting poor Enos with the "thighs" and "legs" of her fried chicken), Jesse smells a rat as Gaylord mentions family members. Sure enough, this "cousin" is a con, Jesse learns when he sends a telegram to the real cousins. The real Gaylord Duke had his important papers come up missing, just as this con man got out of prison. *L.B. Davenport makes a rare appearance. Boss is shown trying to work out, first with an exercise bike, then with weights.*

"The Runaway," January 11, 1980
Powerful business magnate C.J. Holmes has forbid his daughter Suzy from marrying "just a farmer," so the pretty blond runs away from the hired goons who are watching her (actually escorting her to leave on a cruise). Where Suzy ends up is the backseat of the General, and who ends up chasing them are Rosco and Boss. The Duke family helps out by hiding Suzy away. Boss is seeing dollar signs if he can get C.J. Holmes' daughter back to him. Holmes' goons drop by the switchboard offices and bribe some info out of Mabel, then head over to the Duke farm. Daisy zooms off with Suzy and helps her get away. Boss trumps up kidnapping charges on Bo and Luke. Later, mechanic L.B. Davenport hides out the Duke boys and Suzy at his shop. C.J. Holmes himself arrives to sort this matter. At the end, C.J. graciously replaces Daisy's yellow Plymouth Road Runner (which went over a cliff — yikes) with Dixie, the cute little Jeep. *Mabel Tillingham may be a young, pretty blond, but she's sure taking after her kin J.D. Hogg by being so easily bribed by C.J. Holmes' goons. L.B. Davenport is shown working at the same garage, and driving the same truck, as Cooter. So is L.B. a cousin of Cooter's like B.B. or what? Inquiring minds want to know!*

"Follow That Still," January 18, 1980

The Bureau of Alcohol, Tobacco and Firearms is after old Hard Luck Jones, who just can't seem to cure himself of brewin' up his distinctive moonshine. The Dukes try to help him stay on this side of the law, but Hard Luck's not much into growing crops right now. Boss, meanwhile, is working on the J.D. Hogg War Memorial and trying to cut a deal with contraband cigarettes. Soon, Hard Luck's still ends up on the Duke farm, inside an armored personnel carrier *(yes, a tank)* from the war memorial, putting the boys in danger. Hard Luck decides to turn himself in, but then Rosco and Enos run off to chase the tracks of the tank. The Dukes get themselves all loaded up in a tank with Hard Luck, trying to unload that hot still, as the law is in "hot pursuit" — including Agent Buchanon of the ATF. *L.B. Davenport three episodes in a row? Yup, he again lends a hand, on and off the CB, much like Cooter Davenport does in other episodes.*

"Treasure of Hazzard," January 25, 1980

Just as Sheriff Lester Crabbe, a traveling lawman who can make flowers wilt, arrives to fill in for Rosco, Professor Laura Bardsley comes to Hazzard seeking a rumored buried Yankee payroll strongbox from the Civil War. Much to Boss' chagrin, Sheriff Crabbe gives her the tip that the Dukes have been around a long time and might know more about this. Luke likes the looks of that lady, while Bo wrestles a gator underwater to save her life *(a great — and very real — scene nearly marred by the atrocious fake background behind the Dukes in the boat)*. As they make their way to where the strongbox may be, Bo gets snared by Jeb McCobb's very sheltered and rambunctious granddaughters. A couple dastardly types are following Professor Bardsley, and they scoop down and seize the strongbox once the Dukes finally dig it up, after a trip to Colonial City and the historical society. Boss, meanwhile, takes the bait on the fake treasure map the Dukes devised, thinking the treasure is actually buried under the Boar's Nest. *Sheriff Lester Crabbe fills in for Rosco while he's "at the police academy"; James Best took several episodes off in his own unofficial protest of issues with the show. Male viewers are treated to Daisy in a mudfight with the female dastardly type. For the second time, Willow Creek is mentioned in a "Dukes" episode. "Dukes" fans will remember John Schneider and Tom Wopat reuniting in the 1987 TV movie "Christmas Comes to Willow Creek" (though that was a different Willow Creek!).*

"Officer Daisy Duke," February 1, 1980

Boss fires Daisy from her Boar's Nest job when she (with the help of Bo and Luke) dares to ask for a raise. Undaunted, she trains up and gets a job as a deputy, fair and square, in the Hazzard County Sheriff's Department. The housework is left in Bo and Luke's not-so-capable hands as Daisy is out working her new job — even enjoying the pleasure of ticketing Boss Hogg's car. The new temporary sheriff, Grady Byrd, fumbles and bumbles (a lot like somebody else we know) as he nabs a couple bank robbers, Floyd Baker and Molly Harmon, for the $10,000 in reward money, but then they escape from the jail. Even though Boss has had Grady reassign Daisy to indoor work like mopping, Daisy chases 'em fugitives down, with her two ever-helpful and ever-protective cousins following behind, and amid a tender moment with Enos. She gets commended for the catch. *In this episode and one other, Dick Sargent fills in for Rosco as Grady Byrd. We love how Catherine Bach's demeanor is so calm and reserved as Daisy is in her officer's uniform.*

"Find Loretta Lynn," February 8, 1980

Boss Hogg's slightly unethical roadway detour is enough to get Loretta Lynn's RV into Hazzard, and it's also enough to make a trio of swindlers a little nervous about the job they were going to pull there. They arrive at the Boar's Nest and do a little trash-talking with the Dukes — Luke, in particular — as Cooter and Bo fix Loretta's under-the-weather RV. Pretty soon, the swindlers have hijacked one celebrity singer and her RV, and the Dukes are on the chase — er, we mean, case. Boss claims it was the Dukes who kidnapped the star. Loretta drops out the RV window a trail of 8-by-10 glossies to follow, then creates a diversion of interest in their own music so her road manager can run off. Pretty crafty, that gal. Her manager makes it to the Duke farm, where Daisy dons a Loretta-like outfit as part of a plan. And, of course, Loretta performs at the Boar's Nest at the end. *Enos returns from getting his appendix removed (see "The Meeting"), and this episode predates the one where Daisy gets Dixie, as she's still got the yellow Plymouth Road Runner here. It takes a jump, too.*

"Jude Emery," February 15, 1980

Bo and Luke are changing a flat on the General lickity-split when along comes Texas Ranger Jude Emery, who's looking for a wanted man, Russel "Snake" Harmon. The Dukes try to help Emery out with a ride, but he gets wrongly hauled in by Sheriff Grady Byrd. Emery gets himself out of that mess, then enlists the aid of the Duke boys to catch his man and his man's contraband gang. But Snake is onto them. The Dukes shuck-'n'-jive a couple degenerate rivals, Willie and Patch Loring, who think they're shuckin'-'n'-jivin' them back. They're in league with Snake, and they put Bo and Luke to the test. Eventually, a fistfight ensues! And a little arm-wrestling. Then Daisy steps in undercover. And somehow it all works out in the end. *A touch of drama plays well for this episode, as Daisy takes a rather strong shine to Jude. C. Pete Munro, the guy who plays Willie, happened to star as Cooter in the "Moonrunners" movie, and he played Detective Bigelow in "Enos," as well.*

"Return of the Ridge Raiders," February 22, 1980

Jesse has been actin' awful strange lately, getting all kinds of phone calls and disappearing to parts unknown. The Duke boys try to solve the mystery, and it's all about Boss planning to take state funds from the proposed senior citizens' center to build his new "Playpen" club. The aging Ridge Raiders, including a reluctant Jesse, have secretly regrouped to take matters into their own hands and stop him. When Boss' stuff starts getting dynamited, Boss of course blames Bo and Luke. And when Jesse stops by the telephone office but doesn't agree to have Bo or Luke ask out Mabel, she goes and snitches to her cousin Boss Hogg about him. Bo and Luke visit their reporter friend Coop the Snoop to help, and Amos' old fire engine lends a hand in the action, too. *Sheriff Buster Moon takes over for Rosco, and Daisy shows up in a pink piggy suit a la Playboy to help Boss host his Hazzard beauty pageant. Coop the Snoop is introduced as Charlie in one scene but listed as Virgil in the episode's credits. Different variations of a newspaper friend of the Duke boys named "Coop," "Scoop," "Cooper" or "the Snoop" were utilized during the series.*

BRBTV got the chance to chat with James Hampton, who played Sheriff Buster Moon, at MegaCon in Orlando, Florida, in March 2011. The Oklahoma City-born actor, who filled in as sheriff in Hazzard while Rosco P. Coltrane was out in 1980, has a long list of screen credits that include "F Troop," "The Doris Day Show" and "Gunsmoke," as well as a newer project called "The Association."

"Mason Dixon's Girls," February 29, 1980

Private investigator Mason Dixon and his lovely "associates" Samantha Rose and Tinker Churchill have all kinds of cool toys with their RV as they try to crack a case of Mary-J.-Wanna smuggling at a former copper mine atop Razorback Mountain. They enlist the aid of the Duke boys, in whose General some marijuana was found after they had picked up what they thought was a new hot water heater in town. After shaking the law (as usual), Bo and Luke sneak onto the old mine site in disguise but get caught. Sam and Tinker come to help them but get caught, too. The foursome breaks away, and Luke gets to go hang-gliding with Sam. They land to sabotage the truck that's carrying the bad substance, sending an explosion of bits-o-pot all over the county. Includes a rare glimpse of Cooter's farm. Gotta love the '70s tube socks Sam and Tinker wear as they scale the mountain. Morgan Woodward stars as a bad guy, and James Best returns as Rosco after five episodes of replacement sheriffs (though they were not aired in the order they were shot). And isn't it ironic that for Rosco's first episode back, his sheriff's car is right back in that lake! This episode helps show why the 2005 "Dukes" movie contradicted many of the values expressed in the "Dukes" episodes. Whereas the movie shows Jesse partaking in it, this episode shows the Dukes opposing a marijuana operation.

"R.I.P. Henry Flatt," March 14, 1980

Directed by Denver Pyle.
A spooky shortcut home through the cemetery for the three cousins unearths the supposedly dead Henry Flatt, who snookered Boss Hogg out of $20,000 last year. They learn this con man did his con to build a youth center in Capitol City, where young folks like his lovely gymnast daughter Gail *(played by Audrey Landers)* can hang out and build their athletic skill. Boss Hogg has plans, meanwhile, for a new housing development, Hogg's Heavenly Acres, on the land that now houses "dead" Henry's grave. Because he wants to stay "dead," Henry snatches himself somebody else's body from the morgue. Pretty soon, ole Rosco is on the case of the body-snatchin'. Bo and Luke have to ditch the evidence. They manage to bury the body — and Henry Flatt, so to speak — and even honor him as a "war hero." *Tom Wopat gets to sing in this one.*

"Southern Comfurts," March 21, 1980

The Comfurts, second cousins of the Dukes twice removed, sell their farm for a cool quarter mill, then lavish fabulous gifts on the Dukes. Boss sees the Comfurts' good fortune and plans to scam them. When their new Rolls breaks down, they take it to Cooter's and get a gray sedan loaner. But when Lori and the boys wander off — after Lori has placed the suitcase holding all their cash in the trunk of the sedan — a drunk comes along and takes off in the car. Boss hears the cash has been swiped and goes after the car, too. It changes hands a few times and ends up with some bank robbers. Boss ends up with the bank robbers, too — at gunpoint. *The General gets a temporary green paint job (as a disguise), and Jesse tries to console his cousin Holly about losing track of that cash. But they do get it back. Edward Edwards, who plays John Henry Comfurt, also is Fred Andrews in "The Runaway."*

Now THAT'S worth it! Gy Waldron discusses the ever intriguing Duke family tree in the third-season DVD set.

Season 3

"Carnival of Thrills," Part 1, September 16, 1980
The Dukes attend the Carnival of Thrills show in Cedar City, where they see a car jump go bad. The next stop for the tour is Hazzard, and the lovely owner of the show, Diane Benson *(played by soap-opera favorite Robin Mattson)* is in need of a new stunt driver. That country boy Bo Duke looks pretty good to her. And she looks real good to him. She woos him into entering a stunt-driving demonstration, goads him into signing on to a

dangerous 32-car jump in the General Lee for her Carnival of Thrills, then talks it up around town and sells lots of tickets. Luke sees through Diane's charm, though, figurin' out what her interest is in a country boy like Bo, and Cooter and Daisy don't want Bo to make this jump, either. The Dukes have to rescue the General from the impound yard, but then it comes to blows between the two boys. *Those blessed Duke boys get to take off their shirts again in this one. Boss, meanwhile, is shown trying to lift weights and use a rowing machine, in order to drop a pound or two for his predicted ownership of the Carnival of Thrills show.*

"Carnival of Thrills, Part 2," September 16, 1980

When the Duke fists stop flying, Bo leaves the farm and heads to Diane's RV. Soon, though, each of the boys is arrested for different trumped-up charges by Rosco and Enos, and the feudin' cousins end up sharing a cell. Diane's partner Carl bails out Bo, and Jesse and Daisy raise the cash for Luke. Jesse gives Luke a good talking-to forthwith. An insurance agent then blows into town, and the Dukes learn that the others who've tried this dangerous 32-car jump for the Carnival of Thrills failed by no accident. But bull-headed Bo won't necessarily listen to reason. Finally, the sabotage is exposed, and Luke is by Bo's side in the General Lee as he takes the jump for real, once the danger is removed. *What a way to start out the third season, with a powerful two-parter that's well-remembered by fans. We've even seen a replica of the Carnival of Thrills car at "Dukes" events.*

"Enos Strate to the Top," November 5, 1980

Daisy takes some snapshots of Jesse in front of a bank in Atlanta, and they find out later that the photos include some robbers! No wonder those guys in the big sedan tried to run them off the road! Deputy Enos, who decides he'd like to make a name for himself, is on the case. He's fed up with Boss' dirty tricks and wants to have some self-respect (and Boss just fired him). The bank robbers follow Jesse and Daisy home and menace them there, then manage to kidnap Daisy. Bo and Luke show Rosco the developed photos, but he's not interested in believing their story about the robbers. As he steps in, Enos gets a little help from the Duke boys, but he also attracts the attention of some big-city lawmen. *This episode served as the launch-point for the short-lived spinoff, "Enos." In this episode, we also officially meet the dog that kicks major butt for charm and personality (and fine acting), Flash, and that sweet little Miz Tisdale. Not only does the General jump multiple times in this episode, one of those times is right onto the sedan of the bad guys!*

"The Hazzardville Horror," November 7, 1980

A couple thieves lift Boss Hogg's prized silver collection, and Boss, of course, decides to blame the Dukes. A pal of the Dukes, Mary Lou Pringle, comes to town to see if she can sell the old home of her deceased uncle, Hezekiah Pringle. When she visits the house, though, she's creeped out by flying objects. When the Dukes investigate, they find it's no haunting — and they suspect that the same culprits who stole the silver have taken up residence in the old house for some silver-smeltin'. They find a secret passage downstairs, but then the perps return to the house. Bo gets conked on the head, and even when Rosco and Cletus catch up to the action, they still don't believe it wasn't the Dukes that stole the silver! *Tammy Wynette gets caught in the celebrity speed trap. Cletus is featured prominently, as is our beloved Flash! We talked to Morgan Brittany, who plays Mary Lou Pringle in New Jersey in 2012, and she remembers her "Dukes" episode fondly. It was where she met her husband — Jack Gill, one of the show's stunt drivers.*

"And in This Corner, Luke Duke," November 14, 1980

Luke helps move the mammoth $3,000 mirror Boss Hogg has added to the Boar's Nest, and some greasy out-of-towners decide that boy sure is a strapping one. One of them, Catfish, picks a fight with Luke and gets him landed in the slammer, then the other cuts a deal with Boss to arrange a boxing match for some cash between Catfish and Luke. Boss threatens the Duke farm to make sure Luke is signed on. So after some soul-searching, Luke starts training for the big fight. Then Luke disappears. But he still makes it to the fight. So he starts duking it out in the ring, gets knocked to the ground, but gets back up. *Daisy gets to take a crack (so to speak) at the country's most beloved — and most difficult — song, our national anthem. Oh, and the General? He gets to fly right through a barn. Tom Wopat trained with real-life boxer Sonny Shields, who plays Catfish, a couple days for this episode. "It was hard work," he says in the Season 3 DVD commentary. "I had a headache for two weeks." Especially since Shields would keep hitting after the director yelled "Cut!"*

"The Late J.D. Hogg," November 21, 1980

Boss is busy trying to foreclose on the Duke farm, as usual, having Cletus stall the Dukes so they can't get to the bank in time, then wrongly accusing them of breaking into his bank, but then Doc Carney tells Boss he only has two weeks to live. Boss and Jesse drink to old times, and the two drive around town as Boss goes on a binge of benevolence. The farm is safe again, until the doctor realizes the lab result was somebody else's and tries to call Boss back with the good news. Two shady types, meanwhile, have stolen the car of one of Bo and Luke's buddies, so they chase 'em down in the General. When Boss finally gets the doc's new news, he (of course!) tries to "undo" all his good deeds. He goes after the mail truck that's carrying the nice letters he mailed, but the mail truck done got stolen by the two shady types. The Dukes inadvertently help the mail truck stay stolen, at least for a little while. BRBTV favorite scene: Flash takes a little ride, cuddled under her seatbelt like a good doggie, in Rosco's runaway squad car — which chases Rosco down a hill! *In this one and in "Baa, Baa White Sheep," Rosco refers to Flash as he, something that would change in later episodes. Dennis Haskins of "Saved by the Bell" makes his second of four appearances in the episodes here, playing a customer (thanks to our buddy Brian Lombard, author of the "Bradypalooza" guide to "The Brady Bunch," for pointing that out to us!).*

"Baa, Baa White Sheep," December 5, 1980
Boss' twin brother, Abraham Lincoln Hogg, whom he had declared legally dead five years ago, is sweet and upstanding and believes in the good of every human being, clad all in black and riding in a black Caddy convertible. He comes to town for the reading of their great-aunt's will, in which he happens to share a property deed (for property that Boss happens to have already sold). Flash even likes Abe, whereas she can't stand ole Boss. In between charging Luke in the bad-check-writin' of Benny the Quill (and Daisy's bout in the quicksand), that rascally J.D. tries to swindle Abe out of his share by framing him for crimes in Finchburg and having his signature forged. But at the reading of the will, Boss doesn't get away with posing as Abe. There's just one sweet little soul that knows the difference between 'em, without a doubt! *Bo is off with the Marine Corps Reserve for this one, by the way. One of BRBTV's two favorite episodes! Especially since Flash gets to save the day! Did you ever wonder who narrated the 30-second trailer seen before each episode (it wasn't Waylon). It was actor Ted Gehring, who appears in this episode (and "A Baby for the Dukes") as Judge Druten.*

"Mrs. Rosco P. Coltrane," December 12, 1980
Rosco meets the lovely little Sue Ann Bliss through a computer dating service, and she pops in from Haleyville for a visit, putting the heat on him to get married. He doesn't know that she has plans that go beyond him: She's part of a gang that aims to swindle Boss out of a lot of cash. More specifically, it's a payroll delivery he's expecting from Atlanta the next day.

The Duke boys, meanwhile, have gotten the General run off the road and flipped by a couple slimy types. (And wouldn't you know it, those seemingly unrelated elements are, quite frankly, related!) Amid initial protests from his mother and Boss, Rosco makes quick wedding plans, and Lulu even steps in to help, but then the Dukes dig into his intended's background. *This episode features some nice glimpses into the character of Rosco: a rare appearance of Mama Coltrane (though in the previous episode we did get to see Rosco's mailbox that lists "and Mother"), as well as Bo's fabulous phone imitation of Rosco, which he'll repeat for "Sky Bandits Over Hazzard," and the mention of what the "P" in Rosco's name stands for, as Sue Ann calls her fiancé by it. Also, Rosco gives his age as 40 here. On his office door, interestingly, his first name is misspelled with an "e" on the end. Once again, Flash is referred to as a boy here.*

"The Great Santa Claus Chase." December 19, 1980
Directed by Denver Pyle.
Bo and Luke are transporting Christmas trees in a truck from Central City when they stop to investigate a laundry bag in the road. Inside is a man with a gun, who, with his buddy, ties them up and hijacks their shipment. Then a crook disguised as a reverend (and under Boss' employ), gives them a lift into town, and promptly frames them for their own hijacking! Word gets around Hazzard, and the boys are feelin' pretty low. But after Jesse bails them out of the pokey, they see that Boss has brought a shipment of trees into town (to sell!) that they discover were their own meant for the Scouts, and they know something's up but just can't prove it. They try to turn things around by posing as Scrooge's Christmas ghosts during Boss' naptime, with great voicework by the trio of cousins, though that doesn't work. The three bad guys are lifting cash from Boss' safe. Wearing Santa Claus suits. And did we mention that Bo, Luke and Cooter are dressed as Santa, too? They're determined those Christmas trees are going to get to the right places. When things finally get sorted out, there's just something about that whole Scrooge tale that strikes a chord with Boss, and he makes a surprise appearance at a Duke house full of holiday cheer. *You get to see ole Cooter as a Scout leader in this one. And Heavens to Betsy — Bo and Luke actually wear some different shirts in the final scene! We love a Christmas episode! Wish they would've done one every year! And just to give another Flash gender update: The lovable little hound seems to have adopted her new gender in this one; Rosco refers to her as a "her."*

BEHIND THE SCENES

> "Two years before 'The Dukes of Hazzard' started, I was 245 pounds with a 44-inch waist."
>
> — John Schneider, on TV-now.com

"Good Neighbors, Duke," January 2, 1981
There's something a little unusual about Adam Venable and his daughter Esther, who are new to town and just bought the Gaylord farm. Two bad guys are secretly tailing them, for one thing. The Duke boys do a little diggin' in the back issues of the newspaper and learn about a case of stolen diamonds. Adam asks Daisy to hang onto a briefcase that he values, and two thugs try to shake her down for it. The Dukes wonder just what's in that briefcase, and Adam reveals that his real name is Josiah Benson and he and his daughter have been in the government's relocation program and have been tailed by bounty hunters. The Dukes decide that faking the Venables' deaths will make the thugs stay away. Boss, meanwhile, hears a rumor about uranium and wants the mineral rights of the Gaylord farm. He builds a toll bridge that proves largely ineffective, though he manages to catch Hoyt Axton in the celebrity speed trap.

"State of the County," January 9, 1981
The Duke boys are off to get the tax return in the mail for Uncle Jesse, as Daisy is making the kind acquaintance of a handsome stranger, Earl Becket. Then, J.W. Hickman of Clarence County is trying to shake down Boss, who's only concerned about his State of the County speech. Hickman's handy-dandy henchman, it turns out, is Daisy's new friend, who handily lifts the check to the IRS out of the General. Daisy gets Earl a job at Cooter's, and a bomb goes off in Boss' office at the Boar's Nest, and Boss frames Bo and Luke for it. Boss is also trying to deal with a driver who's hauling electric typewriters for him. Bo and Luke try to clue Daisy in about Earl, but she has to find out about Earl on her own. He holds her hostage, as a bomb is rigged to explode all over Boss' anticipated speech. *The Oak Ridge Boys get caught in the celebrity speed trap for a second time.*

"The Legacy," January 16, 1981

The Dukes run into Uncle Jesse's former sweetheart Lucinda Meadows, who has a message from her late husband for Jesse — a message that leads the Dukes to the old Rainbow Mine. Cletus is named acting sheriff while Rosco is out of town with Flash for "obedience training," and Wilbur Fudge, the county controller, is made acting deputy. Bo and Luke find nine full barrels of 'shine at the bottom of the mine, and Lucinda decides that since it's aged so badly, its only value is in a sale to Boss, who reneged on his age-old I.O.U. to Lucinda's husband Cyrus. He jumps at the offer to buy so much 'shine, even at $600 a barrel, then arranges to resell it to Mean Joe Hatcher at a nice profit, plotting, meanwhile, to catch the Duke boys delivering the 'shine to him and violating their parole. Boss sends Cletus skulking around the Dukes farm to plant a tracker on the General, then rushes over to bust 'em. *A sheriff's car is actually sawed in half for this one; interesting trick. Kinda matches the fact that Boss Hogg chops in half the stack of $5,400 in bills he pledges to Lucinda for the 'shine. Jesse mentions his wife who passed away as Martha, a bit of continuity that would be contradicted in a future episode.*

"Duke vs. Duke," January 23, 1981

Boss Hogg's first Hazzard Derby sets the boys a-racin' — Bo is hot to get the General Lee through the finish line first, but Cooter has a cool, new souped-up car with a Cale Yarborough engine. When Cooter is injured after a little test race with the boys, Bo and Luke are then squaring off for the race, while Boss has entered Rosco and placed a $10,000 bet on him to win with the infamous Ma Harper and her boys, Billy Gene, Billy Boy and Junior. Ma comes to Hazzard to look into things a bit, shuckin'-'n'-jivin' Cooter to lift his cool car. Meanwhile, Daisy has overheard Boss telling Rosco about how anybody who loses the race surrenders their car ownership to Boss (part of the fine print of the sign-up agreement). Boss has arranged for a secret weapon for Rosco's car: nitrous oxide. Bo and Luke learn, once again, they're much better riding in the same car. So who wins the derby? Well, everybody, really! *Stunt man Al Wyatt Jr. plays Junior Harper.*

"My Son, Bo Hogg," January 30, 1981

What could be more preposterous than a Hogg and a Duke related? When our Bo hits his head on a log and gets amnesia, Boss decides it could be profitable to claim the sweet blond boy is his son. Boss then sends his new "son" on a 'shine run, since he's got C.V. Gumble desperately requesting a shipment into Chickasaw and willing to pay much more than the going rate. And Chickasaw does have that really mean sheriff, after all. So pretty soon he's taking Bo under his wing, feeding him hog jowls and such, while the Dukes are wondering where Bo went. Boss also brainwashes Bo against that awful Duke family, just as Luke and Daisy search all the back roads for their cousin. When the cousins see him, he wants nothing to do with them and hurries off. The Dukes spot Bo again, with Boss, and wonder what on earth is going on. Then they have to chase their cousin down before he reaches the Chickasaw County line with a load of 'shine. *We get introduced to that wonderfully intimidating Sheriff Ed Little in this one — and even get a brief glimpse at his daughter as he writes her a ticket! Don Pedro Colley does have a daughter in real life, and we can tell ya, from hearing him talk, that he treasures her much more! In this one we also get Luke's fab imitation of Boss Hogg over the CB (seriously).*

"To Catch a Duke," February 6, 1981
Directed by Denver Pyle.
A husband-and-wife thievery team, $200,000 worth of jewels in their possession, blow into town with a broken fan belt and hang out awhile as Cooter fixes it up. They get caught "osculating" in public by Rosco, whom, along with Cletus, Boss has sent out on a ticket-writing frenzy to generate some revenue for the coffers. As Rosco is processing the paperwork at the courthouse, Flash takes a potty break outside and finds the robbers' pouch of jewels, forcing Boss to oust Rosco from his job. The Dukes have also fallen prey to the ticket blitz — and have been implicated in the jewel theft. Rosco and Flash try to adjust to life without the uniform, no longer even welcome at the Boar's Nest. Bo and Luke finally use some dangerous driving and an open CB channel to clear themselves. *Daisy does not appear in this episode (visiting Aunt Kate for a couple days).*

"Along Came a Duke," February 13, 1981
Boss is mighty proud of his Stonewall Jackson Day, and he secures a "loan" of the famous general's sword for his bank's display. The curator of the Atlanta Museum is impressed by the hospitality of the Duke boys (they just saved him from two ruffians on the road) and taps them to transport the special sword. Boss wears a Confederate uniform like a Butterball turkey as he wheels and deals with fence Beauregard Mason to sell the sword he's "borrowing" from the museum. Those two ruffians from the road were really his hired thugs. Bo and Luke battle a sick radiator in the General on their journey with the sword, in addition to the ruffians — again. Long-lost cousin Jeb Stuart Duke then rides his dirt bike onto the scene to help. When Bo and Luke deliver the sword to Boss, he switches it with a fake and

accuses them of stealing the real one. The Dukes decide to get an upper hand by having Jeb pose as Mason's son, to cut the deal with Boss.

"By-Line, Daisy Duke," February 20, 1981

Bo and Luke encounter a road-hogging truck while they're strolling along in the General, not knowing the truck is hauling another stolen tractor in a recent rash of them. Daisy, meanwhile, is moonlighting at the Hazzard County Gazette to earn some money for modeling school, to help her future singing career, of course. She's sent off to cover a meeting regarding the tractor thefts. And who's secretly behind the thefts? You guessed it. Bo and Luke are accused of stealing the tractors (when Boss arranges for the evidence to be planted right behind the Duke barn!), and as such, they're caught right in the crosshairs … of Daisy's camera lens. But Daisy gets the real story after the Dukes make Boss think his tractor-thieving partners have double-crossed him. *Dottie West gets caught in the celebrity speed trap, and Boss is exercising but still gaining weight. "Little House on the Prairie" fans will recognize Farmer Perkins as Kevin Hagen, who portrayed Doc Baker. The Duke boys appear shirtless early on in the episode. How many times has that happened now? Not that we're complaining …*

"The Return of Hughie Hogg," March 6, 1981

After the donation of a new fire engine, and a little car-chasin' through the back roads, the Internal Revenue Service drops in on Boss with some threatening news. Boss' darling nephew cons him into signing over his assets to pass the IRS' inspection. Hughie is certainly just running a scam, and Bo and Luke spy Hughie talking on the sly to this "IRS agent." Lulu's skinny sister Hortense drops in to keep an eye on Boss while Lulu is at the "fat farm." Bo and Luke get locked up on trumped-up charges, and they shyster Cletus to escape, but then they get caught again, but then Rosco helps them escape when Hughie tries to jail him, too! Hughie starts taking over the town, renaming everything after himself. Boss and the Dukes unite to take on their common enemy, sending Daisy in for a little distractionary measure. *The Oak Ridge Boys are making a habit of that speed-trap thing. We get to see a sheriff's car jump through a wagon full of hay in this one, as well as two sheriff's cars jumping right at each other in midair, and we get to hear Bo refer to Hughie as a "pint-sized polecat." Love it.*

"Bye, Bye Boss," March 13, 1981
Directed by Denver Pyle.
Bo and Luke are heading into town for some screen for Uncle Jesse's farmwork when they're hijacked by escaped convict Digger Jackson and tied up by the roadside. The convict then robs Homer Griggs' general store, and as Homer sees the General drive away, he (of course!) thinks it's the boys. Bo and Luke get a lift into town from the moonshine-swigging Hobie Harkens, just as Cletus gets the order from Rosco to get them Duke boys. Boss hears about Digger's escape and realizes he's come after him, as Boss helped put him away a decade ago. Lulu tries to help calm poor J.D.'s nerves, but then Digger takes him hostage. Jesse helps Lulu take up a collection in town when she can't get to J.D.'s funds. The Duke cousins do a little horse-ridin', since the con has the General Lee. *A quite grumpy Freddy Fender gets caught in the celebrity speed trap. Maybe he's grumpy because his first name is misspelled on the poster at the Boar's Nest.*

"The Great Hazzard Hijack," March 27, 1981
Bo and Luke find $1,000 in cold, hard cash in the creek, and soon Luke's ole Marine buddy Phil Ackley comes a-calling with his sister Kate and friend Tom Dunkirk. They say that Kate was wrongly accused of stealing this cash, which was part of the haul of an armored truck heist, and that some weird types have been following Kate. The Dukes offer to help the trio find the rest of the cash. Luke gets sweet on Kate, but Jesse sees these "siblings" Kate and Phil kissing. Jesse does a little digging into this armored car heist that took place five years ago and finds out Phil and his friends were the hijackers, and that Kate's real name is Sandra Rhodes. He confronts "Kate," while Bo and Luke are out at the creek helping Phil look for the cash. Luke starts to get a little suspicious of his buddy. Then they find the rest of the cash. *This storyline was no doubt inspired by the real-life case of D.B. Cooper. The celebrity-speed-trapped Roy Orbison performs his famous "Pretty Woman" with Daisy perched nearby. That ruggedly handsome Sam Melville, who stars as Tom in this episode, also plays Snake in "Jude Emery" and Rick in "Happy Birthday, General Lee."*

"The Hack of Hazzard," April 3, 1981
The Dukes fill in for Miz Tisdale's taxi business while she visits her mother, and they actually get a fare (a rarity in Hazzard) — they pick up two out-of-towners whose car has broken down. The two guys are carrying a $100,000 gold bank certificate, and when they see Rosco skulking around writing tickets, they get nervous and leave the certificate in the backseat of the

taxi. It then finds its way into Cooter's mail after Bo and Luke have to take out the backseat to be reupholstered. Rosco, of course, locks up the boys in suspicion of stealing the gold certificate (and he and Boss try a dramatic "interrogation" with bright light at the jail), then try to reclaim it from the cracked upholstery of the taxi's backseat, which is then being fixed over at Uncle Charlie's upholstering shop. The two goons check with Cooter and learn the certificate went out with the mail. And who's carrying the mail? Miss Daisy, filling in for Miz Tisdale's job at the post office! *James Best's daughter JoJami appears in this one.*

"The Canterbury Crock," April 10, 1981

The Dukes' friend Emma Partridge is having a barn sale of her late husband's "junk," because she's got to meet the mortgage. When she doesn't get any good offers, she sells the whole lot to Boss Hogg for a low sum. Among the items left over is a vase her husband bought in Canterbury, England, which no one at first realizes came from ancient Egypt. Daisy buys that one. Two out-of-towners, Beckman and Maury, show an interest in the vase, offering a cool grand to Emma for that piece of "junk," and it changes hands more times than the Dukes, Boss Hogg or these out-of-town swindlers can imagine (most of the time under the camouflage of some pretty flowers Daisy picked!). Boss accuses the Dukes of passing counterfeit bills, and Bo and Luke get shot at by Beckman and Maury. Cletus wants a raise from Rosco, meanwhile, and Cooter wears a snazzy three-piece suit for his birthday. Bo and Luke look into the history of this vase with Miss Emma, learning it has a connection with Cleopatra. They wheel and deal with Boss before revealing the crock's location to him. *With Luke behind the wheel, the General chases Rosco's sheriff's car — backward.*

Tom Wopat, John Schneider and Catherine Bach offer commentary on the "Double Dukes" episode on the fourth-season DVD set.

Season 4

"Mrs. Daisy Hogg," October 9, 1981

Jonathan Frakes blows into town as Boss' baby brother's boy Jamie Lee Hogg of Atlanta in a riveting episode of love and heartbreak. *(Four stars! Sob!)* He takes a liking to Daisy's fire, as she calls him to task for the fact that Bo and Luke are being blamed for a crash with his car. Jamie Lee drops the charges against the boys. Soon, he and Daisy are inseparable, and Boss and Uncle Jesse work from each side trying to break them up. Luke even calls his buddy Norman ("Scoop") Scroggs at the Atlanta paper for the goods on the silver-tongued Jamie Lee, who, despite the fact that he cut a deal with Uncle Jefferson on the grits mill in Hazzard just to smuggle funny-money inside the grits, really has fallen in love with Daisy. The heavies he's working with are none too happy about that. When Daisy spots some of the funny-money, Jamie Lee decides that the most savory way to protect his interests is to marry her, so she can't testify against him. The announcement at the Boar's Nest goes over about as well as a mouthful of root canals, as Waylon puts it. *What a way to start off the fourth season — BRBTV's very favorite episode!!!!*

"Double Dukes," October 16, 1981

Two creepy guys, Turk and Moody, stir up some trouble at the Boar's Nest when they hit on Daisy. Cooter doesn't like that, and neither do Bo and Luke. Fists fly. Come to find out, Boss has hired the gruesome twosome to pose as Bo and Luke in clever peel-away masks, and rob an armored truck! Turk and Moody capture Bo and Luke after a little car chase. They rob the armored truck right there in broad daylight in Hazzard, in front of bunch of people, framing the Dukes — even with a duplicate of the General (only, its doors open!!!). Daisy, Cooter and Jesse witness this and take off after the boys, then encounter the real boys, who have no idea why ole Rosco is pinching Luke's cheek like it's going to come off. Soon, Sheriff Little of Chickasaw County is chasing a General Lee, then another General Lee, and everyone's confused about who's who and what's going on, as the Dukes avoid crossing the county line to violate probation. *Donna Fargo gets caught in the celebrity speed trap. The Dixie Jeep does a little jump in this one. In the Season 4 DVD commentary, Catherine Bach remarks that her "hair was all broke off" because she'd just gotten divorced and showed up to the set as a blonde. This one was filmed near the "most exclusive golf course in California," as John Schneider says, Lake Sherwood.*

"Diamonds in the Rough," October 23, 1981

Directed by James Best.

Bo and Luke are testing out a new sway bar on the General when a Bugs Bunny stuffed animal parachutes out of a plane with a belly full of diamonds. The Dukes intercept it, thinking they're being good neighbors, but they then get shot at by a couple "rabbit hunters." At the Boar's Nest, Rosco and Cletus are testing out an electric changing speed-limit sign in the back office when the bar's payphone, arcade games and cash register start going haywire and spewing out cash! The FBI calls the Dukes and explains where the diamonds came from, but while the Dukes are trying to hang onto them, Rosco and Boss bust in with a phony search — and then that lady who says she's an Atlanta Tribune reporter is really one of the con artists pursuing the hot rocks. Daisy has invited her home for her alleged "research on moonshine." She's not the only one posing. About as soon as the Dukes think they've shaken the cons, a fake FBI agent comes by to fetch the hot rocks. Understand? Good. *James Best talks in his autobiography, "Best in Hollywood," about how he used this first opportunity to direct an episode as an opportunity to also give Catherine Bach a time to shine. He writes that she hadn't been given many meaty lines up to that point in the series, so he told her beforehand that she was really going to act in this one, and that he was going to protect her in it.*

"Coltrane vs. Duke," October 30, 1981
Boss plans to sell the Dukes' property to a businessman who wants to build a brewery on it, Mr. Crystal, but when Boss can't manage to prevent the Dukes from getting their tax payment in on time, he has Rosco fake a serious injury from the crash the Dukes caused in their hurry. Boss calls in a snake-charmer, Slick, to pose as the doctor, while Jesse calls on his own Doc Appleby. It's too late, though; the judge finds for Rosco, to the tune of $50,000, after that ole Sheriff Little has chased Bo and Luke in the General. Emery Potter is sworn in to help the side of the "law." The Dukes concoct a scheme to prove Rosco isn't injured, dognapping Flash and making Boss think that Crystal is no longer interested in the Duke farm. *Sheriff Little appears again, as the boys have to cross into Chickasaw County to chase down the judge and show him the evidence they've gathered. You might recognize the actor who plays Judge Buford Potts, Barney Phillips, from several episodes of vintage "The Twilight Zone," notably the wonderful "Will the Real Martian Please Stand Up?" where he plays the alien with the third eye. Slick is played by Bob Hastings.*

"The Fugitive," November 3, 1981
Bo is trying out for the annual Tri-County Motocross. Motorbikes are disappearing all around town, meanwhile, and you just know Boss and Rosco are behind it. When a pretty blond gal wanders by and might have overheard their conversation about the thefts, Rosco sets off to arrest her, and she ends up with the Dukes. Her name is Mindy Lou, and she's trying to raise cash for nursing school by selling T-shirts at the Motocross. The Dukes try to figure out why Boss and Rosco are after her. They lay a trap for Rosco over the CB and just confuse up things in general on the road, between their various vehicles and Boss and Rosco. In his own "hot pursuit," even Boss takes to a motorbike to get that poor girl. But Rosco thinks she's at the Motocross, but Daisy has given out all of her shirts to other gals, so it's a little hard to tell which one is her! In the end, it's back to the Boar's Nest for Johnny Paycheck singing about taking that job and you-know-whatting it. *Mindy Lou is played by Laurette Spang, who starred in the original "Battlestar Galactica" series and was also featured in an episode of our beloved "The Secrets of Isis" Saturday morning series of the '70s.*

"The Great Bank Robbery," November 6, 1981
Directed by Denver Pyle.
On orders from Boss, Cletus chases after the Dukes to give them a ticket but heads straight into the pond instead. Then just one day shy of his pension, faithful 30-year bank employee Clarence Stovall gets canned by Boss Hogg. He's angry enough to haul off with a suitcase of the bank's cash, equal to his pension amount, which the Dukes discover by accident when Clarence stops by. The Dukes help him realize the error of his ways and decide to return the cash. The problem is, they have to "unrob" the bank — which Boss doesn't even know has been robbed — despite the vault's time-release lock that won't open until 8 a.m. Monday. Boss gets wise to the possibility that the bank's been robbed and calls in the sheriff's reserve. Cletus, meanwhile, is making a habit of that pond thing. Bo, Luke, Daisy and Cooter keep Rosco and Cletus coming and going *(love Cooter and Daisy posing as Luke and Bo!)* while Jesse makes it look like there's a fire in town to draw the reserves away to their firefighter duty. Bo, Luke and Clarence head to the bank to put the cash back.

"Sadie Hogg Day," November 13, 1981
It's April 1, when the government is turned over to the females of Hazzard County. As the gals gather around in their short-shorts to draw for various jobs, Boss gets a call from the state bank examiner, L.S. Handley, who's doing a sweep of the tri-county area looking for embezzlement activities. Since Boss has been dipping into official funds for his various "business ventures," he decides that he'll make sure Daisy gets the job as county treasurer, so he can pin his own embezzlement charges on her. He then promptly has his bank robbed of six figures in county funds. That means it's actually Daisy's turn to take the common Duke position behind bars! And Boss and Rosco aim to nail Bo and Luke, as well. Jesse comes to the jail with flowers for the guard — Miz Tisdale — so Daisy can bust out. Bo and Luke see Rosco fiddling with two sets of books for the county finances, then hear Boss telling Rosco to burn one of them. *Lulu dons her own three-piece white suit (with skirt) for her job as honorary Boss for a day. It's interestingly accessorized by that big box of chocolates!*

"10 Million Dollar Sheriff," Part 1, November 20, 1981
After yet another car chase, Rosco is getting sick and tired of them Duke boys making him the laughingstock of Hazzard County. Boss is pretty fed up, too. Then a lawyer from Atlanta drops in on Rosco to tell him he has inherited $10 million from his great uncle Hosiah P. Coltrane's will. With his

newfound prosperity, Rosco bargains with private investigator / bounty hunter Jason Steele to get them Duke boys once and for all. He also goes on a spending spree, and even Flash gets a manicure. Bo and Luke get wind of the Jason Steele thing and dial up Norman Scroggs at the newspaper to find out about him. The bounty hunter chases the boys, and they almost cross the county line, where the salivating Sheriff Little is waiting. The Dukes then enlist the help of hillbilly hermit Ben Wilkenson, who's about the only one who's ever seen this Jason Steele character. Boss is sick of hearing how rich Rosco is and takes him on in a high-stakes game of cards. *The Duke boys take off those shirts in a scene (they sure are makin' a habit of that, aren't they? and really, do any of us chicks mind?).* Rosco gets himself a Rolls Royce sheriff's car; we know a "Dukes" fan who's making a mini-replica of that car!

"10 Million Dollar Sheriff," Part 2, November 20, 1981

Thick into his garish rhinestone outfits and lavish feasts, Rosco has only get-even animosity for his old boss, Boss, and even recruits him as his patsy — er, we mean, deputy. Jesse has been seriously injured in the struggle to find Jason Steele and keep the boys safe, and Boss offers a tender visit to his bedside. Bo and Luke are in their own pursuit of this bounty hunter and finally confront him face to face. The meaner that things get in Steele's pursuit of the boys, the more Rosco begins to feel remorse. Bo and Luke get thrown in jail, then trick Cletus to get out again. Then, lo and behold — the Atlanta lawyer returns to say it was all a computer error, and Rosco inherited $10, not $10 million! With true heart, the boys then work to keep Rosco safe from the bounty hunter, who's now kidnapped him Steele wants that hundred grand Rosco owes him for the bounty. And Uncle Jesse gets back on his feet. *James Best tells BRBTV this two-part episode is among his favorites.*

The prototype of the 12-inch Luke Duke action figure announced by Figures Toy Co. in 2013; see more in the Merchandise chapter. Photo courtesy of Figures Toy Co.

"Trouble at Cooter's," November 27, 1981

Cooter has a run-in with a brown van carrying a load of ladies' fur coats, then Bo and Luke find a mink coat along the road, and it soon becomes evident that there are some shenanigans going on. The fur trader, Russ, has been dealin' with Boss Hogg, who's been dealing with Harvey Dunsmore of Atlanta. His stop-off at the Boar's Nest raises Daisy's suspicions. The fur swindler has his girlfriend Bonnie Lane distract poor old Cooter, who has his car in the garage, while he breaks in to where Boss has the furs stored. Bonnie and Russ then tie up Luke and Bo, after a robust fistfight among the boys, and when the boys break free they have the task of telling Cooter that his new love interest isn't quite what she says she is. *In a touch of irony, the episode opens with the two boys in the front seat of the General Lee singing "Take it Easy," and Waylon calls it "sorta" singing. Didn't he know those boys were going on to successful singing careers???? We get to hear Rosco say "there's a flaw in the slaw" in this one. Colleen Camp plays Bonnie Lane; we remember her as one of the Jenna Wades on "Dallas."*

"Goodbye, General Lee," December 4, 1981

Directed by Denver Pyle.

Luke gets injured under the General Lee while he and Bo are preparing to run the car in Boss' first annual Drag 'n' Fly car race, and Boss sees this as an opportunity to win the race for himself and make a little profit, even though he's the sponsor. Boss hires NASCAR drivers for the derby, then has his buddy the Professor hypnotize Luke. Boss feeds him rotten thoughts about the General Lee, like it's always breaking down and ready for the junk heap. Luke then starts trashing the General's good name to Bo. Them's fightin' words, but Jesse talks the boys into settling their differences with some archery. The boys then unload the "ailing" car on 'shiner Hobie Harkens, who then turns to Boss to broker a deal. Boss hopes to demolish the General once and for all. Cooter happens to be in the right place to save the car. Luke, thankfully, snaps out of his hypnosis, with the snap of a finger from Jesse. A drunken Hobie does a turn-about on Boss and tells Bo and Luke what he's up to, and Bo and Luke are able to make it to the derby, 01 helmets and all.

"Cletus Falls in Love," December 11, 1981

... with Daisy, no less! It all starts when Daisy sweet-talks Cletus out of writing a ticket to Bo. Pretty soon, he's bringing her flowers, but she's busy trying to have "a little talk" with him — except when it suits the Dukes' purposes for Cletus to be distracted. Boss, meanwhile, is feelin' the heat from a new state probations officer. He accuses Bo and Luke of writing a bounced check (he added a few digits onto their check, of course). The boys are soon jailed. And they just as soon slip away. Cletus loses his job, but he's too lovesick to care anyway. Luke tries to help Daisy out by having his own little talk with Cletus, but to no avail. Boss then hires Sheriff Little to nab the boys, and right back in the jail they go. In the end, Flash saves the day by disposing of the allegedly rubber check in her cute little doggie way. *Cletus is making a habit of his "buzzards on a buzzsaw!" phrase. In this one he mentions his "one-eighth" Hogg blood. Miz Tisdale appears on her motorbike. Don Pedro Colley gets some good time as "Big Ed" Little. Stunt man Al Wyatt Jr. appears as a put-upon delivery guy for pies; he keeps getting run off.*

"Hughie Hogg Strikes Again," December 18, 1981
The title explains it all, as the runt blows into town — in disguise at first — with a vision for "Hogg's Happy Hacienda" condominiums at 100 Hazzard Square. Cooter's Garage is in the line of fire of this happy plan. Hughie dons his grandfatherly disguise to frame Cooter for stealing, and Cooter lands in jail. Jesse tries to get him out on bail with the pink slip to the farm pickup, but Boss refuses. When the Dukes pitch in at Cooter's Garage and it doesn't look like he'll be able to foreclose on the mortgage, Hughie tries to frame Jesse for moonshining, hooking Revenuer Roy Winters into coming to Hazzard. Bo and Luke have discovered the plan for the Happy Hacienda, though, and eventually figure out who this grandfatherly guy who's causing all the trouble really is. *Buck Owens gets caught in the celebrity speed trap. We see Cooter use his yellow tow truck in this one, we get a good shot of the "Hoggoco Gasoline" pump at Cooter's (not often seen), and we see again the technique of driving a car through a big stack of hay (or was it straw? J). Plus, Luke surfs the hood of a fast-moving General at one point. Action-packed!*

"Dukescam Scam," January 1, 1982
Directed by Denver Pyle.
The Dukes are rushing the monthly farm mortgage check to the bank when they learn that the bank's been robbed. It appears that Boss did it — and Rosco arrests him! A $10,000 bail is set. Boss uses an emotional Ridge Runner plea on Jesse to put up his bail money. Of course, it's all just a scam to get the Dukes' money so they cannot cover the mortgage. Boss sneaks out of town; the boys follow him and learn of the scam. The Dukes rush to the court of Buford Potts for Boss' hearing, wanting to plead their own case about the scam on the farm. Somehow in all of this mess, Boss and Jesse get themselves locked in the bank vault, with Boss trying to sign the vault

lock combination to Rosco, Cooter, Daisy, Bo and Luke through the closed circuit camera. No go on that. It gives Boss enough time for an attack of conscience as he and Jesse think about old times. And who are Bo and Luke busy finding, in the meantime? Ole Emery Potter, to get that bank vault combination entered before the air runs out.

"The Sound of Music — Hazzard Style," January 8, 1982
Mickey Gilley comes to town, along with some recording industry pirates, Heep and Morton. As they try to escape Gilley's concert, the pirates hijack the General Lee — just in time for that bright orange car to be seen by the feds who are pursuing them. The boys are able to strand them and take off in the car, but the feds have already spoken to Boss about that car and the pirates. Bo and Luke catch on to that and take a look around Hazzard for the pirates' hangout, all the while dodging the two feds. Boss, who's actually working with the record pirates, sees his opportunity to pin the evil deed on Bo and Luke. The pirates double-cross Boss, though, as he was thinking they might. They kidnap him when he says that Rosco has photos of them committing their piracy at the concert. Guess it didn't matter that Rosco never got to take those pictures. Rosco turns down Bo and Luke's offer to help find Boss, but Cletus takes them up on it. Good thing, because Rosco ends up a hostage, too. *Love how Bo and Luke grab the bars on the Dixie Jeep as Daisy flies by, to escape the federal agent and his gun. You might recognize the guy who plays Heep, Burton Gilliam, as the bad guy who fakes the plague in "Double Sting."*

"Shine on Hazzard Moon," January 15, 1982
Boss is trying to cut a deal with D. Jasper Fenwick for his moonshine, but Jasper has more of a taste for Jesse's well-regarded brew. Boss fixes to nab Jesse's recipe, sending Rosco into the Dukes kitchen where Jesse evidently has it hidden. But it's the wrong recipe. Boss wants to set up Bo and Luke, using their incarceration as leverage. He gets Rayford Flicker to give a charity shuck-'n'-jive and soon has the boys behind bars for stealing from the orphans' fund. Forced into a corner, Jesse pretends to make some 'shine for Boss, as Bo and Luke, with Cooter's help, flee the jail. Bo and Luke go after Flicker to get him to confess. Then Boss wants Jesse to truck the still across the county line into Chickasaw where, of course, Sheriff Little is obediently waiting. Luckily, Cooter overhears Boss giving Sheriff Little the heads-up over the CB.

"Pin the Tail on the Dukes," January 22, 1982
Jesse's friend Hector Farley returns after 10 years in prison, and Boss tries to pin some trumped-up charges on him. Hector takes off in the van for Rhuebottom's General Store. Rosco has a new radar gun, sorta (it's really a hair dryer in disguise), and he accuses the Dukes of blowing it up after he points it at the General and it just accidentally gets splashed. Hector is fuming about the thing with Boss, but the Dukes stop him from doing something dire. The Dukes are also being pursued for aiding and abetting Hector. Boss then tells Hector he's going to give him back the $25,000 he took from him, but it's just to lure Hector — and the Duke boys — to where he and Rosco can nab 'em for stealing the county payroll. Doesn't work — Bo and Luke intervene again. The Dukes find out what this "radar gun" really is and get a hold of it, using it as leverage. *Bo and Luke are often shown climbing across the tops of buildings in the Hazzard Square, and Luke does it again in this one.*

"Miz Tisdale on the Lam," January 29, 1982
Miz Tisdale observes a strange feller coming into the post office every day, not knowing that he's executing a mail fraud scheme with Boss and Rosco. Bo and Luke meet Sue-Ann Blake, who says she's bought some land as part of the "Hazzard Highlands." She's a U.S. postal inspector. When she uncovers the mail fraud, Rosco implicates Miz Tisdale, whom the Dukes then convince to hide out at the farm. They're figuring Boss must be in this somehow. They convince Billy Joe Fong to take Emma's place on her motor-sickle then smuggle her out of town. Boss sends Rosco over to the Duke farm to plant incriminating evidence. Luke calls Scoop Whitman at the Capitol City Gazette to find out more about this mythical land development. There's some possible mail theft, and there's Jesse riding in Emma's sidecar! When everything is all sorted out, "Emmer" even gets an invite from Jesse to go catfishin'. *"Hazzard's oldest and only Chinese family," the Fongs, make an appearance. How hilarious to see Miz Tisdale stuffed into the back of the General.*

"Nothin' But the Truth," February 5, 1982
Boss sets up a casino in the old Hazzard livery stable, then learns that the state's Crime Commission is sending an investigator into Hazzard to sniff around. He decides to fix it so the Dukes will take the fall, having the gambling equipment planted in their barn, then bringing them up on charges and locking them up. Rosco and Flash return from a sheriff's convention in Atlanta, meanwhile, with all sorts of cool new gadgets,

including a hypodermic needle filled with sodium pentothal — truth serum — which Boss accidentally sits on. Boss goes on a confession binge. He even calls the IRS! The Dukes try to track down these tour buses coming into town then realize all the action going down at the livery stable — even the kidnapping of Boss by his cohorts. The Dukes eventually are able to utilize Boss' newfound truthfulness to clear themselves. *The theme of Boss confessing his misdeeds is utilized in another episode, of course, though without the truth serum. And here, Daisy again dons her familiar red bikini, this time to distract Cletus. Another amusing note: When a sign in Hazzard says "FALLING ROCK," it really means falling rock!!!*

"Dear Diary," February 12, 1982
Rosco has this little book, see, that just happens to document every highly illegal, unethical and immoral caper he and Boss Hogg have ever pulled. That rascally and playful hound Flash buries Rosco's incriminating diary on the Duke farm just as Rosco is trying to nail Bo and Luke for a busted brake light. Boss then gets wind of the book being missing, and accuses the Duke boys of taking it, threatening to jail them if they don't return it. Then Jesse accidentally finds the diary on the farm (well, Bonnie Mae the goat found it, actually). He dials up J.D. to make a deal to get the charges against the boys dropped. Two "business associates" the Boss just double-crossed overhear and decide to complicate matters, stealing the diary themselves and blackmailing Boss with it. *Ernie Hudson, who's made more movies than anyone can count and starred more recently in shows like "Stargate SG-1" and the WB's "Everwood," plays Avery, one of the bad guys. Bo sure is making a habit of that hood slide in this season.*

"New Deputy in Town," February 19, 1982
Directed by Denver Pyle.
The cash flow in Hazzard has dwindled down to a drip, Boss reports to Rosco during a regular meeting. Then a young, beautiful blond, Linda May Barnes, is the new temporary officer in town (she's a sheriff's deputy from Roseville, they say). Even Boss is intrigued by her. Young punk Denny is her slimy associate. They're really in town, however, to bust another slimy guy out of custody, Denny's brother, Linda May's boyfriend and the second most wanted man in the South, Rafe Logan, who's being transported, top-secret-like, for a grand jury date in Atlanta. Rosco tries to amp up the charges against the Dukes to amp up the coffers. Boss then promotes Linda May to acting sheriff. Bo and Luke are interested in this new acting sheriff — even more interested when they learn she's a fake. Meanwhile, Lulu is

BEHIND THE SCENES

Ernie Hudson appeared at Awesome Con in Washington, D.C. in April 2014. "Dukes" fan Brian Lombard asked Hudson, in his Q&A session, about the "Dear Diary" episode, in particular about when the car goes off the cliff and explodes in mid-air. Brian wondered if it was an accident or planned that way. At first Hudson quipped that he didn't know because he hadn't seen the episode. As the laughter died down, he said, "I don't watch everything I do. I'm not embarrassed to say that. Well, the part I wanted to play was the bad guy. I found out great, I got the job. And then they handed me the script. I thought, oh no. And the guy who was playing the part wasn't really an actor, so I was kinda disappointed. Then when I got there, they had a tank top and some baby oil for me. I don't think I had hardly any lines. Maybe one line or something. So they wanted me to oil up. I'm thinking, this is 'Dukes of Hazzard.' And I was like, no, no. First off, the day I was working, I drove to the set, and as I was coming in to the driveway, there was a Confederate flag. It didn't start the day off right." (OK, he's kinda joking with that.) "Then I get there and I see the baby oil and the tank top. Then I go, 'No, I want to see the director.' I went, 'No, no. This ain't gonna happen.' I'm walking to see the director and I go past the one other black guy in the entire room, and he's telling a black joke. So now I'm like, OK, this is getting bad. So now I'm going to see the director, I'm going to say I'm not wearing this thing. And he's going to say something, and I'm going to knock him. You know how you're thinking in your head, when he says this, I'm going to say that. Then something said, just let it go, whatever happens. You can deal with it. And then I just ... " (spreading hands) "And I saw the director, and I said listen, and he said, no, it's OK, it's over. And then I did show up in one of the funniest experiences I've ever had. With Tom, and in fact I just worked with John Schneider again." (in "Doonby") "That was a really big learning experience for me. Because sometimes you're acting on the emotion of what you're expecting to happen. And none of that happened. It actually turned out nice."

Ernie Hudson, left, at his April 2014 Awesome Con discussion panel, moderated by Ulysses Campbell, producer of the D.C.-based "Fantastic Forum" TV show of which this author is a part.

more irate than usual with that rat J.D., and even manages to drive the crooks a little crazy, too, when they force her into their car — then dump her back out! *Tracy Scoggins plays Linda May, blond rather than the brunette she has been in so many other screen appearances since then, and Gary Graham is Denny.*

"Birds Gotta Fly," February 26, 1982
A female champion NASCAR driver, Molly Hargrove, sees Daisy's skilled driving while passing through Hazzard, and tells the young girl she's good enough to join the circuit. Molly has Daisy take a turn behind the wheel of her car, for which the pink slip is secretly in the hands of Boss Hogg because of some silly loan situation Molly has with him. Daisy doesn't want to drive on the NASCAR circuit at first, feeling a loyalty to Hazzard and her family. Boss then fires her. Daisy changes her mind about the circuit, with some coaxing from her cousins. Luke checks in with Charlie Cooper Jr. of the Tri-State Press to learn more about Molly and her not-so-spotless "track record." Soon, Boss Hogg has his own grimy hands on Daisy's racing contract. In the end, though, Daisy realizes she has nothing more to prove — and there's no place like home.

"Bad Day in Hazzard," March 5, 1982
A refined and slightly snobby out-of-towner named Thackery and his men scheme to rob an armored car carrying $10 million. They duke it out with the Dukes, hold them hostage at the Boar's Nest, along with Boss, Cletus and Rosco (and Flash!) and force Boss Hogg to bust in on the local radio to call for a town evacuation because of "insect spraying" for a fruit fly. Cooter arrives at the Boar's Nest and gets caught in the mess, then everybody puts their heads together. After hearing Jesse's tale of a tunnel under the bar from his Ridge-Running days, Bo and Luke conspire to be locked up in the storeroom, under which they know there is said tunnel they can escape out of. But despite the distracting noise of Daisy and others dancing to the jukebox, the thugs still break in and find the boys digging away under the floorboards. M.C. Gainey (so young and fresh-faced!) plays Peters — he went on to star as Rosco in the 2005 "Dukes of Hazzard" movie. Tim O'Conner, who is Thackery here, was not only Dr. Huer on "Buck Rogers in the 25th Century," but also the original Andros the alien on the 1970s "Wonder Woman" series.

"Miss Tri-Counties," March 12, 1982
It's time for the Miss Tri-Counties beauty pageant once again, and we just know that our little Daisy is favored to win. Boss is blackmailed by Big Jim Mathers to fix the beauty contest for another contestant, Melanie DuBois. He tries to prevent Daisy from entering, but she still manages that. For part of the contest, Daisy races the others at putting together a carburetor, and she nails it but forfeits it because of some missing parts. Our girl then needs to get her driver's license renewed for the driving contest. Boss diverts her to Chickasaw County, then gives Sheriff Little the heads-up that the Dukes will be breaking their probation to get her there. Cooter overhears the conspirin' against Daisy and tries to warn the Dukes. After things go around a bit, with Boss feeling some heat from Big Jim Mathers, and then all gets settled, it's Daisy in her sleek blue bathing suit who nails the title. *"The Big Valley"* fixture Joe Higgins plays Big Jim Mathers. Melanie DuBois is Danone Simpson, who was secretary Kendall on "Dallas."

"Share and Share Alike," March 19, 1982
Directed by Denver Pyle.
As Lulu engages in the Hazzard Equal Rights Society (HERS), the scheme for Boss this time is stolen bank credit cards, which he plans to sell and make a cool profit from. Bo and Luke find the stolen cards on the road, where two bad guys just dumped them, and Uncle Jesse urges the boys to turn them in to Rosco. Lulu hires up Daisy as an assistant after she informs J.D. she's now

his equal partner. Rosco thinks with this whole credit card thing that he's finally got the evidence to do in Bo and Luke, even as he and Boss have to tread carefully to not implicate themselves. Sheriff Little comes a-shopping with Lulu and Daisy for a good used patrol car for a new officer he just hired. And what does the good sheriff take away but a card holding some stolen credit cards! When it all gets sorted out, Lulu has such a nice thank-you for Daisy and the rest of the Dukes — as well as the announcement that she's going to run for county commissioner! *David Hayward, who was bad-guy Dickens here, was also Turk Moody in "Luke's Love Story."*

"The Law and Jesse Duke," March 26, 1982
Rosco and Cletus get turned down for a raise by Boss, and they decide to go on strike. Boss tracks down the Jones gang — Simon, Floyd and sister Alabama — to make a move on the unprotected Hazzard. Bo and Luke get themselves apprehended by the Jones trio and tied up in Boss' warehouse, so some false charges can get piled on them. Alabama takes some incriminating photos of them, just before Bo and Luke escape in the General. Boss then appoints Jesse as sheriff to force him to arrest the Duke boys on charges of robbing a store — with Alabama's photos as evidence. It's up to the Dukes to track down the evidence and implicate the real perps — the Jones trio. Jesse's first and only arrest as sheriff ends up being the Jones trio, and Rosco and Cletus are soon back from their time on the picket line. Jesse was happy to resign that job!

"Dukes in Danger," April 2, 1982
Bo and Luke are rolling along in the General when they see a traffic light pop out of nowhere. Yup, it's Rosco, who promptly gets himself "treed" (after driving backward). Jesse and Daisy are then off to the bank with the monthly mortgage check when they get intercepted by a couple prison escapees. They're held hostage, while Boss Hogg, devoid of his mortgage cash, celebrates foreclosure on the Duke farm. He hops in his white convertible and heads to the farm to check out his new prize, becoming ensnared, of course, in the cons' web. Rosco soon inadvertently joins the party. Then along comes Cooter, whom the Dukes do manage to shoo away unharmed — and with a secretly scribbled note in his pocket. Wonder if he'll notice it, with that kiss Daisy planted on him. The hostage crew gets locked up in the barn, but it all works out, ya know. *Love how Boss, under duress of the prison escapees, asks Mabel on the switchboard to put in a call to Cletus and automatically tacks on a "Hey from Rosco" without any prompting or without Rosco even being there.*

John Schneider and Tom Wopat left the set in May 1982 and filed a $25 million lawsuit against the WB regarding royalties from merchandising, according to TNN's special "The Life and Times of the Dukes of Hazzard." Schneider said in the special, "We'd had a Bo and Luke moment, because we felt that we had some discrepancies in accounting procedures — put it that way — with regard to merchandising. And we were kinda brushed off, and brushed off, and we figured well, the way to get somebody's attention is to just leave. So we did." Wopat said, "We felt we had been treated unfairly." In her own interview, Catherine Bach had this view: "And I said, well, OK, do you want me to come with you? 'No, this is a man's work. This is man's work.'" She shook her head. "Yea, whatever." WB ended up countersuing Schneider and Wopat for $200 million. The legal dispute dragged on through most of the fifth season.

A season to remember? Just sweet Daisy went on the cover of the fifth-season DVD. Hmm ... wonder why ...

Season 5

Enter Byron Cherry and Christopher Mayer as the "other" Duke boys. Vance is a former Merchant Marine, and Coy worked as a test car driver in Detroit. Sonny Shroyer is back as Enos.

"The New Dukes," September 24, 1982
Bo and Luke depart to work their dream on the NASCAR circuit, and, after six years away, Coy and Vance Duke return to Hazzard County to help look after things. Enos also returns with a commendation — and the boot — from the governor of California. He also gets a welcome-back kiss from Daisy. Boss introduces a hideous bank-robbing tank he calls the Mean Green Machine. With Boss' two bad-guy associates, the MGM terrorizes Capitol City and its bank. The three Duke cousins catch sight of that action and get their blue car blown up as a result. When Boss and Rosco won't listen to their report of the MGM, what else can they do but dust off the ole General? The Dukes then get framed for the robbery, get thrown behind bars, see evidence of currency counterfeiting and really catch on when they find out some $100 plates are on tour in the South. *Coy and Vance promptly jump into that whole shirtless Duke boy thing (we don't mind), and with their introduction here, the script is littered with references to try to make them fit in. We're pretty sure we've seen Capitol City spelled with an "a" in previous episodes, but we'll defer to what the signs in town say in this one and spell it with an "o."*

"Dukes Strike it Rich," October 1, 1982
With some fence-mending to be done after a run-in with the local law enforcement, it's an opening scene that just goes to show ya them Duke boys are always looking for a chance to take off their shirts. Plus, Daisy redefines that whole tight-jeans concept. Beyond that, though, Boss cheats young newlyweds Jeb and Carrie Morton on some swampland that he promised as farmland. Coy and Vance break into Boss' office to have a look at the contract the Mortons signed, and land themselves behind bars, then bust out. The whole Duke clan fools Boss into thinking there's gold in that-thar creek that runs through both the Duke and Morton properties. They paint up some rocks a pretty gold, then parade around in some glitzy duds. Boss takes the bait and gets the property back from the Mortons. *Cooter has a cousin who's an undertaker, called Earl in another episode but referred to as Tyrone here (unless he has more than one cousin who's an undertaker!).*

Is that the same red sequined gown Daisy wore in "Route 7-11"? Uncle Jesse says here that she needs to sew it up a little, but it's smashing.

"Lawman of the Year," October 8, 1982
Directed by Denver Pyle.
Daisy gets caught in Rosco's speed trap, as Coy and Vance stop to help a couple rude guys with a hidden gun along the roadside. Boss is hiring these two goons to rob his jewelry store. The opportunistic Rosco preens for the Lawman of the Year contest, releasing Daisy from jail. Coy and Vance learn from Rhuebottom that those two guys also tried to buy some dynamite, and they find out who the guys are through the wanted posters at the post office. The cousins drive a big monkey wrench into Boss' robbery plans after they discover the robbers' hangout. Then Rosco goes and loses that Lawman of the Year contest. Rats. Cletus and Enos, meanwhile, spend plenty of time in the mud or in the pond. Things just ain't workin' out, all the way around.

"Coy Meets Girl," October 15, 1982
Boss arranges for a sly hijacking of the Dukes' rental truck full of family antiques, planning then to jail the Duke boys for the deed! An orphan runaway named Bobbie Lee witnesses Boss' goons making their move on the truck. She runs off and finds herself in quicksand, and Coy arrives to pull her out. They arrive back at the Duke farm, where Bobbie Lee tells a couple white lies. Boss realizes the girl could thwart his plans and sends Enos and Cletus out looking for her. Bobbie Lee has developed a crush on Coy. When Daisy drops her off at the bus station, two guys try to abduct the girl. Coy and Vance realize Boss was the one who had their truck hijacked. Bobbie Lee then works with the Dukes to clear their name and expose Boss, doing what she can to attract the winsome Coy all the while. *You might recognize Michele Greene, who plays Bobbie Lee, as Jill from ABC's "Eight is Enough."*

"The Hazzardgate Tape," October 22, 1982
The Dukes help Boss fend off rival crime bosses from other counties in a plot worthy of a "Godfather" movie (*well, OK, not quite, but it's fun nonetheless*). Coy and Vance are coming home after earning a little extra chore money when Enos sets off after them, but they get stuck in the mud. Boss, meanwhile, is having a meeting with Boss Bowman of Choctaw County, Boss Sharkey of Wiriga, and Boss Hopkins of Hatchapee, and it's not going well. They want a new deal with him that includes a piece of the Hazzard action. Boss Hogg refuses. The other bosses then have their own

private meeting at another location, and Coy and Vance happen upon them and overhear their plotting to take out J.D. Hogg. The bosses realize the boys have overheard and send two goons after them and after Boss Hogg, who ends up in the backseat of the General then at the Duke farm before all this gets sorted out. *Mel Tillis performs, and he's feeling like himself this time, not a character named Burl Tolliver, as he was in an earlier episode. (Say, did anyone on the show even notice the resemblance?) Cletus is on vacation in this one.*

"Big Daddy," October 29, 1982
Oh, haven't you always wondered what kind of man could father a cretin like Boss Hogg? Here's your chance to find out: Boss' father, Big Daddy Hogg, comes to Hazzard — and promptly swindles him. Boss gets word that Big Daddy is coming to town and worries, because Big Daddy wants J.D. to be "lovable and honest" like him. Boss arranges with Rosco for a big public spectacle in town to show how "loved" he is. Rosco heads to the Duke farm to plant a stolen license plate on the General, followed promptly by Cletus and Enos arriving to the farm to arrest Coy and Vance, but they run off. The General's plate has found its way on the car of a guy, Jenkins, who stops at Cooter's garage. This guy Jenkins recognizes Big Daddy Hogg's driver Ernie as someone he did time with. That can't be good. He tips off the Dukes. Later Ernie gets a gun on Coy and Vance in the General, then takes off in the General himself. In the end, J.D.'s image of his daddy is shattered — and that's a good thing. *We're seeing a lot of Boss' lush house this season. Boss' papa is the London-born Les Tremayne of classic films like "North by Northwest" and "The War of the Worlds," as well as the wonderful "Shazam!" live-action 1970s Saturday morning series.*

"Vance's Lady," November 5, 1982
As a secretary in state Sen. Jason W. Maynard's office, Vance's former flame Jenny finds evidence of embezzlement — and a whole heap of trouble. She comes to Hazzard and tries to get help, reuniting with Vance after three years, as the embezzlement charges point to her. One of her coworkers, Dugan, is hot on her trail, and when Boss finds out he's got someone from the senator's office in Hazzard, he rapidly develops delusions of political grandeur. He also points things in the direction of the Dukes, as far as guilty parties and such. Boss, Rosco and Enos arrive at the farm, and Coy scrams out of there, then meets Vance and Jenny by the lake. Jenny changes her mind about dragging Vance into this mess and tries to leave town, but the Duke boys find her and work to help her expose the wrongdoing and get

herself safe. We love Coy's little hop over the General's hood in this one; it's a sort of prelude to his gymnastic flip in a future episode. He can also jump through the General's window like nobody's business. In fact, this author has a friend who drove his own General to pick up Byron Cherry from the airport for an appearance a few years back, and Byron jumped right in through the window "without touching the paint," the friend says. Bessie Lou is minding the switchboard in this episode rather than Mabel.

"Hazzard Hustle," November 12, 1982

Over in Rapaho County, Boss and Rosco are working on an illegal horse-betting outfit. Boss sets it up so the Dukes phone line is connected to all this so they'll be implicated if the heat goes down. The Dukes then keep hearing their phone ring, but nobody's there. The three Duke cousins run into Enos and coerce him into revealing that Boss and Rosco are in Rapaho. The cousins head over to investigate. Big Billie Tucker in Rapaho is none too happy to hear someone is cutting into her business there. She and her thug Bull drop by for a visit, and under a certain amount of pressure, Boss points the finger at the Dukes. Big Billie heads over to the Duke farm, then Coy and Vance run off and find the evidence of the operation at a warehouse in Rapaho. But Boss has slyly moved the operation somewhere else. Coy and Vance turn their attention to the local phone wires and find out more about the operation, while Jesse and Daisy locate the new betting room. Time for a little fixin' of the bettin.' Bruce M. Fischer, who is Bull here, also plays Buck in the episode "Gold Fever." Cletus and Cooter are both on vacation here. In a new twist — literally — Vance swiftly rolls over the roof of the General as he and Coy are racing to get inside. Good thing those guys aren't on probation — they've got no issue crossing the county line into Rapaho.

"Enos in Trouble," November 19, 1982

Some big, dark emeralds are in Enos' foot locker, which finally arrives from his former job in California. But sssshhhh — he doesn't know that yet. A couple thugs are after the foot locker. They accost Coy, Vance and Enos, shoot at them, and just all-around menace them. The Dukes decide to have a look at the foot locker, and amid the polka-dotted nightshirt and framed photo of Daisy and other odd artifacts, there's not much there. Boss gets wind of the two guys' pursuit of Enos and orders Enos to his office forthwith. Another look at the foot locker at the Duke farm reveals the emeralds. Boss Hogg, of course, tries to confiscate the jewels. Jesse and Daisy see the two thugs drop by the farm and ransack it. The Dukes bury the emeralds to hide them, but then Enos runs off to turn himself in. Boss turns

Have we mentioned that Byron Cherry is a ham? We really should. Here he is sharing a ride on the Hazzard Sheriff's boat with BRB at the Hair Dare Dukes Days event in Ontario, Canada, in 2008.

the interrogation lamp on Enos, but his lips are sealed. The two thugs, who incidentally are the ones who stole the emeralds in the first place, arrive at the police station and grab Enos. Rosco's car ends up in a tree after a jump in this one and has to be lifted out with a crane.

"The Great Insurance Fraud," November 26, 1982
Directed by Denver Pyle.
Boss has devised an insurance scam called Hoggoco, and he's got Rosco out there selling as much of it as he can. A couple "flimflammers," though, have a scam for the scam, planning to fake an accident. Pretty soon, the truly distraught Coy thinks he's caused a car to go over a cliff, but it's really the scammers' $1-million scam. The female flammer threatens to turn Boss in to the state insurance commission if he doesn't pay up on her "deceased" loved one. Coy and Vance look around Bottomless Lake, where the car went

in, and almost get hit by falling rock as the alleged accident victim watches them. Vance finds the female flammer to ask her some questions, but that doesn't go well. Vance then gets to go for a harrowing hanging helicopter ride in the Dukes' efforts to expose the flimflammers and put Coy's conscience to rest. *The male flimflammer, Ward S. Davis, is referred to as Wade in the credits.*

"A Little Game of Pool," December 3, 1982
A couple of crooks, under Boss' employ, have their eyes on the General Lee, and soon, while the Dukes are out in the barn practicing for the 37th annual Hazzard pool tournament, their faithful orange family member gets "kidnapped." They get the car back, then Boss makes them an offer for it, which they refuse. The two crooks are sitting in jail, and Enos tries to send their fingerprints to D.C. to do a check on their record, but the "facsimile machine" isn't working. He finally does find out who they are through the Capitol City cop shop, though. Jesse and Boss are about to go head-to-head at the pool tournament for their car titles (General and Caddy), when Boss fakes an arm injury and calls in "Chickasaw Thins" the pool hustler as a sub. The Dukes finally are able to expose the crooks for what they are, but not before the General gets a new black coat of paint. *The Duke boys utilize yet another opportunity to take off the shirts.*

"The Treasure of Soggy Marsh," December 10, 1982
Two cons bring Boss a map depicting where a bank robber's half-mill treasure is buried in Soggy Marsh. He just has to supply the diving equipment and send Enos to a far corner of the county to stay busy and out of the way. Boss also sends the Dukes to Chickasaw to pick up some menus for the Boar's Nest. When they get there, they realize there are no menus to be found, and good ole Sheriff Little is just a-waitin' to search the General Lee and find Boss' allegedly stolen cufflinks. The three Duke cousins are jailed, and Jesse tries to bail them out but can't for a few days, so they bust out instead (with a little help from Daisy's feminine wiles). They track Boss' recent purchases of diving equipment and check all the local bodies of water, with Daisy finally discovering the site of the diving escapades. Unfortunately, the divers discover her, too. *We see a really nice jump in this one of the General with the Chickasaw County sheriff's car right behind it in the air. Stunt guy Al Wyatt Jr. appears again as a pie delivery guy who has some messy encounters with passing vehicles! The Chickasaw street where the Dukes talk with Sheriff Little is the same street that runs behind the Hazzard courthouse. It also served as Capitol City during the Mean Green Machine's*

assault in "The New Dukes." And it's the same street that the Batmobile used to pull up on in the opening of every episode of the old Adam West "Batman" TV series. (Thanks, Brian Lombard!)

"The Revenge of Hughie Hogg," December 17, 1982
When Rosco comes up for reelection, Hughie blackmails Boss into backing him for sheriff instead, showing evidence of his uncle committing some acts not so legal. The Dukes, meanwhile, back Rosco, figurin' that option is the lesser of two evils. Lulu also jumps up to support her brother in the race. When Hughie's demands and shenanigans get too hot to handle, Boss confesses to Rosco that he was planning to cut him out of a deal. Hughie gets more and more threatening, and the Dukes send in a skunk to do the job, then they have to send in Daisy (in her swimsuit) to get the goods on him. The audio tape she has with her doesn't catch it all, though, and the Dukes have to do some shuck-'n'-jive to make Hughie fall for the bluff, meeting him at a secret location and getting him to confess to much more on tape this time.

"The Return of the Mean Green Machine," January 7, 1983
Coy and Vance are doing a little romancing with Ellie May and Bonnie when Vance sees some tracks in the mud that leave him unnerved. Looks like the Mean Green Machine is out and about again. It seems Boss is after some valuable gold coins at the Hazzard Gold and Silver Emporium, coins that are worth a million bucks. He gets the Mean Green Machine out of its semiretirement, unfortunately, to accomplish this goal. It has the enhancement of magnetically attracting metal. The creator of the machine apparently wants his invention back, however. Off it goes, from under Boss' nose, then Coy and Vance see it on the country roads and try to disarm it, so to speak. The two bad guys end up at Cooter's garage, where they do a little slugging with Cooter and Jesse. They take Cooter hostage. Vance enlists the aid of Bonnie, who works at WHOGG Radio, while Enos has an encounter with the MGM and has to get a lift from Miz Tisdale on her bike. *We get a shot of Enos' pink "underdrawers," as Waylon puts it. They're long like thermals. And yes, pink.*

"Ding, Dong, the Boss is Dead," January 21, 1983
Coy and Vance stop to help a couple people broken down on the roadside. They're really a couple criminals posing as brother and sister as they plot to do Boss in. The sister, Lorna Mallory, acts all sweet on Vance. The Duke boys then save Boss and Rosco from a falling scaffolding, and they suspect

something's up. Next, it's a little sabotage of Boss' car. Boss thinks the brake failure is Cooter's fault, but then he gets a tipoff from some conversation heard on the switchboard. He takes on Coy and Vance as bodyguards and hides out at the Duke farm. Soon, Hazzard fakes Boss Hogg's death to save him from the real enemy, Floyd Calloway, a moonshiner Boss turned state's evidence against. Floyd's been waitin' 20 years to do in that "double-crossin' water buffalo." The Dukes put on a showy funeral for Boss at the Boar's Nest, but then the casket rolls out of the hearse! *Gussie Peabody is minding the switchboard in this one.*

"Coy vs. Vance," February 4, 1983
Directed by Sorrell Booke.
The state fair has come to Hatchapee County, which everybody knows is right next to Hazzard County. Coy has lost himself over Billie Ann Baxley, who, with her equally fast-acting, stunt-racing sister Kate, has been dressing up as a cop and robbing people at the fair in their off-time from being the "Biking Baxleys" (or the Famous Flying Baxley Sisters, as their van proclaims). They hit up Boss and Rosco on the road. Vance doesn't have such a good feeling about Billie Ann, and we think we've seen this cousin-vs.-cousin thing before. Kate doesn't much like Billie Ann hanging out with Coy, either. When Vance's suspicions grow, Coy gets fed up and leaves the farm, then Daisy has to break up a fistfight between the two. Meanwhile Boss promotes Enos to sheriff and demotes Rosco to his deputy. Vance continues his digging on the sisters, and it leads to a confrontation with the two in an old cow shed, then Daisy, Coy and Jesse must track him down. *The 1980 Miss Universe Shawn Weatherly plays Billie Ann. Nice and ironic that these stunt gals have the last name Baxley, isn't it? Cooter mentions an uncle named Earl in this one. Guess that must be the dad of his cousin Earl the undertaker? And there's ole Al Wyatt Jr. again in this one, playing a role on the sidelines, this time fishing down at the pond when Enos' patrol car goes in.*

"Comrade Duke," February 11, 1983
After a little maintenance of a tour bus at Cooter's garage, a Russian gymnast named Natasha defects into the back of Jesse's pickup. While Coy takes a shine to her, and the Dukes try to figure out whether to appeal to the police or to the FBI in Atlanta, the girl's Russian caretakers have raised a stink with Boss, who is happy to point the blame to the Dukes and demands the girl's return. There's a lot of shuffling around of the poor girl, as she tells Coy more about her life back in Russia. Coy sneaks her into Cooter's to try to call the FBI, but none of the lines out of Hazzard are working. He's trying

to get her to the state department in Atlanta, even if by air, but then the poor girl is apprehended and put behind bars in Hazzard, with only Enos and his "possum on a gumbush"es to comfort her. Eventually, both Coy and Daisy have taken to the air for Natasha: Coy in his showoff gymnastic flip, and Daisy in piloting a plane to help her escape to Atlanta. *Byron Cherry tells BRBTV he had to do that aerial flip 28 times for 28 takes of that scene. In this one we see Darcy, the flight instructor and crop duster who has a liking for Daisy.*

"Witness: Jesse Duke," February 18, 1983

Jesse is on his way to the bank in Capitol City to take out a loan for farm equipment when he gets a serious blow from a jewelry-store thief. He loses his eyesight. The three cousins speed to the hospital, and Enos even gives them a pass when he hears the news. Enos passes along the news to Boss and Rosco. One of the crooks, afraid Jesse will regain his sight and be able to ID him, poses as a reporter to get to him. Boss then takes Jesse in at his and Lulu's luxurious pad (Lulu is visiting Hortense in Decatur). Having Jesse there cramps Boss' style a bit — he's got to make a meeting with his associate Hanson for some short-changing gas pumps. The crooks track Jesse down there after a quick and fruitless stop at the farm. Jesse proves he can still find his way around them woods blindfolded (though not with one hand tied behind his back). His family members, who've been praying for him, are thrilled to see his eyesight come back — and the crooks caught. *This is one of those episodes where Boss shows genuine concern for his old friend Jesse. Judson Scott is familiar as Parker, the crook who hits Jesse. He had a key role in "Star Trek: The Wrath of Khan." He'll be back in the "Sittin' Dukes" episode.*

It just wasn't the same; Schneider and Wopat realize what a good thing they had going and return to the set in January 1983, with both them and WB dropping their lawsuits, according to the TNN special "The Life and Times of the Dukes of Hazzard."

"Welcome Back, Bo 'n' Luke," February 25, 1983

Bo and Luke return from the NASCAR circuit and get the General Lee's keys — and the show — back from Coy and Vance. You'll see all four boys in the opening credits, but it's the Bo and Luke Show, once again. Soon, Coy and Vance are off in the yellow Mustang that Bo and Luke arrived in. The Miss Tri-County pageant is also on again when they make their surprise return, and Daisy is ready to relinquish her own crown. Boss Hogg has some development plans that don't include Cooter's Garage, and the balloon payments Cooter's having to make on his place are making that abundantly clear. He's surly to the Dukes and everyone else, and he won't ask anybody for help. The Duke boys still figure it out, though, as Boss closes in on Cooter's Garage. Racer Petey Willis and his daughter Sarah-Ann are in town, to boot. Cooter works on Willis' car, then it crashes, so Cooter caves to Boss' demands. *The reason Coy and Vance leave is given as their Aunt Bessie needing help on the farm since Uncle Albert got sick. We're assuming with the way it's discussed that this an extension of the Duke family (not family on the boys' moms' side, on the other hand, which might not make much sense for the both of them, anyway). So that makes how many brothers in Uncle Jesse's family now? Gotta be at least eight boys, at our count, remembering Phillip, who we're assuming, when he was mentioned, was not the dad of Coy or Vance. Of course, there is the possibility that one or more of the cousins has a mom who's a Duke instead of a dad and just has the Duke name. Confused yet? Yea, really.*

"Big Brothers, Duke," March 4, 1983
Directed by Denver Pyle.
Bo and Luke take on a problem teen, Andy Slocum, as a little brother. To make his introduction, the little crook-in-training steals the General Lee. Luke doesn't want to file charges. They take him for some new clothes, and he lifts some extra outfits from Rhuebottom's store. Then he steals a bunch of hubcaps, which Bo and Luke have him replace one by one. They finally tame him down a bit with some good, honest farmwork. He goes looking for a lost baby billy goat and finds a bag of money from the Atlanta National Bank, making him a target for some crooks. Boss, meanwhile, has been dropping some weight, and he doesn't much like that. It's all that stress from lost crooked business deals, though he did manage to cut a deal with the robber of the Atlanta bank, along with Bad Barney. *Sorrell Booke takes out some padding for this one! Didya catch Waylon's "Reckon he's been kidnapped?" joke about the lost baby goat? Rosco is shown giving Flash a bath in this one. Good thing — Catherine Bach, John Schneider and Tom Wopat have joked in their DVD commentaries about the dog's smell.*

"Farewell, Hazzard," March 11, 1983
The Dukes are on the way to pay the mortgage, as usual, when they get sidetracked by car trouble from a menacing helicopter and have to have Cooter come pick them up. Boss is trying out various odd hairpieces and partnering with the shrewd L.S. Pritchard of Dallas to buy up massive land in

Hazzard and develop a "New Hazzard." The Duke farm, unfortunately, falls prey to the scheme, as the Dukes don't make the mortgage payment on time, thanks to that copter. They see it again, and Daisy gets hurt as they try to dodge it. Pritchard turns out to be a "she," not a "he," and to help the situation, Luke pours on the ... charm? (At least the closest thing a by-the-book boy like Luke can come to it!) But the shrewd L.S. can see him a-comin'. Strip-mining for coal is what Pritchard is interested in *(a theme that would be repeated in the reunion movies)*. Jesse gives some Duke history: five generations of Dukes have lived at the farmhouse, Jesse was born there, his wife Lavinia died there, Daisy came there when she was 6, and the boys were little tykes when they arrived, too.

"Daisy's Shotgun Wedding," March 25, 1983

The awful "200 proof" Beaudry brothers and their skanky pa blow into town, dealing 'shine with Boss. One of 'em just *loooooves* Daisy. Pretty soon, some brawlin' ensues at the Boar's Nest. Meanwhile, Daisy's been feeling that Bo and Luke's watchful eyes have become a little too watchful. When Bo and Luke spy on her goodnight kiss with Darcy Kincaid, she's fed up. She decides to move into town with her friend Sally Jo. Bo and Luke's buddies Vern and Skip glide on by the farm in their ultralights, and when Rosco and Enos also come by, Bo and Luke hop off in those ultralights. Then the Beaudrys manage to kidnap not just Daisy — but Flash, too! Big ole Milo Beaudry figures he's got himself a bride. That bride turns into a runaway one, but doesn't get far. Bo and Luke are on the hunt for her, though, in those fabulous ultralights. When they finally find her, it's country boy against country boy, and those Beaudrys are pretty tough. *Milo Beaudry is played by Richard Moll of "Night Court."*

Back to the roots: Season 6 includes "Back Where We Started: The Real Hazzard County," a mini-tour of the original filming sites in Georgia with Ben Jones and Sonny Shroyer. The segment was shot in Covington in late 2005 (we remember Jo McLaney mentioning it to us when she saw part of it being shot in downtown Covington). Jones and Shroyer begin at the Holiday Inn in Conyers where the cast and crew stayed for a couple months, saying that Catherine Bach stayed in room 228 and John Schneider in 112.

Season 6

"Lulu's Gone Away," September 23, 1983
Directed by Tom Wopat.
After that dang Jefferson fails to get her car fixed for the umpteenth time, a fed-up Lulu takes refuge at the Duke farm, even taking a turn in the driver's seat of the General Lee (and executing two rapid-fire jumps, with her bro close behind)! After their argument at the Boar's Nest, J.D. is mighty perplexed to get home and find his wife gone — and no dinner. Unfortunately, Lulu then gets kidnapped by a trio of hoods who've been watching her. Boss frets after getting contacted by the kidnappers, but the Dukes are on the case. Lulu helps by leaving a clue or two as she is moved to and fro. When her captors are surprised by the Dukes, Lulu sits on the female of the bad bunch to detain her! Before long, it's a grand reunion between Lulu and J.D. It's just precious when Bo and Luke are trying to stuff Lulu into the General through the window. Chris Mulkey, who plays bad guy Billy Ray here, appeared in another episode along with a whole lotta other stuff over the years, often as a bad guy.

"A Baby for the Dukes," September 30, 1983
Bo, Luke and Daisy open the episode by singing "Mama, Don't Let Your Babies Grow Up to be Cowboys," then lo and behold, a woman drops off her baby boy Jamie in the General Lee. Bo and Luke encounter two goons who seem to be looking for the baby. Emerson P. Craig then drops in after Boss' county budget meeting ("Hoggonomics") with Enos and Rosco to tell Boss he's looking for the missing baby, which is his grandchild. He tells the story of how his son married a country girl he deemed "unfit," who, after his son died, took off with the child. The baby's mother, Mary Lou, says she wanted to bring Jamie to Hazzard so he could grow up around nice people. Bo and Luke look into the legalities of the situation. Daisy goes into hiding with the child at the old sawmill, while the boys and Mary Lou try to sort out the mess. And even Boss is tiring of Craig's snobby attitude. As part of his Hoggonomics, meanwhile, Boss has Rosco and Enos riding horses instead of driving the patrol cars they keep wrecking. *James Best's daughter Janeen plays Mary Lou.*

"Too Many Roscos," October 7, 1983
James Best gets to show his acting range: First Rosco is kidnapped, but everyone assumes he's dead when his squad car is found in the lake, and then they have this big wake and everybody cries, and then he shows up, but it's really not Rosco because it's the crook Woody impersonating Rosco, and the real Rosco is being held captive by the other crooks, and the Rosco that everyone thinks is Rosco is sure acting strange. Understand? And at the heart of all of this is a shipment of $1 million in federal reserve cash in an armored car that's due into Hazzard from Atlanta. Woody and his crooked friends have their eyes on that, and finally Bo and Luke get the real deal when Woody and his guys have them at gunpoint. *Bo does a nice little imitation of Rosco's "coo-coo!" We just love how Flash mournfully barks in this one. And when James Best as the crook Woody says he's been associated with the theater for 20 years, he really means it. Clancy Brown, such a young-un here, plays Kelly, one of Woody's associates.*

"Brotherly Love," October 14, 1983
Luke's baby brother, Jud Kane, who was assumed dead in a fire when he was just two weeks old, surfaces, for real, and he's gotten himself into a heapin' helpin' of trouble. He tells the Dukes that he has some gamblers chasing him because he refused to throw a boxing match. Lo and behold, those crooks come knocking on Boss Hogg's door, talking of reward cash for Jud's return but then locking Rosco and Boss into the jail cell. Luke

concocts a scheme to get the crooks off Jud's back, but Luke ends up at Tri-County Hospital with a concussion. When Enos gets a look at those two crooks, they seem awfully familiar. And it's up to Bo to do a daring dive to save the day. *Flash gets the best actor award for this episode, for picking up the keys that would free Rosco and Boss from the jail cell but then turning around and leaving when Boss won't apologize to her for being mean.*

"The Boar's Nest Bears," October 21, 1983
Directed by Tom Wopat.
Hazzard's annual pee-wee hoops game against the Chickasaw County youngsters is on its way, and Boss is without a decent coach for his Boar's Nest Bears. (Rosco just can't cut it.) The Duke boys volunteer themselves, in exchange for dropped charges for when they were late for their probation meeting. They also have a "secret weapon" for the team — family friend Rod Moffet, who just lost his dad but sure is great with the ball. But Bo and Luke have good ole Sheriff Little of Chickasaw to contend with first. A.C. Tate Jr. of Chickasaw County tries to intervene with Rod, threatening him. When Bo and Luke finally convince the boy to play, the grimy Tate decides to thwart the "secret weapon" by claiming he's not the right age to play. Courthouse documents back it up. Boss is hot and bothered by that, as he has a huge bet riding on the game. Daisy rushes off to get the correct documentation on Rod's age. *Jason Lively, who also appeared in the series pilot, plays Rod Moffet.*

"Boss Behind Bars," November 4, 1983
It's time for the Ridge Runners Old Timer's Race once again, and NASCAR vets Bo and Luke draw up the course. The bad old Beaudrys are back in town, though, and this time they want to nab Boss' still. At the Boar's Nest, Rosco is taking bets on the race, and Jesse is favored. In the race, Jesse crashes but is not hurt. Evidence of the sabotage of Jesse's car is planted on Boss (and even Rosco turns against his little fat buddy), but we know it was those ole Beaudrys. Landing in jail, Boss keeps insisting he's been framed and finally escapes to try to prove it. Bo and Luke are on the case — whether they realize it or not — as they try to keep track of them Beaudrys. *Richard Moll reprises his role as Milo, the Beaudry with a thing for Daisy. Rosco continues his "Say hello from Rosco" theme while Daisy is calling her cousins on the CB. The Ridge Runners' name is not consistent in the series — sometimes it's the Ridge Raiders.*

"A Boy's Best Friend," November 11, 1983
Directed by Sorrell Booke.
The Duke boys help out a sad orphan boy, Terry Lee, giving him a dog that looks amazingly like Flash, not knowing it's a valuable show dog that just escaped out of the back of a van. Flash then gets dognapped when crooks think she's the show dog (whose name is Maxine). Rosco is distraught. Boss catches wind of the $10,000 reward for Maxine's return and secretly swipes her out of Terry Lee's possession. The Duke boys track down Maxine's real owners, the John J. Hoopers of Chickasaw, and offer to buy the dog no matter the price. The Hoopers get to meet Terry Lee, and that changes things quite a bit. *Terry Lee was the very first credited role for Danny Cooksey, who went on to a robust singing and voice acting career, which is rather ironic since his voice is so clearly dubbed in this episode. The dubbed voice sounds like June Foray, though we haven't found it documented anywhere.*

"Targets: Daisy and Lulu," November 18, 1983
For the Hoggs' 25th wedding anniversary, Boss lets Lulu and Daisy go to New Orleans to buy a dress, but a case of mistaken suitcases on the way back reveals a stolen diamond necklace worth more than $200,000. Jefferson is all too interested in that necklace and a possible reward for its return. The crooks try to kidnap Lulu and Daisy in their quest to regain the jewelry, then later succeed at it. Bo and Luke hear about the theft of this Osborn necklace and realize what's up. They bargain with the kidnappers. Boss has his chubby little hands on the necklace and fences it to his cousin Big Dan Hogg, but then must get it back. So then Bo and Luke are able to get the girls back, too. But even though the two kidnappers have been caught, their ringleader Lipton is still out there. Finally, in a memorable turn, Boss and Rosco do a drag-thang to pose as Lulu and Daisy and sting the crooks. *Sometimes '68 Dodge Chargers were used for the General, as you can see at the beginning of this episode. Bruce Glover, who portrays Lipton's associate Wilbur here, has done just about any '70s-'80s TV show you can name and was in the movie "Diamonds are Forever."*

"Twin Trouble," November 25, 1983
Blond, jewelry-nabbing twins divide Bo and Luke. One is fleeing the scene in Capitol City and being chased down by Luke, while the other is hitting up Bo with the whole "broken-down car" routine in Hazzard. Luke then sees what he thinks is his pretty little jewelry-robbing buddy with Bo. He confronts them unsuccessfully then dials up Sheriff Floyd in Hatchapee to turn her in. Bo is mad as his new lady friend is arrested. Sheriff Floyd is trying to

investigate, having connected with Rosco about it, while the girls, Cindy and Sandy, work on getting those jewels fenced. Rosco and Enos, meanwhile, are tooling around on three-wheelers after their patrol cars get wrecked once again. And Boss is interested in the loot that those little ladies have, so he has Cindy followed. Finally Luke comes face to face with both girls and realizes what the deal is. *The twins in this one, Candi and Randi Brough, also appear in "Arrest Jesse Duke."*

"Enos' Last Chance," December 2, 1983
The Dukes pick up a hitchhiker, Lynn Brady, who's really a hit man, Frank Scanlon, whom Enos helped incarcerate in L.A. — and who has revenge on his mind. After an altercation near the general store, Enos apprehends him and brings him in, then he escapes custody and takes off in a police car, and a fed-up Boss fires Enos. The saddened Enos is about to leave town, but the Dukes talk him into staying with them. But Scanlon has his eyes on things. He puts explosives in Enos' car, and Enos and Daisy narrowly miss that danger. The Dukes devise a plot to flush out Scanlon, with a little help from Enos' buddy at the radio station, Elton, announcing Enos' appearance on the radio show. The Ridge Runners lend a hand. But the plan backfires, and Scanlon kidnaps Daisy. Enos puts himself up for Scanlon, to get Daisy back, but which one is really Enos? There are several of 'em!

"High Flyin' Dukes," December 9, 1983
Daisy gives a hand to her buddy Joe Ward the crop-duster (who bought out Darcy the crop duster, by the way) when Joe has to be taken to the hospital. The three cousins offer to cover his crop dustin' work. Boss is connivin' with a couple crooks to put lye in the crop pesticide, then he frames Joe and the Dukes for it. The crooks, Hector and Percy, are worried Boss is going to double-cross them, so they have a tape that implicates Boss and Rosco. So that helps immensely when the Dukes get wise enough to make a citizen's arrest on them for the lye sabotage. The crooks then steal Joe Ward's plane and start up a protection racket in Hazzard, shaking down the local farmers. The Dukes decide to use Daisy's tape recorder to make a tape of their own, with Jesse posing as one of his fellow farmers. But even that doesn't stick. *Love how Uncle Jesse leaves the phone in the windowsill so it can be answered inside or outside. Phones had cords back then, ya know.*

"Cooter's Girl," December 30, 1983

Just as Bo and Luke are taking a spin in Darcy's plane (*lots of flying going on lately!*), Cooter's 18-year-old daughter Nancylou Nelson— a daughter he doesn't know, you understand — shows up to see just what kind of dad she has. She gets to the Boar's Nest just in time to see Cooter in a big brawl. The Dukes help out to try to cast Cooter in a better light. It's also Health Week in Hazzard, and Boss leads the aerobic charge, with his sheriff and deputy in tow. Despite some more bad luck and trouble, like a couple swindlers who envision turning Hazzard into a toxic waste dump, Cooter is still able to show his good, honest self to Nancylou. *It was nice to see the long-faithful Cooter come off the sidelines and into center stage for this one. The gal who plays his daughter, Kim Richards, starred as Tia in Disney's "Witch Mountain" movies and is aunt to Paris and Nicky Hilton, nowadays.*

"Heiress Daisy Duke," January 6, 1984

It's time for Rosco's performance evaluation, so Boss does a ride-along with him. They both learn about Georgia tycoon Carter Stewart, who has some kin who decide they'd rather see his heiress and granddaughter Vivian dead than alive. It just so happens that Daisy is the very image of Vivian's dead mom, and so could be thought to be Vivian. Especially if she thought it! Boss has Daisy hypnotized to believe she's actually this wealthy chick named Vivian — because, of course, he wants the hefty $200,000 finder's fee for ... er, finding ... her. And soon Bo, Luke and Jesse are wondering why their girl is acting so weird. They do a little digging and find out more, just as Boss introduces Carter to "Vivian." *Walker Edmiston reprises his role as Professor Crandall from "Goodbye, General Lee," and his other appearance is referenced by Bo and Luke in this episode (and that time, his last name was spelled Cradall).*

"Dead and Alive," January 20, 1984

Directed by James Best.
An armored truck moving through Chickasaw County gets robbed, and Artie Bender inadvertently points Sheriff Little toward Bo and Luke, really meaning to point him toward the crooks Bo and Luke are following. Boss then pays talented artist Artie to be "dead" so his paintings will be more valuable. So the only eye witness who could help out Bo and Luke is ... the deceased Artie Bender. Boss Hogg brings in an Atlanta art dealer to clean house on Artie's art. The Dukes have to flee the Chickasaw jail, investigate this sudden "death" of Artie's with Doc Appleby (who says Artie wasn't ailing at all), and chase down the real crooks — and they get a great family

portrait, too. *Sheriff Little plays big (so to speak) in this episode. To see him hunting and pecking at the typewriter in his office is precious, and in another scene he hangs Rosco up on a pole.*

"Play it Again, Luke," January 27, 1984
Luke meets up again with his old flame, budding singer Candy Dix, when she tries out some new material at the "out of the way" Boar's Nest. Her stern manager, Eddie Lee, though, has financial trouble going on, and he's salivating over her $75,000 life insurance policy. And Eddie Lee doesn't miss the fondness Candy has for Luke. The two trade blows, and Eddie Lee and his cousin Hoby try to force Candy to stay with them. Eddie Lee has been stealing from her, she later tells Luke. Candy goes on the lam with the Dukes while they try to figure out how they're going to get her out of this mess — namely by getting Eddie Lee in jail. And Boss Hogg? Well, he's cutting a deal on the side with Eddie Lee. The Dukes hide out Candy at Cooter's garage, but then she gets an attack of conscience for all the trouble she's causing and sneaks off. *Tom Wopat sings and plays guitar at the end with the actress who portrays Candy, Roberta Leighton. Rosco's car lands in a tree after a jump in this one, and we also get a jump of the General over some bales of straw. We get a rare glimpse of the loft living area above Cooter's garage.*

"Undercover Dukes, Part 1," February 3, 1984
Bo and Luke meet a pretty little female racecar owner, Mary Beth Carver, whose Daddy just happens to be mobster J.J. Carver. She asks them to return to the NASCAR circuit and drive for her. As enticing as that is, they're not interested. J.J. Carver then comes to town to have a conference with J.D. Hogg, and with these Duke boys who turned down his daughter. He tries to throw more money at Bo and Luke, and they still turn it down. The feds, however, manage to successfully recruit the Dukes to investigate Carver. The boys are sworn to secrecy, so they can't tell Daisy and Jesse. Daisy is distressed with the boys because she thinks they're neglecting Uncle Jesse on his birthday. Bo and Luke progress with the plan, moving in at the Carver estate and preparing to race the mobster's car. *Lydia Cornell, the buxom blond of ABC's "Too Close for Comfort," plays Mary Beth. Stepfanie Kramer is her right-hand gal Anna Louise. Special agent Walden is portrayed by Herbert Jefferson Jr. "Saved By The Bell"'s Dennis Haskins puts in his third "Dukes" appearance, though this one is uncredited. He plays a security guard at Carver's front gate. Thanks to our fellow author Brian Lombard for that tip-off!*

"Undercover Dukes, Part 2," February 10, 1984

Daisy's Jeep Dixie comes in handy, and even Flash lends a hand, in this second half of the story. Bo and Luke are keeping their eyes and ears open at the Carver estate, realizing J.J. Carver is planning a big coup in a meeting with mobsters from other regions of the U.S. Boss and Rosco are on their own stakeout and camp-out, following around the boys and thinking, as they see them talking to the federal agent, that they've caught them doing something illegal. Carver decides the best Duke is a dead Duke. Bo and Luke prepare for the race, while Daisy and Cooter hold a surprise birthday party for Uncle Jesse at the Boar's Nest. Uncle Jesse's too worried about the boys, though, to really enjoy it. Boss and Rosco muck things up and get themselves and Luke apprehended by Carver's goons, then Bo must bust them out. The Dukes' car pulls out in front at the race, and Bo comes running up on foot to clear out the goon before the guy takes a shot at the driver — who is actually Daisy.

"How to Succeed in Hazzard," February 17, 1984

There's a Dewey Hogg sighting in Hazzard — "There goes the neighborhood," as Cooter says. Dewey feigns terminal illness and proposes building a medical clinic in Hazzard, with a county fundraiser to foot some of the bill. Jesse's savings-deposit box holds the cash. Luke decides to use Daisy as bait to get Dewey to mess up and reveal the truth about his "illness." Sure enough, it works, and then Daisy must fight him off! But Dewey squirms away from that situation and furthers his schemes to lift the raised funds. But the Dukes have another trick up their sleeve, plotting with Boss and Rosco and some allegedly tainted champagne. Dewey believes it and thinks he may be dying for real. *Bo is gone in this episode, and Cooter fills the void with the Dukes. Loving AMC's "Mad Men" so much, we were rather shocked and amazed to see Dewey Hogg — Robert Morse — show up as Bertram Cooper, one of the bigshot owners of the ad agency. Though Dewey Hogg seems older than the Duke cousins in this episode, Luke remarks that he once beat Daisy "out of first prize in the old school spelling bee." Fellow author Brian Lombard wonders if this episode was originally written for Hughie, though the title could be a nod to Morse's 1967 film, "How to Succeed in Business Without Really Trying."*

"Close Call for Daisy," February 24, 1984
As she's dressed as a nurse for the church play, Daisy inadvertently picks up the little black book of an ailing and nervous gangster, Norman Willis, when she thinks it is her own pocketbook. Nervous Norman and his goon Jake take potshots at Bo and Luke, then pursue Daisy. Boss gets involved and tries to get the book back himself. He thinks Norman might be looking for that take he's been withholding from him. That just makes Boss a liability with Nervous Norman. Daisy, meanwhile, hides out at Enos' house (Enos is rather nervous himself, hurriedly removing his numerous photos of Daisy from the mirror). And of course, he's a perfect gentleman! Rosco finds out Daisy is there and blabs to Nervous Norman and Boss, and Nervous Norman and Jake kidnap Daisy. Bo and Luke try to cut a deal for Daisy with Norman's little black book.

"The Ransom of Hazzard County," March 2, 1984
Boss Hogg decides Enos is too gentle a soul, especially when dealing with the Dukes, so he "promotes" him to an office job of "commissioner of records" and hires tough new deputy Billy Joe Coogan. Boss then sets about getting all his fabulous scams up and running, targeting the Dukes, of course. Billy Joe ends up threatening (under the guise of the "Doomsday Gang") to open the dam on Hazzard if he doesn't get $150,000. The Dukes discover the plot through a map found in a patrol car. Enos learns that Coogan is behind the scheme, and he, Boss and Rosco get locked in the jail cell by Coogan. The Dukes must fight to expose this blackmailer and close the dam back down. *The stunt of setting Boss Hogg's hat on fire as he's trying to light his cigar was James Best's idea, and Sorrell Booke never flinched as the fire grew and grew on his hat, Best says in his autobiography.*

"The Fortune Tellers," March 23, 1984
A couple of flimflamming fortune-tellers, Madame Delilah and her flunky Three Pack, roll into Hazzard looking for easy prey. Luke and Daisy encounter them on the road after an altercation with Rosco. Madame Delilah and Three-Pack head to the Boar's Nest to put on their act, then Daisy is framed for stealing money from the Boar's Nest. Lulu is looking to finally cash in on the bonds her Uncle Jasper left her, not knowing that Boss nabbed 'em years ago. Boss then pours on the charm (sexy smoking jacket, gooseberry wine) to love up to Lulu and get her safe combination so he can get the fake bonds out. He decides the flimflamming fortune-tellers might be able to help. The Dukes, meanwhile, have caught on to the fact that these fortune-tellers had something to do with the missing cash. *This*

episode has enough derogatory references to the little person, Three Pack, to inflame any politically correct person. Waylon is quite funny in this one ("Thanks for the warning, Enos!" after Enos yells out to Daisy that he's got to arrest her). And Bo is out racing on the NASCAR circuit, by the way, and is shown at the end for a minute.

"Cooter's Confession," March 24, 1984

Cooter's old friend, Jonas Jones, who served time for armed robbery in another state, has his truck hijacked and is in trouble. His lunch pail ends up in the wrong place, and the hijackers are happy to implicate him with it. Good-hearted Cooter believes in his buddy and doesn't want to see him get punished for something he didn't do — especially since Jonas once saved Cooter's life. Cooter confesses to the truck hijacking and gets himself locked up. Bo and Luke, who are the ones who brought in the lunch pail, catch on to this and plan to clear both Cooter and Jonas — by setting themselves up as bait to the real hijackers. Daisy keeps Enos busy with her "broken-down" Dixie while Bo and Luke go to bust out Cooter. *We love how the show utilizes Georgia place references, like when Enos tells the Dukes he's on Peachtree Lane here. This episode marks the beginning of the usage of miniatures for the car jumps.*

End of the line: A cozy family scene went onto the cover of the seventh and final DVD set. The special features include a tribute to Waylon Jennings.

Season 7

"Happy Birthday, General Lee," September 21, 1984
The Dukes remember when they first built the General, eight years earlier, when Bo was fresh out of high school and Luke right out of the military (and Boss was thinner and Rosco sporting a thick moustache). In the flashback, Bo and Luke are needin' some wheels for the road race, so Jesse appeals to Boss for a loan. Daisy and her beautiful legs start working at the Boar's Nest as a bargaining chip. The boys get their eyes around a promising-looking black Charger at the junkyard. They buy it, and then two strangers (who happen to be robbers) are claiming the car is theirs. But dressed in a coat of the only color paint Cooter has in his garage — orange — and the "fighting spirit of the South" with the rebel flag and Dixie horn, the newly christened General Lee is ready to rumble. It takes its very first jump as Bo and Luke are fleeing the two crooks, then it takes on Hazzard's big race. *Bo and Luke start out the show's final season by jumping the General through a drain pipe at a construction site. As we then go into the flashback, it almost feels like a tribute to the show itself, which nearly spans that time, and we realize that in the timeframe in which the show began, the General had only been around a year or two.*

"Welcome, Waylon Jennings," September 28, 1984
The balladeer himself brings his semitruck country-western museum through Hazzard for a visit, staying with the Dukes and enjoying his time. His female partner Betty Jo, though, is suspicious after their empty decoy semi is hijacked. She decides to investigate the Duke boys. The Dukes fall prey to the real hijackers as the museum disappears for real, on Enos' watch. And Boss and Rosco? They're busy cutting letters out of the newspaper for the ransom note. Bo and Luke get held against their will but then escape by pulling a fast one on Rosco and Enos, and even Betty Jo. They even employ the "Hazzard Homing Device" to track the criminals. Before it's all said and done, Waylon gets to be in on one of those General jumps he's been narrating for so many years. *Waylon adopts the first person in referring to his true self on-screen as he narrates this one. Betty Jo is played by Shannon Tweed, known, of course, for being Gene Simmons' wife.*

"Dr. Jekyll and Mr. Duke," October 5, 1984
Excitement is in the air for the annual Hazzard Hayride. A van carrying genetic research materials accidentally dumps a vial into the Hazzard pond, right before Luke takes a quick drink while filling a gallon jug for the General's radiator. It's a mind altering-chemical, and it makes Luke a mite-bit ornery for the hayride. After he spouts off to everyone he encounters, he tears off in the General to vandalize some property. Bank robbers Ben and Hurley arrive in town, meanwhile, and see Luke's fancy driving. They figure they've got themselves a nice local patsy. Boss and Rosco observe Luke getting money from the two and of course get suspicious. Pretty soon, Luke's got a pistol in his hand practicing for his own bank robbery. Bo, Daisy and Jesse investigate Luke's personality change, but the Genetic Research Corp. they visit in Atlanta just wants to sweep it under the rug.

"Robot P. Coltrane," October 12, 1984
A couple of robot rustlers run the Dukes off the road on their way into town to demonstrate their new acquisition, Bobby Joe. Rosco brings the two in for speeding. Boss is so impressed with Bobby Joe that he "hires" the robot to replace Rosco as sheriff. The Duke boys sense that something's funny with these robot peddlers, so they investigate. They find the rustlers' hideout but get apprehended and tied up. The robot rustlers then trick Rosco into becoming involved in their plot to rob the bank and frame the robot for it. The Dukes finally learn that the robot is stolen merchandise, and they have to free Rosco from its grasp at the bank. *The General lands on a semitruck and drives through fire in this one. James Best writes in his autobiography, "Best in Hollywood," that he had pitched this idea of Boss Hogg replacing Rosco with a robot to the show's writers, and they brushed it off as a bad idea, then later, lo and behold, this script appeared. He says the same thing about the idea of an alien visitor to Hazzard.*

"No More Mr. Nice Guy," October 19, 1984
Boss sets up the Dukes by fooling them into thinking Daisy won a department store contest by being the one-millionth customer, having his partners Stoney, Billie Jean and Zack dole out stolen gifts to her like a fabulous mink coat and a hot yellow Mustang. Rosco then shows up with stolen goods charges. It's all for Boss to impress a senator who's cracking down on crime. But then Boss goes and gets amnesia and doesn't understand why these "nice young men" Bo and Luke are being harassed. Then he regains his memory. Then he gets amnesia again. And it all gets real confusin'. *Audrey Landers plays the swindler Billie Jean. It's funny how Bo*

makes reference to Daisy's car from early in the season, noting that both that one and this Mustang are yellow. And speaking of references, artist Artie Bender, who appeared in an earlier episode, is mentioned here though he doesn't appear.

"The Dukes in Hollywood," November 2, 1984
A Hollywood crew comes to Hazzard to film a flick — complete with heartthrob Brock Curtis. But there's a plot by producer Jason Dillard to cash in on the $5-million insurance policy of the big star. The Dukes manage to save Brock's life when his car speeds out of control, putting themselves square in the center of the mess, especially since Brock and the director, Billy, insist that Bo, Luke and Daisy come to Hollywood and appear in the film, too! Boss and Rosco scam their way to California, also, with Boss trying to get somebody to listen to his great movie idea: his life story. On the movie set, more attempts on Brock's life occur, so Bo and Luke do some poking around, irking the on-set security (who's even more irked by Boss and Rosco in wacky costumes). Pretty soon, the General and the Dukes are in danger. *Dick Van Dyke's hunky son Barry, who would go on to star in CBS' "Diagnosis: Murder," plays Brock. Flash gets discovered (we always knew she was a star). And of course, the Dukes would return to Hollywood in the second reunion movie in 2000.*

"Cool Hands, Luke and Bo," November 9, 1984
Bo and Luke are venturing into Osage County — all legal-like on an errand — and the sheriff pulls them over. Boss' rival in that county, Col. Cassius Claibourne, throws the Dukes on the chain gang. Jesse and Daisy come to Osage to plead their case, to no avail. Claibourne dials up Boss Hogg to make a deal, but Boss won't have it. Meanwhile, Lulu returns early from the fat farm (she gained weight) and rallies her J.D. for the Dukes. Claibourne then manages to put Boss and Rosco into custody, as well, blackmailing them with sumptuous food to get his hands on Hazzard goodies such as the Boar's Nest. Bo and Luke get into lots of tussles on the chain gang and are tossed into solitary confinement. Daisy has to bust the General out of its own confinement (doing a big jump in that thing!) and do that whole tail-flappin' thing that she does best. *James Avery and Morgan Woodward star.*

"Go West, Young Dukes," November 16, 1984
Boss is fishing through the old "junk" his great-granddaddy Thadius left him and he finds the deed to the Duke farm, dated June 13, 1872. Looks like this time Boss has finally got 'em. The Dukes start packing. As Jesse reads an old

diary of Jenny Duke, the show travels in time to the Old West as the Hazzard ancestors duke it out over the farm. Meet Jeremiah and Jenny Duke, Bo's great-grandpa Joe Duke, Daisy's great-grandma Dixie Duke, Hank Duke and the ruffians Thadius B. Hogg and Rufus Z. Coltrane, along with a couple gunmen named Frank and Jesse! The James boys hold up the stage carrying Joe and Dixie into town, though unsuccessfully. Dixie gets herself a job at the local saloon. The Dukes know some nefarious plot is afoot. Then Thadius has Hank put in jail, figuring Jeremiah will sign over the Duke farm to free him. Times' was bad back then, too, for sure. But the Dukes end up saving Thadius' life, so Thadius signs the farm back over, and the Dukes buried this deed in a very safe place. *Catherine Bach's fancy saloon gown as Dixie is just lovely, and Denver Pyle gets red hair and beard for the part of Jeremiah. We're wondering, by the way, in this era of miniatures, how many times they're going to do that jump-through-the-silo thing.*

"Cale Yarborough Comes to Hazzard," November 23, 1984
Directed by James Best.
The real-life racecar driver returns to town to visit a sick orphan boy, Robby, who idolizes him. On the way, though, he gets carjacked, and Bo and Luke come along to give him a lift. But then the General's acting up, so they have to take the 'jackers' car. When Rosco catches up to them, he doesn't believe that Cale Yarborough is really Cale Yarborough, plus Cale has the bags of bank money the 'jackers were carrying. Bo, Luke and Cale are thrown in jail, but then are able to get out. Robby brightens at Cale's visit and undergoes his surgery successfully. The carjackers Eddie and Elmo are still after their cash, though. They eventually are caught, fortunately, and hopefully Cale will still be convinced to c'mon back and visit! *Dennis Haskins of "Saved by the Bell" plays Elmo Smith. Fave line, as Rosco is trying to hightail it after the Dukes and has Boss in the passenger seat: "You know when there's flab in the cab it's hard to put the pedal to the metal!"*

"Danger on the Hazzard Express," November 30, 1984
Directed by Sorrell Booke.
Bo, Luke and Daisy are run off the road by another car, which has no driver, and which also gets wrecked. When they try to investigate, they get shot at. Boss and Rosco won't listen to their story. Later on, when they return to the scene, the car is gone — then the General gets stolen on 'em! Come to find out, Boss has employed a train-robbery gang that uses remote-control cars — and the General Lee is their next criminal tool. Boss has got a scheme going related to a shipment going to the Precious Metals Exchange

in Atlanta. Bo and Luke sneak into Boss' office and see a model train setup. Pretty soon, the five o'clock freight train is on its way to Hazzard, and the Dukes have to figure out a way to keep their best orange buddy from being involved in a life of crime. It doesn't help that they're tied up by the crooks.

"Sittin' Dukes," December 14, 1984
Luke's old Marine nemesis, Benson, returns for revenge, escaping from prison in Chickasaw and, with a con buddy, seizing the Duke household. He demands a change of clothes, then takes Luke into town in the General to buy some guns. Lulu, meanwhile, has imposed martial law in the Hogg household as she puts her not-so-little J.D. on a diet, even putting an alarm on the fridge. Boss takes to smuggling in food on the side, even having to navigate past Rosco. Sheriff Little pays a visit to look for his escaped convicts, and the Dukes get implicated. Daisy and Jesse get locked up by Rosco as Luke and Bo are being held by Benson and Hixx. Then Boss, Rosco and Cooter end up in jail, too. For Bo and Luke, it becomes a matter of divide and conquer. *Lulu delivers one of BRBTV's favorite classic lines about J.D.: "Much as I love that apple muffin, I don't like the crust he's showin'." Though Benson is only referred to as Benson in the episode, when Rosco looks at his mugshot, it also includes the name Lee. Jesse does an impression of Sheriff Little over the CB, and the General jumps right on top of another car.*

"Sky Bandits Over Hazzard," December 21, 1984
A foursome of thieves hijack an armored truck and helicopter it away. The news disrupts Boss and Rosco's aerobics routine — especially since Boss' bank money was on that truck. Bo and Luke, who were seen by Enos helping the armored truck out of a ditch earlier, are arrested and jailed in the robbery. When another truck is hit, though, it's obvious the boys aren't guilty, but Boss keeps them thinking they're implicated, then allows them to escape so they'll go after the real crooks to clear themselves. Sure enough, they investigate, followed by Boss and Rosco in disguise, and an errant wristwatch belonging to one of the hijackers helps their cause. Later, Daisy gets kidnapped by the thieves, and the boys take to the sky in their buddy Vern's ultralights to scout out the territory. *This episode includes Bo's A-plus imitation of Rosco over the phone. Bob Hastings is Taylor, one of the hijackers.*

"The Haunting of J.D. Hogg," January 4, 1985
Directed by Tom Wopat.
It's time to read the will of Boss' Uncle Silas. Even though Silas left Jesse as executor of his estate to ensure that his cash goes to charity, Boss engineers a plan to make himself the executor instead. He conspires with a couple thugs to replace the newer printed will with an audio will that's 15 years old. But Silas sent Jesse a letter recently about the will's change, a letter that Boss and Rosco promptly steal and destroy. The crooks then decide to double-cross Boss. The Dukes realize what is going on and call in the local ventriloquist, Mr. Winkle, to help out in their camp. He impersonates Silas Hogg for a good "haunting" of Boss as he visits his uncle's old house to liquidate it. Porch swings and rocking chairs seemingly moving on their own help the cause, too. And that voice from beyond the grave knows the details of Boss' life (because Jesse does!). Boss has a change of heart about Silas' money. Daisy finds herself caught up with the double-crossers, though that works out, too! *Is the Mr. Winkle shown here the same Mr. Winkle who owns the Hazzard Dog Pound, shown in "A Boy's Best Friend"? Why, yes, he is.*

"When You Wish Upon a Hogg," January 11, 1985
Bo and Luke get knocked out when a couple strange men put some noxious gas in the back of the General Lee. As they're snoozing, Daisy is all but run off the road by those same two dudes. Boss' nephew Hughie arrives to town and cons Boss into believing an old lamp is magic — with a lovely female "genie," too. She seems to grant his wish of putting Bo and Luke Duke in jail (they're still asleep!). The boys manage to finagle themselves out of the jail cell while Boss rubs that lamp for another wish forthwith. Getting stacks of cash is next on his wishlist. The Dukes pursue the two baddies and learn about Hughie's scam to get Boss to sign over everything he owns. They get to the courthouse to see Boss and Rosco now jailed, then the two crooks pursue them outta there. Pretty soon, Hughie has his uncle irate at him just in time for him to leave town again. Yet another reference to Willow Creek in this one. Boss worries that the genie will turn him into a warthog. *This may be a direct reference to the animated series from two years earlier, specifically, the episode "Boss O'Hogg and the Little People," wherein J.D. faced that very same fate.*

"Strange Visitor to Hazzard," January 25, 1985
Directed by Sorrell Booke.

UFO sightings abound in Hazzard, then Enos witnesses some funky lights at Skunk Hollow. Boss sees an opportunity in all the hoopla and sets out to shake things up a bit and add some cash to the corrupt — er, we mean, community — coffers. At Skunk Hollow, the Duke cousins investigate Enos' claims — and do a little crabapple pickin' — unknowingly picking up a little alien critter in the back seat of the General. They take him back to the farm to make friends. Two scammers overhear Boss' plot to fake a space invasion and decide to outscam the scammers — hijacking Boss' WHOGG radio station to announce the invasion, then kidnapping the little alien so they can make their own profit from him. *There are a lot of things wrong with this episode, besides the major problem of the premise. Much of the action is awkward and seems thrown together: the two scammers trying to take a snooze out in the open air suddenly shoot at the alien with no transitioning, Daisy flubs her line during the crabapple picking but the scene just charges on, there's truly dreadful, '70s-style, eerie elevator music in the background as the Dukes try to make friends with the alien at their house, and when the alien takes off in a police car the viewer's imagination — and patience — are REALLY stretched. But hey, besides that! ... BRBTV appreciates ANY and ALL "Dukes" episodes, but it's this one that fans might bring to mind when they think of the show's hokey image.*

Veteran actor Felix Silla played the visitor in "Strange Visitor to Hazzard." Silla makes lots of appearances on the con circuit; here he steps away from his autograph table to snag a photo of the Monkeemobile at the Motor City Comic Con in May 2012.

"Enos and Daisy's Wedding," February 1, 1985
Directed by Tom Wopat.
When he's left to guard Boss' bank, Enos is forced by a couple crooks to "rob" it, and the sole witness, Daisy, figures out the only way to save him is to marry him, so she won't have to testify against him. Her family members are a little surprised by this and try to talk some sense into her. Enos has been framed, though, and Bo and Luke get wind of that and get hot on the trail of the framers. Meanwhile, Lulu is signed on to this whole wedding thing and encourages the happy couple along. Everybody gets all gussied up for the nuptials at the Boar's Nest. Bo and Luke hit the road to pursue the bank robbers and a fistfight ensues. When the real crooks are caught, Daisy still feels she should go through with the wedding, but Enos has a frank talk with her. *This plotline is "to be continued," if you watch the reunion movies. Daisy is just resplendent in her wedding dress full of lace and ruffles. Jesse refers to his wife as Lavinia here.*

"Opening Night at the Boar's Nest," February 8, 1985
Directed by John Schneider.
It's time for Lulu's talent review, and the Dukes are comin' out singin'. Rosco is polishing up a magician's routine with his assistant "Flash-o." Bo and Luke try to talk some sense into some crazy drivers they encounter on the road, but that doesn't go too well. These two out-of-towners are targeting Boss, however. They arrive to town and try to run him down. When the Dukes perform at the talent show, it's Bo, Luke, Daisy, Cooter and Jesse. Rosco (in his fabulous sequined suit as "Coltrano the Great") makes Boss disappear — well, really, two men do — the same two men Bo and Luke encountered on the road. One of 'em was incarcerated with Boss' assistance a few years back. Bo and Luke put two and two together, along with Enos, and go after the kidnappers. They want a million bucks in exchange for J.D. Rosco, meanwhile, is distraught because he thinks he really did make Boss disappear! *Wow, look at those legs! We're not talking Daisy here; we're talking Boss in his tutu and tights! Yikes!*

BY THE NUMBERS

7 seasons

147 episodes (S1: 13, S2:23, S3:23, S4:27, S5:22, S6:22, S7:17) (two-parters counted as two eps)

262 General Lee jumps

127 Sheriff's car jumps (not just Hazzard County sheriff's)

12 slides across the hood of the General by a Duke boy (including Luke in "Daisy's Song" and "The Sound of Music — Hazzard Style," Bo in "Shine on Hazzard Moon," "Nothin' But the Truth," "Dear Diary" and "Bye, Bye Boss," with the latter being more like a hood climb than a hood slide, then Vance in "The New Dukes") (not counted: a sort of hood climb by Luke in "Shine on Hazzard Moon" that was not quite a slide and not really seen well on-camera) (plus, Vance has an epic roll over the roof in "Hazzard Hustle" — seriously)

674 times a Duke boy gets into the General through the window (shown on screen, not implied)

312 Yee-haaaas! (sometimes rapid-fire) (sometimes more like a "Yahoo!" or a "Yee-hoo!")

129 Dixie horn blasts from the General

139 times Rosco says "dipstick" (first one: "Swamp Molly") (Boss and Bo said it, too)

54 times Enos says "Possum on a gumbush!" (first one: "Deputy Dukes") (Cooter said it, too)

303 Flash barks (record at one time: 15 or so barking at the alien in "Strange Visitor to Hazzard")

3 Burt Reynolds references ("One Armed Bandits," "Repo Men," "The Dukes in Hollywood")

(The above numbers are not counting the show's intro scenes, since those are taken from the episodes!)

Beyond the Series

"The Dukes of Hazzard: Reunion!"
A CBS-TV movie airing on April 25, 1997.
"It's the 200th anniversary of the founding of Hazzard County," Gy Waldron explained in a April 1997 interview for Country Weekly, "so there's a big homecoming with a possum cookoff and a rattlesnake chili contest." Luke Duke has been working for the forestry service, and Bo Duke has been a racecar driver (surprise, surprise). Daisy? Well, she up and got married, then her fella left her. She got a Ph.D. from Duke (!) University just the same. Cooter has become a congressman (as did the actor who portrayed him!). Rosco now goes by the title "Boss," and the hound dog at his side is Toodles. Enos has been a successful police sergeant in L.A. And the story here? Oh, yea ... Mean old developer Mama Max (played by the exquisite Stella Stevens, so bawdy here in those '90s power suits) wants to build a theme park in Hazzard County, and the Duke Farm is in danger, of course. Mama Max is scheming with Boss Rosco, whom she flatters with the pet name "Clint" (as in Eastwood). The Duke boys plan to run the General Lee in a cross-country moonshine race. But look out — it's the oo car to challenge them, the only car to beat the General in an overland race! Enos, meanwhile, asks Daisy out for a proper date, after all these years, and then asks her to marry him. Mama Max arranges for a kidnap of Daisy, but who's kidnapped whom? Daisy manages to keep her busy with wedding plans.

The original cast is back, except Sorrell Booke, who died in 1994. Gary Hudson plays Riker, and Cynthia Rothrock plays Bertha Jo. We wanted to know where the wonderful portrait of Sorrell Booke as Boss Hogg, hanging in Rosco's office, ended up. It's quite touching as he talks to it in one scene. Well, our fellow author Brian Lombard had an answer (yea, we mention him a lot — he's like a "Dukes" computer!). "It was temporarily loaned to the production by Sorrell's daughter," Brian says. "Sorrell kept it when the series ended. It used to hang in Boss's living room (see 'The Revenge of Hughie Hogg,' 'Ding Dong, The Boss is Dead'). Speaking of Sorrell, his name is misspelled in the tribute. Also, the year before this movie aired, Gy Waldron produced a TV movie called 'Smoke Jumpers,' which no doubt influenced Luke's profession here." Thanks again, Brian! And by the way, as of presstime of this book, you could go on YouTube and watch John Schneider's behind-the-scenes filming of this reunion movie's production, featuring the lucky contest winner who got to travel to the set, Schneider's own General Lee, chats with cast members on the set, and advertising for Schneider's FaithWorks company.

Whenever anybody asks this author what her favorite star car is, she'll say the "00" Mustang from the "Dukes" reunion movie. Well, one fellow "Dukes" fan even painted this beauty. He's Jim Wilson of Ontario, and you'll see more of his wonderful "Dukes" paintings later in the book. BRBTV is proud to own the original of Jim's painting of the 00, hanging right here on the wall of the BRBTV Batcave. Next to it is a print of Jim's painting of the Duke farmhouse, by the way.

"The Dukes of Hazzard: Hazzard in Hollywood"
A CBS-TV movie airing on May 19, 2000.
Hazzard County needs a new hospital, and the Dukes pitch in to raise money for the efforts. It helps to have Toby Keith appearing (early on in his career). Businessman Ezra Bushmaster has pledged to add to the funds they raise, so they travel to Hollywood to see if some of their songs will fetch a decent price. They get hit by thieves though, and lose both their music and their cash, encountering some Russian gangsters and international loan sharks. This is Enos' neck of the woods, so the rest of the gang gets to see him in his element (with his fellow officer calling him a "studmuffin"). In fact, everywhere he goes, women are fawning over him! And as for Luke, the lady he was once involved with has become country star Anita Blackwood.

This time around, Uncle Jesse is missing from the lineup along with Boss Hogg. George Temple Hammett stars as Ty, Sven Holmberg as Serge and Kristof Konrad as Misha. Nicolas Coster, one of BRBTV's favorite actors, plays crooked businessman Ezra. Patricia Manterola plays Bo's love interest, Gabriela. We love how in the opening scene Cooter is wearing a hat from Ben Jones' own Cooter's Place. Amaury Nolasco, who portrayed Sucre on "Prison Break," appears in this one, as Bo and Luke encounter some Hispanic kids and go to one of their neighborhood parties. Meow on him! Patricia Belcher of "Bones" also appears as the feisty Deacon.

"The Dukes of Hazzard"
A theatrical movie released on August 5, 2005.
The Hazzard gang is completely recast for this big-screen remake. Johnny Knoxville is Luke Duke, Seann William Scott is Bo Duke and Jessica Simpson is Daisy, with Willie Nelson as Uncle Jesse, Burt Reynolds as Boss Hogg and the totally creepy M.C. Gainey (who starred in the original episode, "Bad Day in Hazzard") as a darker Rosco P. Coltrane. James Roday of "Psych" is almost recognizable as Billy Prickett.

Hazzard's hometown hero Billy Prickett comes back to town to run one of his old racing events, but he's really been hired by Boss Hogg to provide just the right ruse to distract the whole town. What Boss is planning is strip-mining in Hazzard (a premise borrowed from one of the original episodes, only it was an out-of-town developer that time), and Bo and Luke soon catch on to the scheme. The General Lee is sabotaged, however, and it's up to Cooter to get it back into racing form. Rosco busts Jesse for moonshinin' by planting a still (because he was "too dumb to find the real one") and, of course, takes away the Duke farm.

The movie seems to start out right, with the General Lee racing across the countryside delivering 'shine, but things quickly go south from there. (And that could mean something good here, but it just doesn't.) To say that this theatrical release was not well-received by "Dukes" fans is an understatement. That's a bit ironic, since there were some hard-core "Dukes" fans who worked as extras on the film. Lynda Carter of "Wonder Woman" is a bright spot — though it's a curious career move — as Jesse's girlfriend Pauline. Boss and Rosco are both dark and creepy, surprisingly, since this movie is such a lighthearted parody. There are plenty of elements you wouldn't have found in the regular series: the f-word, the s-word, Jesse's dirty jokes, pot-smoking, nudity (we watched the unrated version — billed as "Hog

This "Hog-Wild Edition" DVD set includes the unrated versions of both the 2005 "Dukes of Hazzard" theatrical release and the "The Dukes of Hazzard: The Beginning" 2007 release.

Wild" on the DVD"). No wonder Ben Jones spoke out publicly against the film. Still, the director says in the DVD extras that he grew up with the original series, and it does include some pretty big jumping and racing (25 Dodge Chargers were purchased for the movie, from scouring sites like eBay, even).

"The Dukes of Hazzard: The Beginning"

A straight-to-DVD movie released in 2007.

This "prequel" of the 2005 "Dukes" movie get a new cast: Jonathan Bennett as Bo Duke, Randy Wayne as Luke Duke, April Scott as Daisy Duke, with Chris McDonald as Boss Hogg. Willie Nelson hangs onto the role of Uncle Jesse from the 2005 movie. The movie explores the point in time when Bo and Luke first move into the Duke farm, years before the series takes place.

Sherilyn Fenn of "Twin Peaks" fame bravely took on the role of Lulu Hogg in "The Dukes of Hazzard: The Beginning," glamming things up a bit for J.D.'s wife. Here, she makes an appearance at the 2012 Motor City Comic Con in Novi, Michigan.

In the story, the boys each got into trouble, so their parents decided they should go work for Uncle Jesse. J.D. Hogg and Jesse are still friends, and J.D. has been looking the other way from Jesse's 'shine activities, but then he tries to shake Jesse down for some more cash. To raise funds, Bo and Luke decide to go into the 'shine-runnin' biz, but they need a fast car for that. With the help of Cooter (too young in the movie for the continuity of the regular series, especially considering his daughter Nancy Lou), they discover a '69 Dodge Charger at the bottom of a pond. Daisy, meanwhile, has just turned 18 and decides to go from a plain-Jane to her sexy self after developing a crush on the manager of the Boar's Nest — none other than Hughie Hogg, quite hunky in this incarnation. Flash is just a pup here, and Lulu Hogg (as played by Sherilyn Fenn) is rather luscious — and hitting on Luke like crazy.

The movie is farcical and rather raunchy, and wasn't any better received by hard-core fans than the 2005 version. There are bare female breasts and hind-ends here, which, of course, you never would've seen in the series, and plenty of swearing: the s-word comes out of the narrator's mouth twice in just the introduction, and there's the usage of the G-d phrase. (BRBTV reviewed the unrated version.)

"The Dukes" Animated Series

An animated series airing on CBS from February 5, 1983, to October 29, 1983.

The cartoon, which aired during the live-action series' fifth and sixth seasons, took the characters where the limitations of production budgets couldn't, to all sorts of exotic global locales under the premise of a race around the world to save the Duke farm. In this setting, the General Lee gets stolen from outside the Roman Coliseum, Rosco gets hold of Aladdin's Lamp, the Dukes encounter pirates and all kinds of other exciting stuff happens. It's not your usual Hazzard County fare! The cast was the same as for the live-action show, with Coy and Vance being utilized while Byron Cherry and Christopher Mayer were behind the wheel on the live-action show, and John Schneider and Tom Wopat later replacing their voices. Frank Welker voiced Flash and the General Lee. The character of Smokey the Raccoon was added, as Uncle Jesse's pet.

Season 1

"Put Up Your Dukes," February 5, 1983
After Boss tries to slow 'em down by trapping the Dukes in the General Lee high atop a garage mechanic's hydro-lift, they power on to Australia, just the same. There, they meet their cousin Willie and his boxing kangaroo Benny (who puts up his dukes!). Boss is interested in this cash cow ... er, we mean, kangaroo, and so are some criminals. It's Smokey the Raccoon's birthday, by the way.

"Jungle Jitters," February 12, 1983
In the South American jungle, the Dukes run low on gas and discover their extra gas supply is missing from the trunk (Boss!). They take a shortcut, where they find an ancient stone monument and some curious natives, who see the General as some sort of god, at first, but are none too friendly. They imprison the Duke trio, then Boss and Rosco when they arrive, as well. Then they figure on sacrificing the General to the big volcano they worship.

"The Dukes of Venice," February 19, 1983
After successfully navigating a closing drawbridge, the Dukes head to Rome, on the way to Venice after that. While they're checking out the Coliseum, the General attracts the eyes of a couple Italian criminals. The pair

steal the car, then rob a bank with it, on their own way to Venice. The Dukes must chase 'em down and try to save the General from this life of crime!

"Morocco Bound," February 26, 1983
The Dukes are about to take the ferry at Gibraltar, but Boss cuts a deal with the ferry captain to leave the Dukes behind. They could miss the race at Cairo! Daisy takes matters — and the wheel of the General Lee — into her own hands. Later, in their hotel in the Middle Eastern desert, Rosco is intrigued by a "Sharif" (he says he's a "Sher-iff" back home), and he winds up with the Sharif's suitcase, which contains a genie's magic lamp.

"The Secret Satellite," March 5, 1983
This time, they're in the Arctic Circle, and a U.S. satellite has gone astray. The Dukes decide to do a good deed and find the satellite, and Boss sees this as his chance to push on and get ahead in the race — until he hears that the U.S. government is offering a $100,000 reward for recovery of the satellite. In an amusing reference to Ronald Reagan, Boss cons an Eskimo boy out of the satellite by offering him jellybeans that he says he got from the president of the U.S.

"The Dukes of London," March 12, 1983
The race reaches England, and Boss gives new meaning to the term "sidewinder" as he destroys the General Lee's tires. Flash meets a look-alike doggie buddy as Boss and Rosco make a stop — and a case of mistaken identity ensues as they get started on their way again. Flash's buddy just happens to be the queen's pet, and the queen is definitely wondering why her doggie came back with all them fleas! The Dukes get thrown in the British brig.

"The Greece Fleece," March 19, 1983
Falling a bit behind in the race, Boss calls up a buddy in Greece and arranges for some traffic violations and other trumped-up charges for the Dukes. Daisy and the boys are jailed. They try to call Uncle Jesse back in Hazzard for some drachmas for bail, but then they must resort to diggin' into the bricks of their cell floor to try to escape. Boss, meanwhile, is fixin' to marry the niece of his buddy Nick, for a big dowry, of course.

"The Dukes in India," March 26, 1983
Boss and Rosco are behind in the race again (or is that still?). Boss calls up a buddy in India this time to slow the Dukes down. While Vance steps away to

use a phone, he's abducted, then a prince who looks a whole lot like him meets up with Daisy and Coy. That prince is in danger, though, as a leadership coup is being planned. As with Flash in London, it's a case of mistaken identity.

"The Dukes in Urbekistan," April 2, 1983
This episode is also listed as "The Dukes in Uzbekistan." Though Uzbekistan is a real country in central Asia, near Afghanistan, the term "Urbekistan" is used throughout this episode and on the title screen of the original television-station cut. The Dukes encounter a twister in Urbekistan, and even Boss and his bologna sandwich get caught up in it. Daisy and the boys then meet a London girl searching for her father, a geologist who disappeared mysteriously while looking for a diamond mine with an ancient map. As Daisy, Coy and Vance try to help her, the General Lee takes a float across a wild river —with the help of a huge wolf — and Boss takes a shine to that diamond mine, himself.

"The Dukes in Hong Kong," April 9, 1983
This episode is also called "A Hogg in Hong Kong."
Boss fakes out the Dukes to think he and Rosco are out of the race, but he's really trickin' up his Caddy for a big shortcut while the Dukes go sightseeing. Again, he calls a local criminal contact for help, this time in China. He employs a ship captain to trap the Dukes to get them out of the way. Coy, Vance and Daisy are imprisoned, but Daisy tricks the guard and they escape, just in time to find a nasty pirate trying to sell the General Lee!

"The Dukes in Scotland," April 16, 1983
Boss is talking over the radio to a Scottish shepherd in his scheming against the Dukes, who are on their way to visit old Hazzard friends Billy-Bob and June Stewart in their inherited Scottish castle. Daisy's driving, and she even spots the Loch Ness monster on the way. When they arrive, their friends tell them the castle is haunted by its previous owner, Angus McCavish, who went out looking for the Loch Ness monster and never returned. Boss and Rosco arrive to the castle, as well, to visit for a spell.

"The Dukes Do Paris," April 23, 1983
Boss and Rosco use their secret weapon, a cloud-maker, to divert the General Lee off the race path, while Boss radios ahead to his criminal contact in Paris, Mr. Blankie LeBlanc. But Daisy accidentally intercepts the rare blue Wazoo (bird) stamp that Boss has arranged to fetch. Boss

convinces the local police inspector that the Dukes are a notorious gang, and they're jailed.

"The Dukes in Switzerland," April 30, 1983
Coy, Vance and Daisy pull over to help Boss and Rosco when their Caddy is broken down in the snowy mountains of Switzerland. But it's just a ruse so Rosco can plant a listening device in the General. Boss hires a snowplow to bury the Dukes and the General, though that doesn't last long. The Dukes then pick up a female skier who's being chased. It turns out her father is a scientist whose latest invention — a way to turn seawater into gasoline — has sparked the interest of some dastardly spies.

Season 2

"Boss O'Hogg and the Little People," September 17, 1983
Boss Hogg steals the General's registration form then tells the police in Ireland that the blazing orange beauty is a stolen car. Bo, Luke and Daisy are pulled over, then jailed. Boss meets a leprechaun and wants his gold. The Dukes get out of jail, crash the General, then are helped by some leprechauns, themselves. The "little people" enlist their help to save their friend from the evil Boss Hogg who's trying to take his gold.

After the DVD set came out in 2010, FlickAttack.com asked James Best what were his memories of doing the animated series. "Of course, we were shooting 'The Dukes of Hazzard' at that time," Best said. "They called up and said Hanna-Barbera — I love cartoons, and I had never done any work for cartoons. We went over to the animation studio — it was very comfortable — and they just gave us scripts and we went into the regular characters as we did on the regular show. I think the cartoons were on for two years, then they took them off for some reason, but now they're bringing them back, so now there's a new generation of young people who will be introduced to 'The Dukes of Hazzard.'"

"Tales of the Vienna Hoods," September 24, 1983

While in Austria, Boss is stuck with babysitting his 10-year-old niece Cindy Sue, who watches his every move and is rather concerned with his immoral activities. Boss talks the Dukes into babysitting Cindy Sue while he cuts a deal with an illicit contact for some crown jewels. The Dukes, though, see sinister characters following them around town and try to elude them. No such luck — they all end up kidnapped, because Cindy Sue just happens to be the daughter of the very wealthy Willington P. Hogg.

"The Kid From Madrid," October 1, 1983

"There ain't nobody that can outdrive a Duke boy at the wheel of the General Lee," Uncle Jesse tells Smokey as he reads Daisy's latest postcard about the Dukes runnin' neck-and-neck with Boss and Rosco through Spain. The Dukes meet a young boy, Beppino, who's an expert horseman. Boss calls up an "amigo" to arrange for the Dukes to be out of the way for a while, and in exchange this amigo wants Boss to ensure that his boy wins the horserace he's riding in the next day. That boy happens to be riding against Beppino.

"A Dickens of a Christmas," October 8, 1983

Just as the live-action series features a Christmas episode, the cartoon follows suit ... The contest rules say there's no racing on Christmas, so the Dukes invite Boss and Rosco to join them for some holiday cheer. Boss turns 'em down because he's planning on cheating the race rules. As he hunkers down for the evening, though — you guessed it — he's visited by some spirits. It's Big Jake Marley, the one who taught Boss all his dirty tricks in Hazzard. Then, of course, it's the Ghost of Christmas Past, who shows Boss himself as a boy getting his first piggy bank, then as a young man dating Elsie McCoy, who would go on to marry Jesse Duke (*and that's three different names the two shows have given for Uncle Jesse's deceased wife, by the way*). This episode, voted the best of this series by BRBTV, offers the only glimpse at the Boar's Nest back home.

"The Canadian Caper," October 15, 1983

The Dukes race across northern Canada on the way to Quebec. But then they crash the General Lee near a wildlife preserve and meet a little girl. Boss, meanwhile, is calling a Canadian buddy who's a fur poacher, who just happens to be poaching at the wildlife preserve where the Dukes have made their new friend. The Dukes investigate the poaching, and soon the Royal Mounties have another closed case.

"The Dukes in Hollywood," October 22, 1983

In Tinseltown, a stunt guy doesn't want to go through with a dangerous scene. The Dukes drive onto the scene, and the moviemakers are impressed. The bigwigs also recruit a flattered Boss Hogg as executive producer of the film. But it's all a setup; the moviemaking con artist is planning on making off with the payroll and leaving Boss holding the bag, so to speak. Flash is pretty good at charades, but that ole Rosco is just no good guesser.

"A Hogg in the Foggy Bog," October 29, 1983

This episode is sometimes listed with the "Bog" spelled as "Bogg."
Jesse's great-uncle Cyrus — a rare skeleton in the Duke family closet — stole $20 million from an Army payroll train and hid it in the Philippines, where the Dukes are now heading in the race. It's the rainy season there (very muddy!). After he happens upon the old treasure map, Jesse decides to fly over, courtesy of a cousin in the military, to try to recover the treasure. Boss and Rosco spy on the Dukes, then go looking in the foggy bog for the treasure, themselves. The Dukes meet a researcher who offers to help them in their own search. This Duke family reunion is rather appropriate for the final episode of the series.

BEHIND THE SCENES

> "It continues to find a new audience of youngsters, not only in America but throughout the world. There is something really magic about the show."
>
> — Ben Jones, on CootersPlace.com

BRBTV fondly misses Glenn Call of Massachusetts, a wonderful, kind "Dukes" fan we saw at events for many years before his unfortunate passing too soon in 2011. Here, Glenn holds some "Dukes"-character-themed ID cards in Covington, Georgia, on the weekend of DukesFest 2008.

CREDITS

Giving credit where credit is due.

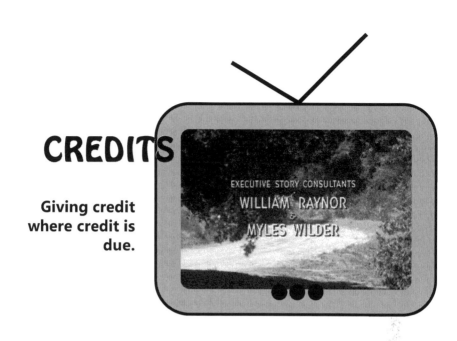

"The Dukes of Hazzard"

"The Dukes of Hazzard" ran for seven seasons, from January 26, 1979 to August 16, 1985 (the last first-run episode was February 8, 1985), Friday nights on CBS, for a total of 147 episodes.

Creator	Gy Waldron
Executive producers	Philip Mandelker, Paul R. Picard
Producers	Bill Kelley, Ralph Riskin, Gy Waldron, Skip Ward, Myles Wilder
Associate producers	Gilles A. de Turenne, Ron Grow, Wes McAfee, Albert J. Salzer, Skip Ward
Supervising producers	Rod Amateau, Hy Averback, Joseph Gantman, Robert Jacks
Directors	Rod Amateau, William Asher, Hy Averback, Allen Baron, Paul Baxley, Gabrielle Beaumont, James Best, Sorrell Booke, George Bowers, Michael Caffey, Bob Claver, William Crain, John Florea, Bob Kelljan, Harvey S. Laidman, Arthur

	Marks, Don McDougall, Bernard McEveety, Dick Moder, Hollingsworth Morse, Ernest Pintoff, Denver Pyle, Ralph Riskin, Ron Satlof, John R. Schneider, James Sheldon, Jack Starrett, Robert Sweeney, Gy Waldron, Jack Whitman, Tom Wopat
Executive story editor	Martin Roth
Story editor	Bruce Howard
Executive story supervisor	Si Rose
Executive story consultants	William Raynor, Myles Wilder
Writers	Bob Clark, Fred Freiberger, Ron Friedman, Herman Groves, Bruce Howard, Stephen Kandel, Len Kaufman, William Kelley, William Keys, Kris Kincade, Nance McCormick, Michael Michaelian, Simon Muntner, Katharyn Powers, William Putman, William Raynor, Jim Rogers, Si Rose, Martin Roth, Paul Savage, John R. Schneider, Michael Sevareid, Gy Waldron, Myles Wilder
Music	Richie Albright, Bruce Babcock, John Beal, Deane Hagen, Earle Hagen, Waylon Jennings, Fred Werner
Cinematographers	Arthur Botham, Dominick R. Palmer Jr., Bradley B. Six, Robert F. Sparks, Jack Whitman
Art directors	James Martin Bachman, Al Rohm
Film editors	Kirk Axtell, Howard Epstein, Robert I. Jillson, Albert P. Wilson
Mechanic / car builder	Tom Sarmento
Transportation director	Don Schisler
Stunt crew	Craig R. Baxley, Gary Baxley, Robert Jon Carlson, Jon H. Epstein, Corey Michael Eubanks (double for Tom Wopat), Debbie Evans, Bob Ivy, Terry James, Monty Jordan, Steve Kelso, Hubie Kerns Jr., Henry Kingi, Hannah Kozak, Gene LeBell, Ray Lykins, Bob Orrison, Eddie Paul, Debby Porter, John Schneider (as a driver), Rich

	Sephton, Tony Snegoff, Jerry Summers, Lance Turner, Renaud Veluzat, Al Wyatt Jr. (double for John Schneider)
Trainer for Flash	**Alvin Mears**

"The Dukes of Hazzard: Reunion!"

A Kudzu production, in association with Warner Bros. television, airing April 25, 1997 on CBS.

Executive producer	**Gy Waldron**
Producers	**Ira Marvin, Skip Ward**
Associate producer	**Russell Livingstone**
Director	**Lewis Teague**
Writer	**Gy Waldron**
Film editor	**Russell Livingstone**
Casting director	**Leslie Litt**
Cinematographer	**Barry M. Wilson**
Music	**Steve Wariner**
Stunt crew	**Paul Baxley, Marian Green, Carrick O'Quinn, Marc Schaffer, Monty L. Simons, Lance Turner, Gary J. Wayton**

"The Dukes of Hazzard: Hazzard in Hollywood"

A Kudzu production, in association with Warner Bros. television, airing May 19, 2000, on CBS.

Executive producers	**Gy Waldron, Bob Clark**
Producer	**Skip Ward**
Associate producer	**Elliot Friedgen**
Director	**Bradford May**
Editor	**Drake P. Silliman**
Music	**David Hoffner, Jim Ed Norman**
Writers	**Gy Waldron, Bob Clark**
Casting director	**Irene Mariano**
Production designer	**Rodger Maus**
Director of photography	**Bradford May**
Stunt crew	**Paul Baxley, Marian Green, Lance Turner, Thom Williams**

"The Dukes of Hazzard"

A motion picture released on August 5, 2005.

Executive producers	**Bruce Berman, Dana Goldberg, Eric McLeod, Greg Silverman**
Producer	**Bill Gerber**
Director	**Jay Chandrasekhar**
Writers	**Jonathan L. Davis, John O'Brien, Gy Waldron**
Film editors	**Jay Chandrasekhar, Lee Haxall, Myron I. Kerstein**
Cinematographer	**Lawrence Sher**
Music	**Nathan Barr**
Production designer	**Jon Gary Steele**
Art director	**Chris Cornwell**
Costume designer	**Genevieve Tyrrell**
Hair and makeup	**Simone Almekias-Siegl, Chris Bingham, Sheri Kornhaber, Gerald Quist, Terrie Velasquez**
Stunt crew	**Hank Amos, Stanton Barrett, Randy Beckman, Troy Brown, John Cade, Andy Dylan, Eddie Fiola, Jeremy Fitzgerald, Tanner Foust, Jeff Galpin, Sean Graham, Tad Griffith, Dean Grimes, Erica Grimes, Mark Hager, Jimmy Hart, Thomas J. Huff, Victor Ivanov, Steve Kelso, David Kilde, David Leitch, Dina Margolin, Eddie Matthews, Rhys Millen, Benjamin Mullens, Cord Newman, Christopher O'Hara, Holly O'Quin, Bobby Ore, Darrin Prescott, Rex Reddick, Tim Rigby, Scott A. Rogers, Rich Rutherford, Felipe Savahge, Bill Scharpf, Kevin C. Scott, Chad Stahelski, Greg Tracy, Tim Walkey**

"The Dukes of Hazzard: The Beginning"
A straight-to-DVD movie released in 2007.

Executive producer	**Alison Semenza**
Producers	**Bill Gerber, Phillip B. Goldfine**
Associate producer	**Taylor Lathem**
Director	**Robert Berlinger**
Writer	**Shane Morris**
Cinematographer	**Roy H. Wagner**
Costume designer	**Tricia Gray**
Stunt crew	**Brian Avery, Joe Bucaro III, Courtney Farnsworth, Nicola C. Hindshaw, Dina L. Margolin, Vanessa Motta, Mike Mukatis**

"The Dukes"
A Hanna-Barbera production, in association with Warner Bros. Television, airing February 5, 1983 to October 29, 1983, on CBS.

Executive producers	**William Hanna, Joseph Barbera**
Producer	**Kay Wright**
Story editor	**Ray Parker**
Writers	**John Bradford, Benny and Clive Ferman, O. Gordy, John Graham, Orville Hampton, Tom Ruegger, David R. Toddman**
Directors	**Oscar Dufau, George Gordon, Carl Urbano, John Walker, Rudy Zamora**
Animation director	**Geoff Collins**
Musical director	**Hoyt Curtin**
Supervising director	**Ray Patterson**
Additional voices	**Jack Angel, Chris Anthony, Jared Barclay, Michael Bell, Phil Clarke, Peter Cullen, Keene Curtis, Dick Erdman, Linda Gary, Joan Gerber, Ernest Harada, Phil Hartman, Bob Holt, Arte Johnson, Stan (Stanley) Jones, Paul Kirby, Peter Leeds, Sherry Lynn, Ken Mars, Edie McClurg, Scott Menville, Larry Moss, Laurel Page, Tony Pope, Phil Proctor, Bob Ridgely, Nelson Ross, Mike Rye, Marilyn Schreffler, Hal**

	Smith, John Stephenson, Janet Waldo, Alan Young
Graphics	**Iraj Paran, Tom Wogatzke**
Title design	**Bill Perez**
Exec. in charge of production	**Jayne Barbera, Margaret Loesch, Jean MacCurdy**

Above, the view across the parking lot at the Professional Stuntman Invitational near Charlotte, North Carolina, in 2009. At top, Byron Cherry and Greg Evigan chat with attendees at the Invitational, including our friend Bill Jennings, second from right. Learn more about the event later in the book.

UP FOR DEBATE

So what do ya think?

We're gonna get ya thinkin' with this stuff. After all, what is life if you can't think about it a little (or overanalyze, in our case)?

Who is the most moral character on "The Dukes of Hazzard," and why?
Uncle Jesse? Abraham Lincoln Hogg? The whole darn Dukes clan? Jesse did teach 'em right, after all.

Who is the least moral character on "The Dukes of Hazzard," and why?
OK, now, don't just fly right off the knee-jerk reaction and say Boss Hogg. We all know J.D. was pretty darn immoral, as the idea goes. But there were a lot of other characters along the way who were pretty despicable — and perhaps to a greater degree.

Is it "yee-haa" or "yee-haw"?
We had to throw this one in there, because we've wondered over the years, as we've heard both phrases out of "Dukes" cast and fans alike. And really, if you listen to John Schneider real close in the earlier episodes, what you hear is more like "yee-hoo!" If you consult the rare "Dukes" novelization by Eric Alter, "Gone Racin'," you'll also see both "yee-haa" and "yee-haw."

Check it out, on pages 61 and 208!

Is Flash a boy or a girl?
You can hear a nice mix of "him"s and "her"s in reference to our poochie in the episodes, even though Daisy very clearly states in "Too Many Roscos" that "Flash is a girl!" In the Eric Alter novelization of the "Dukes" mentioned above, Flash is a boy. (But if BRB does a fabulous imitation of Flash the hound dog — which she does — does that mean Flash is a girl?)

If Flash could speak just one sentence to Rosco, what would it be?
We'll just let y'all run with that one.

FUN & USELESS INFORMATION

You know you've been dying to know!

Sort of a combination of "where are they now?" and "where did we go then, anyway?" — with some other cool stuff thrown in, here's the chapter of what BRBTV fondly terms "fun and useless information" ...

John Schneider

We can't help but begin with John Schneider. *Ahhhh* .... John Schneider. And we have to admit, it didn't really click until we heard the host on Detroit's Fox 2 TV say it after interviewing Schneider on the day that his new role in Tyler Perry's "The Haves and Have Nots" debuted, at the end of May 2013. The host called him suave, and said Schneider was nothing like the Bo Duke he once played, but that now he's more like that smooth guy from the Heineken TV commercials. Yes, indeed. Our Bo Duke has grown up. He's exceedingly tall in person, and has a deep, commanding voice. And he's a good actor, we've noted, from everything we've seen him in: from that recent "Haves and Have Nots" to the controversial and effective movie "October Baby" and even the Syfy crocodile movies and beyond!

A native of Mt. Kisco, New York, Schneider lives just outside of Los Angeles. He and his wife Elly have three kids: Leah, Chasen and Karis.

The 6'3" Schneider, who has owned and restored his own General Lees and has offered DVD "rides" filmed in them benefiting charity, is also a cofounder of the Children's Miracle Network with Marie Osmond, founded in 1983, a life's work he said on a Country Music Television 2005 special that he's most proud of. (Though, we'll note, when he was asked in the aforementioned Fox 2 interview what role he's enjoyed the most, he said "Smallville.")

When he took on the role of Bo Duke, John Richard Schneider was just a young-un, a tender age of 18 and coming off only a spin in a Coors Beer T-shirt, uncredited, in "Smokey and the Bandit" in 1977 (the perfect preparation, it seems, for Hazzard County). Though admittedly not a country boy at the time, he auditioned for the role of Bo sporting stubble, driving a borrowed pickup truck, carrying a six-pack of beer and claiming to be from Snellville, Georgia, an Atlanta suburb not far from the Covington and Conyers areas where the show was initially filmed (Schneider had been living in Georgia for three years at the time of the audition). He says that he was inspired to do that by Sonny Shroyer, who once spit on the ground when auditioning for a role.

Early shot of filming from John Schneider's own collection. Photo courtesy of John Schneider, Chad Collins and JDS.

One good-sized part of John Schneider's life outside of the "Dukes" has definitely been country music; he's done many albums. But he's done some other acting that's absolutely rocked, notably CBS' "Dr. Quinn, Medicine Woman." In his role as Daniel, he first was a rival to Sully for Michaela's affections, and then when it was clear that wasn't going to work, he cooled his jets and provided stable, compassionate support to Michaela and her family. Like the real man he is. *Aaaahhh … swoon!*

Another great TV role for him, of course, was on the WB's popular "Smallville," where he played Jonathan Kent, dad to the future Superman, from 2001 to 2006. (Tom Wopat made a guest appearance on the show as Jonathan's friend, appropriately enough — see the next section.) Schneider has had many other forays into television, like "Grand Slam," a three-month show in 1990 where he played "Hardball" Bakelenoff, a San Diego bounty hunter. He played the title role in the 1999 TV movie about Michael Landon. He starred with other country-music legends such as Johnny Cash in 1986's "Stagecoach" (featuring "Dukes" balladeer Waylon Jennings and his wife, Jessi Colter).

He kept busy with the very typical turns on TV mainstays such as CBS' "Touched By an Angel" and "Diagnosis Murder." He also, it should be noted, did his own stunt driving on the "Dukes" and "Smallville," did some directing on both those shows, too, has done some TV writing, and was executive producer for CBS' "Christy" series and made-for-TV movies. Schneider even starred for quite a while in Tommy Tune's "Grand Hotel" on Broadway.

We keep joking about it on the BRBTV News Blog — it's hard to keep up with Schneider. He's never hard up for roles; they just seem to keep coming out of his ears.

Tom Wopat

For our own Luke Duke, Tom Wopat, life is all about Broadway these days. He's made a huge career, and has enjoyed success in, productions such as "Annie Get Your Gun," "42nd Street," "Chicago" and "Glengarry, Glen Ross." He has split his time between Los Angeles and Nashville. "I sincerely love the town," he has said of Nashville, "because it feels like the

Midwest to me and there's a great climate for writing music."

Wopat grew up on a small dairy farm in Lodi, Wisconsin, with his six brothers and sisters. He was singing and dancing in high school musicals, and he studied music at the University of Wisconsin. As with John Schneider, the "Dukes" launched Wopat into acting. He was on a trip to the West Coast when he auditioned for and won the role of Luke Duke. Both Dennis Quaid and Gerald McRaney were up for the role, according to the IMDb. Lorenzo Lamas is another actor who auditioned for the "Dukes." "I read the script in New York on Tuesday and was on a plane that night for Los Angeles," Wopat says on his official website. He jokes in the Season 3 DVD extras that he met John Schneider in the men's room at Warner Bros., his guitar in tow, and of course the two have remained friends to this day.

"My screen test was on Friday, and 10 days later I was in Georgia for filming," he says. Beyond the "Dukes," Wopat turned in some good time as ex-husband No. 1 on CBS' fine "Cybill," starring Cybill Shepherd. (BRBTV laments the loss of this sitcom; we used to just love the female issues it explored.) As Jeff the hunky Hollywood stunt guy and father of Cybill's older daughter, Wopat popped in now and then to raise some good points. But Wopat's done some other TV work, too. He starred in CBS' short-lived "Blue Skies," playing Frank Cobb in this hourlong drama in the summer of 1988. In 1989, for about the same length of time (two months — yikes!), he played Dr. Jed McFadden in CBS' "A Peaceable Kingdom," set at a zoo. He played Hank Pelham on ABC's "All My Children" in 2001-2002.

He starred with John Schneider in the 1987 TV special "Christmas Comes to Willow Creek." He then shared the screen with his "Dukes" buddy on the WB's "Smallville," in the November 2005 episode "Exposed," playing Jonathan Kent's (Schneider's) best friend of "over 25 years," Sen. Jack Jennings. As Jennings, he rolls onto the show in a blue Charger (color in honor of Superman?) and tells Clark tales of his dad outrunning police "in Chickasaw County" back in the day. And yes, there's a scene where Wopat jumps into the Charger through the window! Schneider also takes the wheel of the Charger, spinning out and loving every second of this tongue-in-cheek reunion. Fabbo!

Like his Duke cousin, Wopat also cut some albums (see our Merchandise chapter). His recording career started in 1983 with a self-titled country album, and continued through several other country albums before a 2000 album, "The Still of the Night" (no, not that kind of still!) reflected his love of standards. In 2005, he released "Tom Wopat sings Harold Arlen — Dissertation on the State of Bliss," and went on tour to promote it. Writer Rex Reed reviewed Wopat's cabaret show "Arci's Place" in the New York Observer: "With his warm, strong baritone and easy soft-spoken manner, Mr. Wopat is no longer a roughneck from 'The Dukes of Hazzard.' Cleanly shaved, trendy and tailored in black, he's still rugged but clean-cut, manly but sensitive, and ready to explore the more intimate and romantic side of his likable personality."

Wopat still ventures into television now and then. We loved him in an episode of the first season of A&E's "Longmire," playing a rival sheriff to the lead character and every bit a country boy all grown up. BRBTV got the chance to chat with Wopat a bit when he was meeting and greeting fans at the 2012 Hazzard Homecoming in Virginia. He told us at the time (a month or so after the "Longmire" episode aired) that he wasn't sure if we was going to appear again on the show. But it's clear to any fan that Wopat's heart is in his singing and on Broadway.

"Fame for me is a tool," Wopat said on the "CMT Insider" 2006 special on the "Dukes," "the more fame I can get, the better parts I can get."

Catherine Bach

Lovely, brunette Catherine Bach, the woman who launched a thousand hind-ends as Daisy Duke in her short-shorts, values her motherhood these days. In 2005, she was working on a book about her entry into Hollywood and was involved in children's charities. She was married Peter Lopez for many years, with whom she had two daughters, Sophia and Laura, before his passing. She lives in California.

Bach was born Catherine Bachman, and on the same day, March 1, 1954, as filmmaker Ron Howard. Originally from Ohio, but spending much of her childhood in South Dakota, Bach's father is German and her mother Hispanic. She has one brother, Philip. After high school, Bach studied acting at UCLA. Just before the "Dukes" hit the airwaves, she starred in a couple episodes of NBC's "Police Woman." She also did some movies in the early and mid-1970s: "Thunderbolt and Lightfoot" (with Clint Eastwood), "The Midnight Man" and "Hustle" (with Burt Reynolds). At the time she was signed on to the "Dukes," she had just written a one-act play and had a writing contract with a network, she says on the show's Season 3 DVD extras. During the "Dukes" run, she did a couple requisite TV appearances on ABC's "The Love Boat" and even crossed over to an episode of the "Dukes" spinoff, "Enos."

Bach designed most of Daisy's wardrobe for the first season, and some beyond, after seeing her initial wardrobe. She cut off a pair of her own pants for the first "Dazzey Duks," according to her publicist. She also has talked about feeling especially nervous as the show first filmed and, at 5'8" and with measurements of 36-23-35, according to Celebrity Sleuth magazine, she kept some modicum of modesty with hosiery under those skimpy shorts. (A story broke in January 2005, by the way, that Bach was in talks with Levi Jeans to create a line of short-shorts, but her publicist told BRBTV for the production of the first edition of this book that this was not the case. Wouldn't ya know it — those CB jeans and short later appeared. Hmmmm....)

Bach said on the "CMT Insider" 2006 special she didn't worry too much about being typecast after the "Dukes" ended: "I really threw myself into the world of Daisy Duke and just needed some time to be regular." She did later star in the 1990s TV series "African Skies," shot in Africa and featuring Robert Mitchum. More recently, she's appeared occasionally on "The Young and the Restless" as Anita, the mom of the character Chelsea.

Bach, who was married to Angela Lansbury's stepson David Shaw in the late '70s, once described her second husband Peter Lopez as "perfect" and knew him off and on for years before they got married in 1991. Lopez died in 2010.

Denver Pyle

Oh ... Uncle Jesse. That great "Dukes" stabilizing agent, Denver Pyle, died of lung cancer on Christmas Day 1997. He left behind a second wife, Tippy.

Pyle was born Denver Dell Pyle in Bethune, Colorado, into a farming family. And yes, he was related to Ernie Pyle — he was his nephew. Denver Pyle did a lot of odd jobs in his younger years, tried college for a while, then was enlisted during World War II. His Naval career was cut short when he was wounded in the Battle of Guadalcanal.

Pyle had reportedly always admired the Hollywood world, so he decided to try to break into it. That trademark white hair was something Pyle wore early on in his life, thanks to the genetics of his family, but it helped get him acting work as Southern / Western / hillbilly / mountain-man types on TV shows such as the syndicated, 30-minute 1951-52 series "The Range Rider," CBS' "Gunsmoke" and NBC's "Bonanza." (It didn't hurt that he became friends with John Wayne.)

Amazingly, he was originally chosen to play Matt Dillon on "Gunsmoke," but James Arness eventually took the role. Interestingly enough, Pyle showed up in CBS' primetime soap "Dallas." He played Blackie Callahan, an old coot of an oilman who helped J.R. Ewing out. But before that, and before the "Dukes," Pyle was a longtime veteran of the small screen. Just get a-load of this partial resume:
• Ben Thompson on "The Life and Legend of Wyatt Earp," ABC, 1955-56
• Grandpa Tarleton on "Tammy," ABC, 1965-66
• Buck Webb on "The Doris Day Show," CBS, 1968-73
• The original Dale Bush on "Karen," ABC, 1975
• Mad Jack on "The Life and Times of Grizzly Adams," NBC, 1977-78 (and in the movie of the same name)

Check out his resume on the IMDb; just his TV appearances number 226! As far as movie appearances, here are some highlights:
• "Streets of San Francisco" (1949), playing Ed Quinn
• "The Alamo" (1960), playing Thimblerig the gambler with his buddy John Wayne in the lead role as Davy Crockett (Wayne reportedly loved Pyle's

photography so much, he made him the photographer on set)
- "The Man Who Shot Liberty Valance" (1962), playing Amos Carruthers
- "Black Like Me" (1964), playing the man in the pickup truck (his "Dukes" costar Sorrell Booke also starred in this groundbreaking movie)
- "Escape to Witch Mountain" (1975) and "Return from Witch Mountain" (1978), playing Uncle Bene

By the time the "Dukes" was hitting it big, Pyle was spending his spare time at his ranch in Texas. Now he's buried near that ranch.

James Best

James Best says he "thanked God every day for the privilege of being on the show." He and his wife Dorothy (who played Sherry Tolliver in the episode "The Rustlers") founded the wholesome Best Friend Films, having soured on the machinations of Hollywood. Best met Dorothy years before she was on the "Dukes," and the two wed in 1986. Besides Dorothy's guest appearance on the show, both of Best's daughters, Janeen and JoJami, also appeared. Best loves fishing, video games and painting, these days. He also has done endorsements for BIOS Fine Nutrients, a natural supplement company based in Tempe, Arizona.

Born Jewel Franklin Guy in Powderly, Kentucky, in 1926, Best grew up in Indiana. The famous Everly Brothers are his cousins. He did some stage work before heading into Hollywood under contract with Universal Studios. He struck up a friendship with Burt Reynolds that meant some behind-the-scenes work directing and writing for some of Reynolds' projects (it was rather ironic when Rosco said in "The Dukes in Hollywood" that he would fancy Reynolds as playing him on the big screen).

By the early '70s, Best actually was considering himself "semiretired" as an artist-in-residence at the University of Mississippi. Besides teaching motion picture and drama, he established the Mississippi Film Commission.

But then ... there was this little matter of a new Warner Bros. TV series taking place in the rural South. Best writes in his autobiography, "Best in Hollywood," that he thought his agent was talking about some gang film when he first told him the title of this new TV show. He found out otherwise, and rode this successful wave for seven seasons, minus a little time off, with the frustrations of the working conditions on the set. "At the time I started work on 'The Dukes of Hazzard,'" he writes, "I was 52 years old. I was falling from trees and crashing and careening around in those cars. It definitely was not all sunglasses and autographs. If I froze in the desert in the morning, I could be sure that I would be burning up by noon. ... I do not think John and Tom minded the hard conditions as much because they were new in the business, and they were just happy to drive the General Lee. Cathy usually worked just a couple days a week. She put on her little shorts and then worked mostly on the air-conditioned soundstage. If the producer had only told me, I would have gladly put on some short-shorts to get some air-conditioning."

Best says he complained to the front office multiple times, asking for a decent dressing room, as well, since stars from TV shows of lesser fame got better dressing rooms than the "Dukes" cast. Finally he left the show, asking Sorrell Booke to go with him. Booke told him he couldn't risk it. So Best ventured out alone, and watched the parade of replacement sheriffs in that second season. "They were all good actors," he writes, "but what the producers had not fully realized was that I adlibbed about three-quarters of my lines. The guys writing the scripts were mostly New York boys, and they did not know the colloquial expressions that I was using on the show."

When Best successfully negotiated his return to the show, he got a motor home for a dressing room, the opportunity to direct episodes, and a little poochie named Flash, who was rescued from euthanasia and for whom Best also fought (for both the dog and her trainer, Alvin Mears, actually).

Best wrote in his book that he was still trying to get (at least as of the book's 2009 release) proper accounting from Warner Bros. about the royalties earned on commodities — merchandise sold with Rosco's image.

Besides the "Dukes," Best's TV appearances have been amazingly numerous, dating from the 1950s to the present day. He's starred in everything from CBS' "The Gene Autry Show" to the syndicated, 30-minute "Death Valley Days" to CBS' 1950s "The Twilight Zone" and 1990s "In the Heat of the Night." His 83 total feature films include five films with Jimmy Stewart, 1954's "The Caine Mutiny" with Humphrey Bogart, five Westerns with Audie Murphy, 1959's "Ride Lonesome" with Randolph Scott, 1968's

"Firecreek" with Henry Fonda and Jimmy Stewart, and Norman Mailer's classic, "The Naked and the Dead" of 1958.

In his 25 total years teaching acting, his students have included, according to his official website, Burt Reynolds, Clint Eastwood, Gary Busey, Teri Garr, Lindsay Wagner, Farrah Fawcett and Quentin Tarantino (the latter of which speaks very well of him).

Like his "Dukes" costar, Ben Jones, Best keeps overall fond memories of his "Dukes" days, and he doesn't see the 2005 film too highly. "We really became a family off and on the screen, in nearly seven years and 150 episodes. 'The Dukes of Hazzard' television series still has maintained its universal popularity. 'Dukes' was a family show with high morals always winning out over the antics of Boss Hogg and his bumbling sheriff, Rosco P. Coltrane. ... 'The Dukes of Hazzard' was meant to entertain, and that was the only reason any of us did the show. We hope it will live on and on, and continue to entertain the world which so badly needs something to laugh at."

Sonny Shroyer

Sonny Shroyer lives with his wife, Paula, in Valdosta, Georgia, where he was born. They have two sons, Christopher and Mark. Shroyer makes a few public appearances here and there (like the one shown on the next page, when BRB had the pleasure to meet him at the Motor City Comic Con in Novi, Michigan, in May 1999).

Shroyer's given name is Otis Burt Shroyer Jr. Growing up, he worked in tobacco warehouses and helped his father in their fruit stand / ice cream parlor business. He attended Florida State University on a football scholarship and, like his "Dukes" costar, James Best, crossed paths with Burt Reynolds and even played football with him in the 1974 film "The Longest Yard." Shroyer did some modeling before breaking into film and television. Strangely enough, through early roles in movies such as 1977's "The Farmer" and "The Lincoln Conspiracy," 1978's "Summer of My German Soldier" and "Million Dollar Dixie Deliverance," he became more popular playing the bad guys. But then the "Dukes" came a-callin' ... and my, my, if

Alright, which one is the real ham? Always in character, Sonny Shroyer poses with BRB at the Motor City Comic Con in Novi, Michigan, in May 1999. Photos by WPY.

he didn't tidy up his manners!

According to his official website, Shroyer was the first one cast for the "Dukes," and Gy Waldron echoes that in the Season 3 DVD extras. Waldron already knew Shroyer. Bumbling and playing pure as Enos Strate got him his own show, CBS' "Enos," in 1981. We all liked him better on the "Dukes," so back he came in the fifth season. Years after the "Dukes," in 1995, Shroyer surfaced in "American Gothic" on CBS. He played Gage Temple, father of a murdered girl who was locked up then driven to suicide by the demented, possessed town sheriff (it was a great show — hats off to producer Shaun Cassidy!). Shroyer took that role and gave it so much deep, desperate pain — and a few facial lines — that we didn't even recognize him at the first viewing! Shroyer played Coach Bear Bryant in "Forrest Gump," and more recently appeared in the 2002 film "Nowhere Road" and even played the bus driver in the ABC movie "The Rosa Parks Story" that same year. He also starred as Governor Jimmie Davis in the well-acclaimed film "Ray" in 2004.

Ben Jones

Nowadays, our favorite mechanic Cooter, Ben Jones, lives in a 250-year-old log cabin in the Blue Ridge Mountains of Virginia, is married to Alma Viator, runs his very own "Cooter's Place" museum and theme stores in Gatlinburg and Nashville, Tennessee and at one time kept the annual, smashingly popular DukesFest events going.

Born in North Carolina and a communications student at the University of North Carolina, Jones did quite a bit of acting before the "Dukes," starring in 80 stage plays and dozens of TV shows and movies. Like his "Dukes" castmate and balladeer Waylon Jennings, he appeared in the 1975 "Dukes"-inspiring "Moonrunners," playing, of all things, a federal agent! Later, he appeared in the 1998 films "Primary Colors" and "Meet Joe Black." He played a sheriff in the TV show "Sliders," in an episode called "Oh Brother, Where Art Thou?" He has even worked on a live production called "Oh Cooter, Where Art Thou?", which is also the title of the third CD of his band, making appearances at fairs and festivals around the country. And, in 2005, he was active with a musical about baseball Hall of Famer Dizzy Dean: It was called "Old Diz," Jones told BRBTV, and he wrote it and starred in it.

Jones is well-known, though, as a congressman. He served from the fourth district of Georgia from 1989 to 1993, despite the "rough and rowdy" life he says he lived before 1977. Redistricting took his seat after two terms. He did run again in 1994, though, against Newt Gingrich for the sixth district seat. He is also a writer, with work appearing in the Washington Post, USA Today and the Weekly Standard.

Jones spoke out publicly against the "Dukes" movie shortly before its release in 2005. "Like our fans, those of us who worked on the show have a special affection for it," he said in his statement. "For over 25 years we have cared about it, nourished it and fought for it. And it seems to me that it is time for us to have our voices heard again. From all I have seen and heard, the 'Dukes' movie is a sleazy insult to all of us who have cared about 'The Dukes of Hazzard' for so long."

Jones wrote an autobiography, "Redneck Boy in the Promised Land," where he chronicles his decades-long struggle with and recovery from

Muggin' it: BRB's assistant, Tara, visited the former location of Cooter's Place in Sperryville, Virginia (which closed in November 2003) and snagged this autographed mug.

alcoholism, as well as his years on the "Dukes" and in politics. He even tells the tale of how DukesFest came about and gives a rather smashing defense of the use of the Confederate flag in the show.

"It's been a good part of my life," Jones has said of the "Dukes," "and obviously going to be a permanent part."

Sorrell Booke

The great Sorrell Booke enjoyed a long and storied career beyond the "Dukes." And that was just in acting — he also enjoyed success in other careers, too! Despite his shuckin'-'n'-jivin' on our favorite show, Booke's intellect was a key part of his personal makeup: He was a student at Yale and Columbia universities, a master of five languages, and a counterintelligence officer during the Korean War. Not much else about his personal life is known, though he did grow up in Buffalo, New York, and did have two children, according to his biographer on the IMDb: Alexandra and Nicholas.

In the TV realm, Booke played Phil Greenberg in ABC's "Rich Man, Poor Man — Book II" in 1976-77. He played Gen. Bradley Barker in the CBS series

Sorrell Booke is buried at Hillside Memorial Park in Culver City, California — complete with a nod to his years as Boss. Photo by fellow author Brian Lombard, who is also a "Dukes" fan and visited this site.

"M*A*S*H," and had a role in CBS' "The Guiding Light" in the 1950s. He took the role of Boss Hogg onto the CBS sitcom "Alice" in October 1983 (can you believe Jolene Hunnicutt is Boss' cousin?). He also did a ton of guest appearances on many TV shows.

On the big screen, he starred in the 1964 movie, "Black Like Me," the story of a reporter who takes drugs to make himself look black and to experience racism firsthand in the Deep South. He played the principal in the 1976 "Freaky Friday" and starred in "The Last Angry Man," "The Take," "Mastermind" and others in the early 1970s before the "Dukes." Booke's last credited role before his February 1994 death of colorectal cancer was a voice on "Captain Planet and the Planeteers" in 1994.

"Sorrell had a heart of gold," James Best writes in his autobiography. Best fished with his costar, made appearances with him, and speaks highly of

Booke's ability to flow effortlessly with Best's own adlibbing on the set. "Sorrell loved to do just about any kind of personal appearance," Best writes. "He loved the adoration, but more than that, he just loved meeting and being with the people who adored Boss Hogg. When we did personal appearances together, I automatically fell into doing Rosco and treating him like Boss Hogg. I opened doors for him and that kind of thing, and he expected it because he was Boss Hogg."

With "Dukes" events over the years bringing the core cast so close to fans on such a regular basis, many fans deeply regret never having the opportunity to meet this great actor. And surely he would've loved what the "Dukes" has become in pop culture in more recent years!

Rick Hurst

Rick Hurst has been layin' pretty low in recent years, acting-wise. He does have a son who's building an acting career, though: Ryan Hurst, of movies such as 2000's "Remember the Titans" and 2002's "We Were Soldiers."

Born in Houston, Texas, Rick Hurst graduated from Temple University in Philadelphia with a theater degree. He started breaking into regular roles in the early 1970s. Before he saddled up as Cletus Hogg, the short arm of the law, Rick Hurst got some airtime as Cleaver in ABC's "On the Rocks" in 1975-76. He played an "eternal optimist" in the series, which was set at a minimum-security prison. In the 1970s, he also did numerous guest appearances on TV shows such as CBS' "Gunsmoke," NBC's "Sanford and Son" and ABC's "Baretta."

Then, after the Dukes hit the dust trail for the last time, Hurst played a chef named Earl Nash in the Bea Arthur series, "Amanda's," on ABC in 1983. And, we must admit, we watched every minute of 1993's Clint Eastwood flick "In the Line of Fire" without spotting his role as the bartender. Hurst also appeared in 1989's "Steel Magnolias" and 1986's "Jackals" and "Blue City." He was the announcer in the third "Karate Kid" movie. He even showed up in a 1993 episode of Fox's wildly popular primetime soap, "Melrose Place," playing a client of Sydney Andrews.

Don Pedro Colley

The lumbering Don Pedro Colley (all 6'4" and 250 pounds of him), stern Sheriff Little from our series, still makes some public appearances these days. He commutes between a home in Los Angeles and his cabin near the shores of Klamath Lake in Southern Oregon, not far from his birthplace, Klamath Falls, according to his official website. Adding to his quality of life: a six-foot in diameter hot tub he built himself in the 1980s from California Redwood. No wonder he retreats to this oasis and only does a few of these kinds of shows a year nowadays.

His hobbies include outdoors recreation, tennis and a stable of classic cars. He has a daughter, Kira Zuleka Zadow-Colley.

Colley has done a lot of other acting besides the "Dukes." He was, notably, in "Beneath the Planet of the Apes" (as one of the powerful, silent, mind-control people living below the planet's surface) and "THX 1138," both from

1970. (BRBTV loves those blessed "Apes" movies and was especially tickled to see Detroit newsman Bill Bonds with a small role in one.) Colley also starred in 1974's "Herbie Rides Again," 1988's "Blue Iguana," 1973's "Black Caesar" and many other films. For TV, he's done guest spots on NBC's 1970s -'80s "Little House on the Prairie," CBS' late-1960s "The Wild Wild West," NBC's early-1970s "Night Gallery" and ABC/NBC's 1970s "The Bionic Woman."

This author had the great pleasure to first meet Colley at Dragon*Con in Atlanta in July 1999 (the photo on the previous page) and has spoken to him many times over the years since then (see the "And Now a Word From ..." chapter). He is a most gracious and personable fellow.

Peggy Rea

We truly loved Peggy Rea as Lulu Hogg. (Didn't ya always just wanna give her a big hug?) In fact, we name her as the official BRBTV role model of "The Dukes of Hazzard."

Originally from Los Angeles and a former saleslady and MGM secretary, Rea had a fine screen career, mostly on television. She was on CBS' "I Love Lucy" and "Have Gun Will Travel," as well as several other early shows. She was the familiar Rose Burton on CBS' "The Waltons," and was a regular on NBC's "The Red Skelton Show" in 1970-71. After the "Dukes," she turned up as Carol's mom, Ivy Baker, on the ABC '90s sitcom, "Step by Step." More recently, Rea played Jean Kelly on the ABC sitcom "Grace Under Fire." In the film world, she showed up in the truly grisly and wonderful Debbie Reynolds / Shelley Winters vehicle, "What's the Matter With Helen?" in 1971. Rea played a vocal coach in 1967's "Valley of the Dolls," and was also in "Strange Bedfellows" and "The Learning Tree" in the 1960s.

Unfortunately, Rea dropped off the acting radar in the 1990s. She did reunite with her "Dukes" castmates for the 20th anniversary barbecue feature on the Season 1 DVD set, however, then later passed away in 2011. Many "Dukes" fans wish they could've met her.

Byron Cherry

Byron Cherry had what some fans would call the misfortune of being a "replacement Duke," and he hasn't done a whole lot of acting besides that. Born in Atlanta (appropriately enough for his spin in Hazzard as Coy Duke), Cherry actually worked as a flight attendant for a major airline. He was in a "Battle of the Network Stars" during the "Dukes," and he did a guest shot on CBS' "Murder, She Wrote" and "In the Heat of the Night."

BRBTV has loved seeing and talking to Cherry at "Dukes" events over the years; read more in our "And Now a Word From ..." chapter.

Christopher Mayer

Byron's on-screen cousin, Vance Duke, aka Christopher Mayer, on the other hand, had a pretty hunky role as the hot young stud T.J. Daniels on NBC's soap "Santa Barbara," in the 1980s. He's also done some hunky other stuff. He was magazine reporter Pete Bozak on ABC's glittery Morgan Brittany-Dave Birney vehicle "Glitter" in the 1980s. He did lots of juicy TV appearances on stuff like the 1990s syndicated "Silk Stalkings," "Baywatch," "Baywatch Nights" and "Sliders." He did the movies "Hard Time" in 1996 and "The Hunted," "Liar, Liar" and "Raven" in 1997.

Born George Charles Mayer III in New York City, he was the oldest of seven kids growing up in Ridgewood, New Jersey. On his Facebook page in 2011, he described himself as "a big crazy boy playing sports, football, wrestling and track and working my butt off to get straight As to seek the approval of my dad, which was slow in coming. A childhood straight out of Pleasantville,

---

Opposite page:
Byron Cherry at the 2008 Hair Dare Dukes Days event in Ontario, Canada, including with the Mego 4" Coy Duke figure (it's mini-Me!!!).

I finally realized life was difficult at age 50, college-educated at Colgate University in New York, where I majored in captaining the rugby team and trying to find a girl that didn't look like me in long hair." Mayer married three times (the second time to another "Santa Barbara" alum, Eileen Davidson). At the time of his death, he was engaged to Catherine Irvine, whom he described as "actress, model, goddess. It's exciting to be 57, still have rather large biceps and meet a girl that helps me touch the face of God! Finally met someone who's like me in a girl's suit. Ahhhh ... now it's Butch and Sundance to the grave."

Mayer had dropped off the radar in 2000 and then resurfaced in 2011, just starting to do appearances with his longtime friend Byron Cherry. Unfortunately he died later that year. It was Catherine Irvine who informed this author of Mayer's death, sad news that was then released on the BRBTV News Blog. See the BRBTV interview with him — which was probably his last — in the "And Now a Word From ... " chapter.

Jeff Altman

We loved to be annoyed by that little Boss-in-Training who often got the drop on his mentor! Jeff Altman is a Syracuse, New York-born actor who after the "Dukes" went on to several roles on "Baywatch" and several more roles on "Late Show with David Letterman." Judging by the latter, it seems comedy was his calling. He also played the comedian on the "Solid Gold" series.

He did quite a few other TV series, including "Nurses" and "The Real Ghostbusters" (Prof. Dweeb — yea, that sounds like Hughie). Altman is also an accomplished magician, Wikipedia says, with one of his effects being included in the famous Tarbell Course in Magic.

General Lee

Our beloved General Lee, of course, has retired into a nice, comfy spot on the car show and convention circuit, among other venues. The car received half the fan mail for the show, it's been reported. The show used more than 300 of these cars (309 is the number Ben Jones gives in the Season 1 DVD extras, and the TNN special "The Life and Times of the Dukes of Hazzard" gives the number of Chargers crashed in the series as 229). Every time you saw the General in the air, show creator Gy Waldron has said, that was another car totaled. The crew of the show had to go out looking for Chargers — sometimes, it's reported, placing notes on owner windshields in parking lots. There were some more technical reasons the Charger was chosen for the role and worked best for the job, which lead mechanic Tom Sarmento and Dodge Charger Registry president Wayne Wooten go into in the Season 6 DVD extras.

According to DualIntake.com, Waldron and an executive producer were driving along a Georgia highway to film the show's first episodes when they heard a Dixie horn on a passing car and decided to use it in the General. John Schneider tells the story a bit differently on the Season 1 DVD extras, saying they were shooting at the Boar's Nest location in Georgia when an El Camino drove by honking the Dixie horn, then Paul Picard had a crew member chase the car down to buy the horn. The horn plays the first 12 notes of the famous song "Dixie." According to About.com, that (now so controversial) Confederate flag on the roof measures 54 inches across, and the black "01" on the side measures 20 inches high, 12 inches wide and four inches thick (but hey, your best source for exact specs is any General Lee owner — they've got 'em, for sure). The General Lee was said to have a 440 cubic inch Magnum V8 engine, though some sources say the engine was most likely a 383. Tom Sarmento says in the DVD extras that it was a mix among the many cars he used.

To see more of this forever-popular car, check out the Meet Some Lees section.

BRB and the General owned by Paul Harrington of Ontario, Canada, at the Motor City Comic Con, May 1999. Photo by WPY.

Star-Spottin'

• Before she was Cat on ABC's "Lois & Clark: The New Adventures of Superman," or Monica on ABC's "Dynasty" spinoff, "The Colbys," the brunette **Tracy Scoggins** was a cute little blond named Linda May Barnes, posing as a sheriff's deputy on the "Dukes" episode, "New Deputy in Town." Scoggins went on to star, incidentally, in the "Dallas" reunion movies.

• Further shades of "Dallas": Perhaps best known as Afton Cooper on CBS' primetime soap (besides the tabloid time she did as one-half of the Landers sisters with Judy), **Audrey Landers** was a swindler in the episode "No More Mr. Nice Guy" and a talented gymnast in "R.I.P. Henry Flatt." Besides other TV appearances over the years, in 2006, Landers was working on the made-for-TV movie "Circus Island" with her whole family (sister Judy, mom Ruth, sons Adam and Daniel, plus Judy's daughters Kristy and Lindsey). "We do not yet have an airdate for 'Circus Island,' " Landers told BRBTV in May 2006, "but we are recording more songs to add to the soundtrack album — songs performed and written by myself, Daniel, my 12-year-old son, who already has hits in Europe, and Lindsey and Kristy, Judy Landers' beautiful and talented daughters."

Original "Dallas" stars Audrey Landers, left, and Morgan Brittany, who both appeared at this event in New Jersey in October 2012, also both appeared in "Dukes" episodes: Landers in "No More Mr. Nice Guy" and "R.I.P. Henry Flatt" and Brittany in "The Hazzardville Horror." BRBTV got to talk to both on camera at this 2012 event, and Brittany had fond memories of the "Dukes," since she met her husband Jack Gill on the set. Photo courtesy of James R. Green Jr.

• Also on the "Dallas" theme: note **Colleen Camp** as Bonnie Lane, the vixen who led Cooter astray in "Trouble at Cooter's." She played one of the Jenna Wades on the primetime soap.

• **Danone Simpson,** who spent several seasons as Kendall Chapman on "Dallas" (as the Ewing receptionist), showed up as Melanie DuBois in the "Dukes" episode, "Miss Tri-Counties."

• AND, to take the "Dallas" theme a little further ... **Morgan Brittany,** the infamous Katherine Wentworth, showed up here as Mary Lou Pringle in "The Hazzardville Horror." She's had a longtime marriage to Jack Gill, who served as a stunt driver on the "Dukes." They married in May 1981, after they'd met on the "Dukes" set.

- **James Avery** was the continually exasperated Philip Banks on NBC's "Fresh Prince of Bel-Air" in the late '80s and early '90s, but long before, he showed up in the "Dukes" episode "Cool Hands, Luke and Bo." Avery died in December 2013.

- The Lively family seemed to have a special interest in the "Dukes." Not only did the father, **Ernie (Brown) Lively,** play Duke buddies Dobro Doolan and Longstreet B. Davenport, but his son, **Jason Lively,** played Rudy in the pilot and Rod Moffet in "The Boar's Nest Bears" episode. BRBTV appreciated Jason's sister, **Robyn,** when she starred as the lovely redhead in the short-lived, Southern-set soap "Savannah" in the 1990s on the WB. Other siblings **Blake, Eric and Lori** have been — er, *lively* — in Hollywood, as has mom **Elaine Lively.**

- In what is BRBTV's absolute favorite "Dukes" episode, "Mrs. Daisy Hogg," a very young **Jonathan Frakes** wooed Daisy Duke as Boss Hogg's baby brother's kid, Jamie Lee Hogg. We cried! Frakes, of course, found great success aboard the Starship Enterprise in the second "Star Trek" series, playing Will Riker. He also did a miniseries in the mid-'80s, "North and South" on ABC, with his wife, Genie Francis of "General Hospital" fame. The two played villains together on an episode of ABC's "Lois and Clark: The New Adventures of Superman."

- *Ahhh ...* **Robin Mattson** was the lovely lady who had Bo jumping through hoops — and over many cars — in the two-parter, "Carnival of Thrills." Mattson is a soap queen who has ruled on ABC's "All My Children" and "General Hospital" (Heather Webber — we loved to hate her), the now-defunct "Santa Barbara" on NBC and "Ryan's Hope" on ABC. Mattson returned to her "GH" role recently.

- After **Morgan Woodward** did two classic "Star Trek" episodes, he had a longtime role as Punk Anderson on "Dallas," and he also appeared in two "Dukes" episodes: "Cool Hands, Luke and Bo" and "Mason Dixon's Girls."

- **Lydia Cornell,** who played the voluptuous and slightly ditzy daughter, Sara Rush, on ABC's "Too Close for Comfort" in the early 1980s, was also a NASCAR owner and the daughter of a dangerous mobster in the "Dukes" two-parter "Undercover Dukes."

Reunited? Lydia Cornell took time out from signing photos to pose with Paul Harrington's General Lee at the Motor City Comic Con in Novi, Michigan, May 2006. Below, she's at her table chatting with BRB and her family. She hugged BRB's niece Veronica — it rocked.

• You might remember **Gary Graham** as that shifty Detective Matthew Sikes on the Fox show "Alien Nation," 1989-91. Graham also shows up as the slimy brother of a con twice in "Dukes" episodes (and both times the episodes have the word "Deputy" in the title ... hmmm ....): He's trying to spring his brother from custody in "New Deputy in Town," and he's the bro of the Public Enemy No. 1 in "Deputy Dukes." Lately, Graham pops up here and there, including as a Vulcan on the most recent "Star Trek" show, UPN's "Enterprise."

• Funnyman **Arte Johnson** played one of the three bumbling crooks in the episode "Double Sting." He's done a lot of other stuff, especially on NBC: "Laugh-In," "Ben Vereen ... Comin' at Ya," "Don't Call Me Charlie" in the 1960s and "Games People Play" in the early 1980s. He also did voicework for the "Dukes" cartoon.

- **Tim O'Connor,** who played Thackery in the episode, "Bad Day in Hazzard," starred as Dr. Huer in NBC's "Buck Rogers in the 25th Century" and Hub Hewitson in NBC's "Wheels," both in the late '70s. Earlier, O'Connor did a spin in ABC's 1960s "Peyton Place" as Elliott Carson.

- Songstress **Stella Parton** of the talented Parton family played an officer with an ulterior motive in the first-season episode "Deputy Dukes." Parton is still performing country music these days, and she's earned herself some accolades with it. The Christian Country Music Association (CCMA) named her Mainstream Country Artist of the Year in 2002 and Female Vocalist of the Year in 2004.

- **Richard Moll,** the big huge (6'8") Bull Shannon on NBC's "Night Court," played a big huge Beaudry brother who had a major thing for Daisy in the episodes "Boss Behind Bars" and "Daisy's Shotgun Wedding."

- **Roz Kelly** had a bit of a hot-driving typecast going there for a while. She played the fast-thinking derby queen Amy in the episode "Luke's Love Story," and you also might recognize her as Fonzie's demolition-derby girlfriend Pinky Tuscadero in ABC's "Happy Days."

- Good grief, it's one of the Darrins! **Dick Sargent,** to be exact. The "Bewitched" star stepped in as Hazzard sheriff Grady Byrd for a couple episodes, even appearing in the opening credits.

- **Simon MacCorkindale** showed up as Duke cousin Gaylord. MacCorkindale, among other things, played the manager of the LaMirage hotel on ABC's "Dynasty."

- "The Dukes of Hazzard" itself was, of course, based on the 1975 film "Moonrunners." It's also been said that "Smokey and the Bandit" was a huge influence (ironic, since its star, Burt Reynolds, went on to play Boss Hogg in the 2005 "Dukes" movie and John Schneider made a brief appearance in "Smokey").

- Ever wondered why the heck those Duke cousins were living with Uncle Jesse, anyway? Creator Gy Waldron said on the DVDs that their parents were killed in a car crash, though it was never mentioned in the show's run. (And really, that was *some* heck of a car crash, killin' at least six people like that! How's-come they were all traveling together, anyhow?)

Deputized: Lovely Stella Parton signs photos at CMT DukesFest 2006.

• And hey — let's pay a little tribute to Boss Hogg's celebrity speed trap, which was responsible for bringing many musical guests to Hazzard County (through his con of tearing up their trumped-up traffic tickets, of course!). Here are some of those "guests," to use the term loosely, as well as some musical folks who actually came along of their own free will!

Mickey Gilley
Oak Ridge Boys
Freddy Fender
Loretta Lynn
Donna Fargo
Buck Owens
Roy Orbison
Mel Tillis
Johnny Paycheck
Dottie West
... and finally ... the great **Waylon Jennings,** who shone as the balladeer through the series' run and actually showed us what he looked like in the episode "Welcome, Waylon Jennings."

Exploring the Show's Roots in Georgia

The first five episodes of "The Dukes of Hazzard" were filmed in the Conyers, Covington and Oxford areas of Georgia, about 45 minutes away from the great city of Atlanta (which, of course, got a lotta mention on the show! BRBTV especially enjoyed when Cooter called it "Hot-lanta," because it is hot!). The first few episodes really established a tone and feel for the show, and one that was never quite duplicated once the film crew relocated to Hollywood.

As a special feature for this Fun & Useless Information chapter, BRBTV offers a modern-day (2005) tour of some of the original filming sites of "The Dukes of Hazzard" ...

Downtown Covington, used for a few shots in the first few episodes of the "Dukes," was also featured in CBS' "In the Heat of the Night." You might recognize that big courthouse below from both shows.

If you wandered to the back of the "A Touch of Country" cafe and store in historic downtown Covington a few years ago, you found the remnants of Jo McLaney's "Dukes of Hazzard" museum, above. The owners of this store, Harold and Dianne Duren, took on the items and gave them a home in June 2003. (See the feature later in this chapter for more about Jo.)

Also at the "A Touch of Country" store in downtown Covington, you could at one time purchase one of these maps for a nominal fee (10 cents for the one at right,

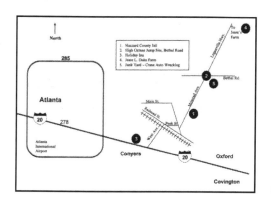

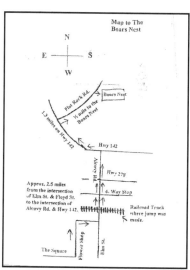

Two maps courtesy of Jo McLaney.

for instance). They clued you in on the "Dukes" filming sites of the Covington and Conyers area.

The "A Touch of Country" store also once contained a replica of the original Boar's Nest sign, shown here mixed in among the store's other offerings. This sign was used in a "Dukes" photo shoot around the show's 25th anniversary. While this surviving "Dukes" museum was located in downtown Covington, in what is called the historic Square, the original Boar's Nest building is a few miles away, on Flat Rock Road off Highway 142 in the Covington-Oxford area.

The building originally used for the Boar's Nest is now ... a church! There aren't many bells or whistles to recommend it, but we understand that it is in operation. (See the photo on opposite page.)

We love what Ben Jones says in his autobiography "Redneck Boy in the Promised Land," about the Boar's Nest and about making the commute from his home in Georgia to the set on the West Coast on a regular basis while he was shooting the show: "Sometimes I would leave the cabin in Georgia at 5 a.m., drive to the Atlanta airport, catch a flight west at 6:30 a.m. EST and arrive at LAX around 7:30 a.m. PST. I kept a car at the airport there and would drive out to the set in time for my first scene. When I left home back in Georgia, I would pass the original Boar's Nest, the roadhouse

from which Boss Hogg ran his operation. And when I arrived at the location, there would be the exact same building. Only now it was not only a replica painted exactly like the original, but simply a façade, behind which was nothing but scrub oak, sandy dirt and a little cactus. There is the saying that 'Hollywood is all front and no back.'"

The intersection below, of Milstead Avenue / Highway 20 / Loganville Highway and Bethel Road north of Conyers, is where the jump was filmed for the early episode "High Octane." In the scene, the General Lee jumps a flat-bed semi carrying a load of what was actually covered-over refrigerator boxes, according to "Dukes" historian Jon Holland of the DukesofHazzard01 website.

To the right of where this photo focuses was originally a general store and gas station that was featured in the early episode "Mary Kaye's Baby." The grocery store is gone, and the gas station has changed quite a lot!

Off Highway 20 in Conyers is the junkyard below, used in the show (Bo and Luke have a powwow there with Cooter, Dobro Doolan and Brodie in the pilot episode). Nowadays, everything's pretty rusted out and run down and ... well ... *junky*. An early version of Cooter's Garage was also located on this site, according to Jack Price of the Hazzard County Directory.

The Rockdale County Hospital, on Milstead Avenue in Conyers, was the building used for the Department of Environmental Protection in the episode "High Octane."

One of the sites marked on the second map on page 211, which was pulled together by Jo McLaney, is the railroad crossing below, on a side street behind the historic Square in Covington, site of a jump in the pilot episode.

In the pilot episode, Bo and Luke foil Boss Hogg's gambling plans for Hazzard, and they donate the cash they collect from Boss' one-armed bandits to the Sheridan Orphans' Home. The structure used for the orphans' home was this beautiful 1854 home, called the Zachary-Echols House and located on Echols Street in Covington.

Jack Price of the Hazzard County Directory website was able to nab the shot at right of the building used for the Hazzard County Jail shortly before it was torn down in 2000. The building, on Milstead Avenue in Conyers, was Rockdale County in real-life, not Hazzard, and the county tore it down to build a newer facility.

Photo by Jack Price of the Hazzard County Directory website.

Bo and Luke start out the episode "Mary Kaye's Baby" runnin' down the road in a car borrowed from Cooter, trying to get rid of the moonshine they discover in the back, so they don't go violatin' their probation and all. They throw one of the jugs out the window and over a bridge, almost igniting some guy down there on the

riverbank when the jug hits his campfire.

This is the bridge, on Lenora Road in Loganville. Just down the gravel road from that bridge was once the site below ... the original Duke farmhouse used for the first five episodes ...

Can you believe this was Uncle Jesse's farmhouse? *Yessiree*, this log cabin on Lenora Road in Loganville, Georgia, was originally covered in asbestos shingles during the filming of the first few episodes.

You would've never known this was the house, if you hadn't known! The road configuration now is confusing, when you try to reconcile it with the farmhouse shots in those five earliest episodes, where the driveway came so close to the house. Plus, there was an additional section of the house that was gone years later when BRBTV took this photo.

The moonshine still used in the series was set up in the woods behind this house. On the opposite page is a more modern photo of the still, as well as a shot of the interior of the house as it sat empty for years after the show went off the air. The house has since been torn down.

"Dukes" historian Jon Holland spoke with the owner of the property several years before the structure was torn down. The owner had intended to tear down the house, which hadn't actually been lived-in for some time, after the filming of the show. When he found the log structure underneath, though, he left it there, figurin' it might hold some historical value. Like Jack Price's Hazzard County Directory, Jon Holland's DukesofHazzard01 site features lots of shots of "Dukes" filming sites like this, yesterday and today.

(Look for Jon's own "Dukes of Hazzard" book, by the way, which he began working on in the late 1990s. It drills down on the original five episodes and will include a ton of photos from the filming in Georgia.)

These two photos courtesy of Jim Wilson.

The Etheredges: Contributing to "Dukes" Culture

Didya ever wonder where those goats came from, that were used in the filming days in Georgia? Or maybe where Uncle Jesse's first white pickup came from? They weren't part of the farm's original filming site, for sure. There are plenty of folks still roaming the Georgia countryside who had a hand — however large or small — in bringing the "Dukes" to life back in 1978-79. That includes the Cecil and Anne Etheredge family of Conyers.

Cecil was hired by Warner Bros. in 1978 to transport a bunch of goats from the home of his neighbor to the site of Uncle Jesse's farm in Loganville. Those goats can be seen in the Georgia episodes, such as at the beginning of "Daisy's Song," when the Dukes are in the front yard talking. Cecil also was hired to transport what was the very original white pickup truck of Uncle Jesse, which belonged to another one of his neighbors, Gwinnett Cox, who is since deceased. Cecil pulled the truck into Uncle Jesse's driveway and parked it, Cecil tells BRBTV, and left it parked there for the filming, at the tune of $50 a day. It was a late-1960s shortbed stepside Ford pickup, while the white truck that took over when the filming relocated to California was a fleetside longbed Ford from the 1970s, recalls Cecil's son Dale, who spent some time riding around in the original pickup in his youth.

Anne Etheredge was a kindergarten teacher at First Baptist Conyers at the time the "Dukes" were filming in November 1978. When the film crew needed children for the orphanage in the pilot episode, Anne supplied 'em. "We gathered up kids from all over the place," Cecil reminisces. "We sure did." Anne says she thought involving the local kids, including some of their neighbors, would be a nice thing. "I got the kids up, and we journeyed over and spent the day there," she says of the orphanage filming site. And you can plainly see, at the end of the pilot episode, when the orphanage is celebrating a picnic and Rosco P. Coltrane arrives and is cheered as a hero, in the closing moments of the show ... right over Rosco's shoulder, there's Anne Etheredge, smiling with her kids, wearing a party hat on her head and a green plastic Hawaiian lei around her neck.

Dale Etheredge also got a little screen time — that's him, just age 18 at the time, on the family's 1954 Ford Jubilee tractor riding around the Covington (Hazzard!) Square, as Bo and Luke in the General Lee whip by in the pilot episode (being chased by Rosco and Enos, of course). At the time, Dale was helping his dad transport the truck and tractor to the film sites. "They

needed me to either deliver the tractor or the truck to the set, and they needed someone to drive it. They said, 'You drive the tractor slow, real slow, and they'll pass you then come around and do a bootleg (a 180) behind you." He laughs, "Of course, I was just thrilled to even be asked to do it. ... I was skippin' work and all that, just to come do it." Like a lot of "Dukes" fans, Dale is amazed at the show's continued popularity, especially locally. "We've got a lot of people here in Covington who are all over it."

Dale also tells about one particular morning on the Square in Covington, when "two of the head guys" of the show were having breakfast, and a kid drove his car up, off Highway 278, playing a Dixie horn. He said the show's producers chased him down and were able to get the horn out of his car and install it into one of three General Lees Dale recalls there being, at that point in the filming. And that, he remembers, was the birth of the General Lee's Dixie horn. (There's a slightly different version of the Dixie horn's incarnation at DualIntake.com; see the info later in this chapter.)

The Etheredges still have their check stubs from Warner Bros. for their contribution to the "Dukes," and that's Cecil and Anne, in the photo above, showing their W-2 forms from the filming's pay. A true family affair — even their daughter helped out behind the scenes.

Where it all Began: Jerry Rushing

In the fabulous late-'50s Chrysler 300D he called the Traveler, Jerry Elijah Rushing, a.k.a. "Snake," of North Carolina ran moonshine, an art he first learned at the tender age of 12, following in the footsteps of his father and grandfather. The powerful machine could run a full load of 'shine at 140 miles an hour, which came in handy, if the Revenuers were on your tail. Rushing even had the car tricked out with a tank of oil, which he would spill out onto the road behind him to get the authorities off his track (sound familiar?). ("Traveler," incidentally, was the name of General Robert E. Lee's horse, if you're a-wonderin', according to TravelerMovie.com.)

Interested in his daring life story, Gy Waldron asked Rushing for more details. On that, he built the 1975 film, "Moonrunners," a project in which Rushing was involved as an actor and stunt man. And from there, our beloved "Dukes" were born, utilizing characters from Rushing's real life. Word has it, Rushing did not get full credit for his contribution to Hazzard County, and he sued Warner Bros., according to TravelerMovie.com.

But the story doesn't end there. Since his free-wheelin', high-rollin', law-fleein' days, Rushing has gone on to discover a richer substance in his life. He found the peace of Christ, and now he's involved in spreading the Gospel through prison ministries and more. He's also written a book, "The Real Duke of Hazzard," with Michael D. Barnes, published by Creation House in August 2005. BRBTV raises a salute to Jerry Rushing for his courage and vigor.

Book-cover image of "The Real Duke of Hazzard" by Jerry Rushing and Michael D. Barnes, courtesy of Creation House / Strang Communications, published August 2005.

Jerry Rushing and his fan-club president Paul Harrington, at the "original" Boar's Nest in Monroe, N.C. Paul Harrington is also president of the Canadian Dukes of Hazzard Fan Club and tours the country with his own General Lee and "Dukes" museum. Photo courtesy of Paul Harrington.

Jerry Rushing took his old Chrysler 300D, "Traveler," to CMT DukesFest 2006, where it even included the requisite (now empty!) jugs in the trunk and backseat.

Keeping the Love Alive: Jo McLaney

Jo McLaney of Covington, Georgia, was a special person in "The Dukes of Hazzard" lore. Not only did she own and display a large collection of "Dukes" memorabilia in her Covington flower shop (part of which was later housed in the A Touch of Country shop), meet most or all of the "Dukes" stars, and lobby her local and state governments in the interest of bringing more TV and movie filming to Covington, she also supplied flowers for the show when it originally filmed!

"This scruffy-looking group came into my flower shop and said they were making a series and it was going to be about Georgia," she told BRBTV. They asked her to make white carnation boutonnieres for Boss Hogg's lapel. That idea was later abandoned, though, because the white flowers weren't showing up on Boss' white suit, she says. Jo and her flower shop went on to serve in other ways during the show's initial filming. "We would send a lot of flowers back to their families," she said of the cast and crew.

It wasn't until years later, though, that her "Dukes" memorabilia collection was born. While NBC/CBS' "In the Heat of the Night" was filming in Covington in the late 1980s, she collected "Heat" memorabilia. One day in September 1996, she saw a man speeding a General Lee around the town's historic Square. Turns out, it was Paul Harrington of the Canadian Dukes of Hazzard Fan Club. As he told it, "All of a sudden, this lady jumps out in front of me; I swerved and went around her." Jo was intrigued by that Lee, but she mused that Harrington must've thought she was trying to tell him he shouldn't be speedin' around the Square in that thing!

She finally flagged Harrington down, he came inside her flower shop, and he was impressed by her "Heat" merchandise. He bartered a trade with his own "Dukes" memorabilia, and that was the first of Jo's collection.

As you saw earlier, the collection includes a chair from the original Boar's Nest. Jo said the pastor of the church that now occupies the original Boar's Nest building was going to throw those chairs away. "He asked me to haul them all off," she said. She took this chair — and gladly made a $100 donation to the church. The pastor also told her he burned the original bar of the Boar's Nest: "He said, 'That weren't no good wood.' " (And "Dukes" fans everywhere heave a collective ... *Sigh* ...)

She met most of 'em: Jo McLaney at the A Touch of Country shop, surrounded by some of the "Dukes" memorabilia she collected over the years, which included signed photos by most or all cast members. The last time we saw Jo, she told us she sold this collection to a friend, who had it displayed in Covington, though not at A Touch of Country, as it has closed.

Jo once held a weekly "Heat" fans meeting at A Touch of Country, but "Dukes" fans often dropped by to catch her, too. "It's like a shrine; they just come in," she said of that collection in the back of the store. "I have a good time with this stuff. At my age, I guess I need something to keep me going a bit." Sadly, Miss Jo passed on in July 2014. We will all miss her!

20 Minutes of Fame: "Dukes" Fans and the 2005 Movie

What a crazy opportunity for avid "Dukes" fans — to show up in the big-screen remake of the series! It happened for several folks in the "Dukes" fan community who got to travel to the Louisiana set of the 2005 feature film and appear as extras. A few of them were Paul Harrington of Ontario, Don Covell Jr. of Michigan, Billy Stephenson of Tennessee, and Scott Romine of Arkansas.

Don Covell, who you can see several times in the stands in the race scenes of the movie, talked to BRBTV about his experience …

OK, Cousin Don, how many days were you on the set of the 2005 "Dukes" movie?
"We filmed for four days, but we were physically on the set, as spectators and stuff, for a total of eight days."

How did you find out about this opportunity and even get involved in this?
"When I heard there was going to be a movie, I said, 'I'm going to be in it.'"

Because you're a big "Dukes" fan!
(Jokingly) "Just a little bit. So I surfed the Internet for a couple of weeks and found the Louisiana tourism bureau, or the film bureau. And they advertised they were looking for extras."

So they actually advertised that they were looking for extras for the "Dukes" movie?
"On the filming site."

Wish I would've known about that!
"So then I said, hey, I'm interested in involving some more people. Getting more people. To get a bunch of my friends to do it, too. I probably had a dozen people that I brought in. From other parts of the country. Originally, they said, well, which scene do you want to do? You can do the courthouse scene, which will have more closeups, or you can do the scenes at the racetrack, which will be more fun, but you won't have as many closeups. So I chose the racetrack scene, and that's a good thing, because they reshot the courthouse scenes in California."

Paul Harrington with his call sheet on the set of the 2005 movie. Photo courtesy of Paul Harrington.

Oh boy, you got lucky with that one. So you were on the set eight days, and you were in that racetrack scene ...
"There were a few different racetrack scenes. They moved us all over the place. It was January. We had to pretend it was summer in Georgia."

How cold was it?
"Forties. So you had girls walking around in bikinis in scenes. And in-between scenes, we had our winter coats on. Literally. You can't tell it by watching it, but we were sitting in the bleachers, and we would take our coats off for the shots, and tuck them down in the footrest area. And they were like, 'Cut!' and you would see like a hundred people all put their coats back on. Then they'd be, 'Coats off!'"

Fun. I know, working on a film set you're waiting around a lot. There's a little bit of camera time, then there's a ton of setup time. How many retakes did you have to do? What was that like?
"About five to eight retakes per shot. And like I said, they moved us around. I'm probably in like, five, six different places, depending on what shot they were doing."

And all of them made it into the cut / the DVD?
"A lot of them. The sad thing is, the one shot, I didn't realize it was for the 'Dukes'; I thought it was 'Jack*ss' or something, because Johnny Knox was filming stuff, so I didn't do what I should have done, and if I would've known it was going to make it into the movie, I would've turned my face more, so I would've had a better shot. Because I had a scene where I had to

act, where I walked up to the bleachers. And it turned out, when I watched the movie, that the camera actually centered on me and panned with me as I walked into the bleachers. And all you can see is the back of my head and my ear. And my butt."

But you're there!
"That's my 'butt shot,' as I call it!"

But why would you have thought they were taping "Jack*ss"? They were only taping "Dukes" there, right?
"They were just filming the movie, but the characters were in a scene where there was nothing that we'd ever heard of. There was a character Sheev, and it was two girls, who, in the normal 'Dukes of Hazzard' world, there was no Sheev. But it turned out he was part of the Broken Lizard Troupe. We reshot that scene about five or six times. So we just thought it was filler stuff they were throwing in, or scenes for some Johnny Knoxville film or something. We were wrong."

So did you get a chance to chat with Johnny Knoxville or any of the other stars?
"Me and a couple friends actually got invited to the wrap party. We stood right next to Johnny Knoxville watching the dailies, which they splice together as a mockup of the movie. And Johnny Knoxville's like, 'Watch this! Watch this part!' So we were standing right next to Johnny Knoxville watching the 'Dukes of Hazzard' movie."

What about Jessica Simpson?
"Never saw her. Never saw Willie, and never saw Lynda Carter."

Awww!!!
"That really bummed me, because I had a folder full of 'Wonder Woman' photos for her to autograph. And the other bummer is I did scenes with Burt Reynolds, I'm on screen with Burt Reynolds, but I didn't get to get his autograph, either, because he actually had sciatica in his back. Because of that, in-between shots, he would go back to his dressing room."

He didn't stick around and chat. Well, what was he like in the scene? That must have been interesting, to actually be in the scene with him.
"That was a lifetime dream, because I've been a Burt Reynolds fan since 1977, 1978 or thereabouts. 'Smokey and the Bandit' I've probably seen a

hundred times at least."

So who's your favorite character from the 'Dukes'?
"General Lee."

What are the best memories from the set?
"Well, I had a bunch of friends there, so that made it awesome. Getting invited to the wrap party was incredible. Being on the set. Doing a scene with Burt Reynolds, my childhood idol. And in-between shots, I actually said, 'Hey, Burt,' and he looked up and said, 'Hey!' So I did 'technically' talk to Burt Reynolds."

Now, what about the fact that when the movie was released, it was not well-received by "Dukes" fans. And of course, Ben Jones spoke openly and publicly about it. How did you feel as a hard-core "Dukes" fan, loving the show, being in this movie ... you could probably tell as the movie was being filmed that it was not being true to the "Dukes" TV show in some way?
"The scenes I did were."

So you felt confidently that OK, this movie might be good?
"I've gotta say the casting wasn't great. I get Johnny Knoxville. He's an awesome guy. He dresses like a hobo, but he's a nice guy. He was awesome. Shouted and waved 'Hey!' as he drove by. Everybody on the set was awesome. And when I talked to Jay Chandrasekhar, I sat and talked to him quite a while, and he talked about how, as a kid, he would sit and watch 'The Dukes of Hazzard' every Friday night. So I said we've got a good man here. But when I watched it, sadly it's one of those movies that is a good movie — on mute."

So the visuals were good ...
"Yea. But the language and the sex jokes were not. And Uncle Jesse being Willie Nelson. The pot jokes. Really was bad. But if you watch it on mute it's a pretty good movie. Also watch the edited version that came out in theaters, because they had, I think, three different versions. The theater version, which had no nudity, then when it came out on DVD, you could get it on full-screen or wide-screen. And the wide-screen, it had a lot more obscene jokes and a lot more nudity. And the full-screen was the only way you could get the 'clean' version."

Don Covell Jr. has some snapshots of his "Dukes" movie set experience framed on the wall of his home.

BRBTV also talked to Billy Stephenson. Here's what he had to say.

How did you first get involved as an extra for the movie?
"Paul (Harrington) had emailed me and he had told me about the movie set down there and asked if I wanted to be in the 'Dukes of Hazzard' movie. And of course, I said yes. I got the details from him, long story short, where it was going to be. He said we wouldn't get paid; it was going to be a walk-on opportunity. Once I got down there, several of the extras that were going to get paid didn't show up. It was unusually cold for Louisiana. There were two lines — one for the ones who would get paid and one for the ones who wouldn't. So we all jumped into the other line when some didn't show up. So once our name was in the pot, we had to call a phone number, telling us who had to show up. We showed up every day anyway, but we didn't have to work it every day. We had a gate pass to get in, so we could go in and hang out, but we weren't paid for every day, if we weren't needed. I don't remember if the number we called was by alphabet, but I remember there was a number to call the night before to see if you should show up the next day."

Billy Stephenson on the set of "The Dukes of Hazzard." Photo courtesy of Billy Stephenson.

So you guys drove there and stayed locally at a hotel?
"We stayed in North Baton Rouge around the LMU campus area. I don't remember the name of the hotel. I want to say it was a Comfort Inn."

How many days were you on the set?
"Altogether, eight."

What was the funnest aspect of being on the set of the movie?
"The Unit 2 stunt team, of course."

Why, what did they do?
"Just all the stunts done by the stunt drivers, the driving. A couple of the jump scenes. All that was just very interesting."

What kind of direction were you given for your scenes?
"In the one scene, they told us to act like we were race fans coming in to the stadium. I had pointed up in the bleachers like, there's a seat. Of course, we weren't speaking. I don't know if that part got caught on film. I did have some props of signs that I was holding up, that I donated to Paul's museum."

Which stars of the movie did you get a chance to talk to or meet?
"Burt Reynolds, Willie Nelson, Johnny Knoxville."

Did you get to talk to Burt Reynolds?
"I spoke to him very briefly. He came out of the trailer and walked by. I also met Joe Don Baker, too. I got to talk with him a little more. I can tell you something that Burt Reynolds did for my mom that impressed me. She's not a big autograph person like I am. She knew Burt Reynolds was going to be in the movie, and she wanted me to get an autographed picture of him. She liked him in 'Smokey and the Bandit' when he was wearing the red jacket. I asked him about this and asked if he had any of those pictures. He didn't have any, but he asked for the address. When I got home, I didn't expect anything from it. But then in the mail, came the picture for my mom."

Billy Stephenson walks up the stands in one scene from "The Dukes of Hazzard." Don Covell Jr. is shown standing to the left of him, in the light shirt and cowboy hat. Photo courtesy of Billy Stephenson.

Here are some more shots of Billy's experience on the set; all photos courtesy of Billy Stephenson.

Have you done any other acting or extras work?
"I have not. I had put my name in for a movie in Louisiana but didn't get called back."

Who's your favorite "Dukes" character?
"I would probably have to say, as a Duke, not as a real-life person, my favorite character is Uncle Jesse. I identify more with Uncle Jesse because he always takes charge and fixes the problem. He has the answers to the problem."

Anything else you want to add about your experience?
"I got a firsthand, birds-eye look at how movies are done, how stunts are done, how cameras are set up. I learned a lot that way. As far as the whole experience, I'm glad I had the experience. I was very amazed at how Hollywood works, at how it all comes together with the crew. They've got their game down pat. I got to see how they create things like dents in cars, for crashes that they have to have for certain shots. I do know that vehicles that appear to be destroyed like racecars, the cars that they were using for the driving shots were not the cars that were in the stunts. They had vehicles that were exact duplicates that they had to be able to tear up. They had so many they used for stunts and so many they used for still shots."

Good Old-Fashioned Faith and Values

Part of the reason Ben Jones and other "Dukes" actors were a bit miffed by the 2005 motion-picture remake of their show was the fact that the movie seemed to leave one crucial aspect of the TV show back in the dust: the good old-fashioned values. Sure enough, you could see a lot of what made Hazzard truly Hazzard in what BRBTV fondly calls these "flashes of faith." This is not a complete list, merely some pleasant observations of how the characters (particularly them Dukes!) reflected honesty, spirituality and the desire to do well by other human beings ...

- The Dukes say grace at the table in "One Armed Bandits," "Money to Burn," "Follow That Still," "Big Brothers, Duke," "The Return of Hughie Hogg," and "Carnival of Thrills," Part 1. It's said in the pilot that Jesse is a religious man.
- In "Luke's Love Story," balladeer Waylon Jennings jokes, as he introduces Uncle Jesse in a nighttime scene, that underneath Jesse's longjohns "you'll find every single one of them Ten Commandments."
- The Dukes start out "The Rustlers" by singing "Amazing Grace."
- In "The Legacy," Lucinda Meadows says she put herself "in the hands of the Lord," and that He put her in the hands of the Dukes, so that's why her car made it to the garage OK.
- In "Along Came a Duke," Luke mentions praying every morning that the radiator will hold out on the General Lee.
- Uncle Jesse says in "The Canterbury Crock" that Boss Hogg has broken "every law in the Bible."
- Sheriff Little is said to "pray every day to his Maker" that he can one day catch the Dukes, in "Coltrane vs. Duke."
- Luke leads a prayer for Jesse's welfare, even acknowledging God's will, in "10 Million Dollar Sheriff," Part 2.
- In "Dukescam Scam," Uncle Jesse says he's "got a friend at the pearly gates," to console Boss Hogg when they're both trapped in the bank vault and thinking they're going to die.
- Daisy prays for Uncle Jesse when he's blinded in "Witness: Jesse Duke."
- In "Big Brothers, Duke," Luke tells Andy Slocum how he and Bo were raised by the Good Book.
- Jesse says the Lord decides when it's time for a person to go, in "Too Many Roscos." Luke later tells the "fake" Rosco that the Dukes were praying for him.

BEHIND THE SCENES

> "'I don't want to do a gang thing,' I told him. My agent said, 'No, this is a good ol' boy thing. They're going to shoot the whole series down around Conyers, Georgia.' I love that area because of the good fishing and the extremely nice people. I told my agent, 'My Lord, if they're going to shoot the whole thing around Conyers, I don't care if it's called "There's Doo-Doo in the Saddlebags" — I'll do it.'"
>
> — James Best, "Best in Hollywood: The Good, the Bad, and the Beautiful"

- When Jesse survives a car crash unscathed in "Boss Behind Bars," Cooter tells him he sure has been saying his prayers lately.
- In "Undercover Dukes" a prayer for safe driving is said before the race.
- In "Dr. Jekyll and Mr. Duke," after Flash chews up the tape that implicated Luke in a bank robbery, Jesse says that the Lord answers prayers in mysterious ways.
- In "The Ghost of General Lee," Jesse proclaims "Praise the Lord" that the boys didn't really get killed.
- In "New Deputy in Town," after the Duke boys survive a near car crash, Bo remarks that he's "going to church this Sunday — early," and Luke echoes with "Amen."

Raise the Flag — and Forget the Flack!

That Confederate flag on the roof of the General may have caused a heap of fuss in these more recent years of political correctness, but any "Dukes" fan knows that the show itself wasn't in any way racist. Ben Jones, who has taken up the cause of civil rights, gives a good explanation of the history of the flag and what it really means in the last chapter of his book, "Redneck Boy in the Promised Land." He writes, "To insist that the 'Battle Flag' is a symbol of bigotry, racism and white supremacy, tantamount to displaying the swastika, is a fallacy, a wrongheaded conclusion based neither on history nor upon any thoughtful social observation. It is an elitist 'canard' and as such has been a very divisive wedge among well-meaning people."

And whether by Jones' own efforts, which he also mentions in his book, or by the efforts of other cast and crew members of the "Dukes," we saw on the show some very consistent scenes and action that were appreciative and representative of multiple ethnicities. Consider these facts:

- First and foremost, the show had a regular cast member of color, Don Pedro Colley as Sheriff Ed Little, and his color was not part of his identity. He was a tall, stern sheriff who had no like of the Duke boys or of Boss Hogg — that was his identity. His color was not referenced.
- The Dukes had a great friend in Brodie, who was black, as shown in the pilot episode and in "High Octane."
- In "Miz Tisdale on the Lam," we meet the Fongs, Billy Joe and Scarlet, who are Asian.

Add that to a whole host of other characters who reflected the show's diversity in casting:

- Doc Homer Willis, the dentist in the RV as seen in "Gold Fever."
- Cale Yarborough's pit guy Chet Garvey in "Dukes Meet Cale Yarborough."
- Big Jim Downey's menacing associate Vic, seen in "Granny Annie."
- In "The Great Santa Claus Chase," one of the three bad guys (the "reverend" who gives Bo and Luke a ride), as well as the young boy Jesse talks to, Otis J.
- In "Good Neighbors, Duke," the government agent.
- In "State of the County," J.W. Hickman's right-hand man Rollo.
- Homer Griggs, owner of the general store, as shown in "Bye, Bye Boss."
- In "Sadie Hogg Day," L.S. Handley, the state bank examiner.

- In "Vance's Lady," the new switchboard operator, Bessie Lou (referenced though not seen in other episodes).
- In "Hazzard Hustle," Boss' right-hand man in the horse-betting operation, Swifty.
- In "Undercover Dukes," special agent Walden.
- Cooter's friend Jonas Jones, shown in "Cooter's Confession."
- The security guard George on the set in "The Dukes in Hollywood."
- The two crooks targeting Boss in "Opening Night at the Boar's Nest."

And in a variety of episodes, you saw diversity where sets of supporting characters were concerned:
- In "Daisy's Song," there are two guys in a car recognized as "the law" — one white and one black.
- In "Repo Men," the three counterfeiter guys are two white, one black.
- In "Route 7-11," Helen Hogan has two associates, one white and one black.
- In "Money to Burn," two guys come in to the Hazzard County Coffin Works to look for a coffin with a false bottom: one white and one black.
- In "Arrest Jesse Duke," the four car-stripping babes are three white, one black.
- In "Along Came a Duke," the ruffians Boss hires are one white, one black.
- In "The Sound of Music — Hazzard Style," one fed is a black male, the other a white female.
- In "Dear Diary," one bad guy is white, the other black (Ernie Hudson).
- In "Dukes in Danger," one prison escapee is white, the other black.
- In "Lawman of the Year," one of the guys Boss hires to rob the jewelry store is black and one white.
- In "A Little Game of Pool," one crook is black and the other white.
- In "High Flyin' Dukes," one of Boss Hogg's crooked associates is black and the other white.
- In "Robot P. Coltrane," one of the robot rustlers is black and the other white.

James Best writes in his autobiography, "I must make it clear that no human or hound in the cast had disregard for any race, creed, color or ethnicity. None of us would have sanctioned the use of the Rebel flag if its intent had anything whatsoever to do with a racial problem. Folks have tried to stir some controversy about it from time to time over the years, but disrespect was the furthest thing from our minds."

The Hazzard County Business Directory

It's a quaint little town, ain't it? And we have to admit we wanted to go live there, as we were originally watching the series. We still do. Here's a glimpse of the businesses you saw on those sweet village streets, and even a couple back roads, in the rough order we noticed 'em in the series:

- Boar's Nest
- Hazzard Garage (called "Hazzard County Garage" on the side of Cooter's truck)
- Ace's Used Cars
- Rhuebottom's General Delivery and Dry Goods
- O'Connor Paint Supply
- Hazzard Courthouse / Hazzard County Court House
- Hazzard Post Office
- Hotel Metropole
- Bank of Hazzard County (J.D. Hogg, President)
- Hazzard County Coffin Works
- Hazzard County Coroner's Office (on the side of the hearse in "Money to Burn")
- Hogg's Heavenly Acres and Mortuary
- Julius Berg
- Mc-something Furniture Mart (!)
- Hazzard Theater / Picture Palace ("Two Features Daily")
- Fanny's Fabrics
- Ice Cream Parlor
- Hazzard County Feed & Grain
- Hazzard Police
- Rick's Pool Room and Lounge
- Hazzard County Telephone Company / Hazzard County Telephone and Telegraph Co.
- Bus Stop
- Drug Store
- Dixie Auto Parts
- Hotchkiss Funeral Home
- Barber Shop
- Hazzard County Gospel Church
- Walter's Auto Paint Shop
- Victor's Bail Bonds

- J.D. Hogg Hotel
- Hazzard Police Impound Yard
- Uncle Charlie's Upholstering
- Julip Mining Co.
- Seth M. Berley Co.
- Hogg Grits Mill
- Bill's Gas
- Sue Ellen's Sweet Shop
- J.D. Hogg Produce Co.
- Hazzard Photo Shop
- Hazzard Jewelry Store
- J.D. Hogg Used Cars
- Otis Plunkett's TV and Appliance Store
- Hazzard Mobile Home Park
- Hazzard Gold and Silver Emporium
- WHOGG Radio
- Hazzard County Orphanage
- Hazzard County Dog Pound
- Cottonwood Boarding House
- Hazzard Airport
- Hogg's Heavenly Haven (cemetery)
- Tri-County Truck Sales & Rentals

BEHIND THE SCENES

> "Without Jesus Christ in your life, it doesn't matter whether you are a moonshiner, bootlegger or Sunday school teacher; your life, too, will be hell and will be without the peace and joy that only Jesus can give."
>
> — Jerry Rushing, author of "The Real Duke of Hazzard"

Don't bust 'im, Enos: Special thanks to Paul Harrington of the Canadian Dukes of Hazzard Fan Club for sendin' this neat shot of Jerry Rushing, the inspiration behind the "Dukes," and Sonny Shroyer, aka Enos Strate, at CMT DukesFest 2006. You'll see lots more goodies from the event as you page onward ...

The 2005 Search for a "Dukes" VP

In 2005, Country Music Television began airing "The Dukes of Hazzard," and with that triumphant return to television (the show was last seen on TNN, back when it was The Nashville Network), CMT decided to host a fun little contest. They put out a call for a "vice president" who would write a blog and make appearances for the brand-new "Dukes of Hazzard Institute," to the tune of $100,000 for a one-year contract. Among the 1,900 candidates who applied, Chris Nelson, a 28-year-old part-time temp worker in New York City, won the title of vice president of the Dukes Institute. Nelson submitted a wealth of ideas for development, such as a Dukes poetry slam and a General Lee-inspired episode of MTV's popular

"Pimp My Ride" called "Duke My Ride."

BRB, who also applied, just got this (very nicely designed!) consolation card in the mail ...

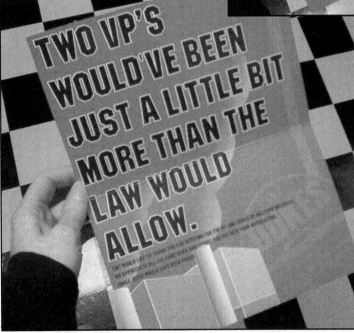

242   THEM DUKES! THEM DUKES!

DukesFest

In 2001, Ben Jones and his wife, Alma Viator, began hosting the annual DukesFest — a time for "Dukes" fans to get together and share their love of the show, listen to great music, watch cool stunts and meet the show's stars. The DukesFests happened over a Saturday-Sunday stretch in the summertime. You could always find 'em promoted on CootersPlace.com. They certainly opened up a whole new world for "Dukes" fandom, and folks will be talkin' about them for generations to come. BRBTV got a little history of the event from Miss Alma, which you'll see below.

DukesFest entry ran about $15-35, depending on if it was for one or two days. Kids 10 and under were free, and active service people and veterans were free. "And we welcome dogs," Alma told BRBTV in 2006. *(Good! Because you never know when Flash might wanna come!)*

- **First annual DukesFest: August 18-19, 2001**
Cooter's Place, Sperryville, Virginia
The tradition began on the grounds of the Virginia (former) Cooter's Place location, featuring original "Dukes" stuntmen and crew members Corey Michael Eubanks, Al Wyatt Jr. and Tom Sarmento, as well as James Best, Rick Hurst and Sonny Shroyer.

- **Second annual DukesFest: August 17-18, 2002**
Cooter's Place, Sperryville, Virginia
Catherine Bach, Sonny Shroyer and Rick Hurst were guests for the second event, held at the same location.

- **Third annual DukesFest: August 9-10, 2003**
Cooter's Place, Sperryville, Virginia
The 2003 event featured the first stunt show, with Tom Sarmento and Gary Baxley. James Best, Sonny Shroyer and Rick Hurst were guests. (About 8,000 to 12,000 people attended each of these first few DukesFests, Alma Viator tells BRBTV.)

- **Fourth annual DukesFest: July 31-August 1, 2004**
Bristol Motor Speedway and Dragway, Bristol, Tennessee
This 25th anniversary celebration featured Catherine Bach, James Best, Sonny Shroyer and Rick Hurst, as well as stuntmen jumping cars, country

music and nearly 50 General Lees. Corey Michael Eubanks, Tom Sarmento and Gary Baxley appeared, along with Waylon Jennings' son Shooter Jennings and widow Jessi Colter. Jerry Rushing, the inspiration for the show, was a guest. About 25,000 people attended.

- **Fifth annual DukesFest: June 4-5, 2005**
Bristol Motor Speedway and Dragway, Bristol, Tennessee
The 2005 event was sponsored by Country Music Television and billed as "A Celebration of America's Family Show" to coincide with the reemergence of the show on CMT. It featured Catherine Bach, John Schneider, James Best and Rick Hurst, along with a tribute to Waylon Jennings by Shooter Jennings. There were stunt shows performed by original "Dukes" drivers (Corey Michael Eubanks, Al Wyatt Jr., Tom Sarmento and Gary Baxley appeared), country music, a Mopar show with two days of drag racing at the Bristol Dragway and a cruise-in featuring dozens of General Lees. Jerry Rushing appeared. (Between 30,000 and 40,000 attended this one, according to Alma.)

- **Sixth annual DukesFest: June 3-4, 2006**
The Music City Motorplex, Nashville, Tennessee
The 2006 event kicked off "Fan Fair Week" in Nashville, as the annual event moved from Bristol to "Music City," with a stunt show and appearances by the entire surviving cast. CMT sponsored the event for the second year, dubbing it CMT DukesFest. Organizers expected 50,000 people, but a mind-blowing 100,000 showed up! It was by far the biggest crowd for DukesFest, and the largest gathering ever at these Tennessee state fairgrounds. The stars were indoors, in air conditioning, for the autograph signing, but the lines swelled to such proportions that the buildings had to be closed down for fire codes! On the pages that follow, BRBTV offers a look at the 2006 event ...

As fans arrived for CMT DukesFest on Saturday, June 3, 2006, around the 8:30 a.m. gate-opening time, it was becoming clear just what kind of crowd this year's event is going to get.

At least four different lines of people snaked up to the entrance of the Music City Motorplex in Nashville on Saturday morning, some folks waiting to exchange an advance ticket for a required wristband, and others lookin' to buy their tickets.

Once inside ... a sea of Lees around the track, in brilliant, blazing orange glory.

Ole Cooter, known to the rest of the world as Ben Jones, stepped up to the stage early on Saturday, ever the gracious DukesFest host. "It's a car show, it's a concert and personal appearances," he said in his introductory remarks. "It's just fun. The best part to me is all these young'uns — like that guy right there," he added, motioning to a young boy. "He thinks 'The Dukes of Hazzard' is a new show!"

The Elvis-inspired performer Paul Casey shared the stage with Cooter's Garage Band during the event, and at one point he paused to present Ben Jones with one of the 400 pairs of aviator glasses that were once specially made for Elvis Presley.

Above, Jessi Colter, wife of the late Waylon Jennings and mom to Shooter Jennings, performed at the trackside stage. (Colter's name, by the way, was mentioned by aspiring singer Daisy on the "Dukes.")

Autograph lines for all the show's stars were several hours long inside the Creative Arts Building, Annex Building and Exhibitors Building of the Music City Motorplex.

Below, Rick Hurst, aka Cletus Hogg, signs for fans.

Rick Hurst was joined by John Schneider, Tom Wopat, Catherine Bach, James Best, Sonny Shroyer and Ben Jones at the event. The stars signed at their tables from 10 a.m. to 5 p.m. both Saturday and Sunday, though James Best's wife Dorothy Collier Best told BRBTV that he began earlier, at 9:30 a.m. Saturday and 8:30 a.m. Sunday, because they'd arrived early and there were already so many people in line. "I'm not going to make people sit around," she said.

At his book-signing table in the Motorplex's Annex Building, Jerry Rushing was joined by Larry Wolfel of Traveler Movie.com, and his DVD of Rushing's life and the real-life story behind the "Dukes" was also featured.

Above, Catherine Bach, who brought her family along, pauses from her signing to reapply her lipstick — while cheers and wolf whistles rise up from her very long line! At right, James Best gives a young fan a Rosco-style treat.

- **Seventh annual DukesFest: June 2-3, 2007**
The Music City Motorplex, Nashville, Tennessee
CMT sponsored the event for the third year, as CMT DukesFest once again. This was the last year an actual DukesFest would be hosted by Ben Jones and Alma Viator.

- **Eighth annual DukesFest: June 28-29, 2008**
Atlanta Motor Speedway, Atlanta, Georgia
For this one, John Schneider took on the mantle of DukesFest and held it south of Atlanta near the show's original Georgia roots. BRBTV attended on the Saturday of the weekend, after enjoying the preceding fun in downtown Covington that Wednesday through Friday before, such as the Hazzard County Cruise-In on the historic town Square.

One of the show's organizers told BRBTV that more than 150 show cars were registered for this DukesFest. You saw not only the many Lees, but some other fun stuff such as Daisy's yellow Road Runner, seen in a few early episodes, and her Dixie Jeep.

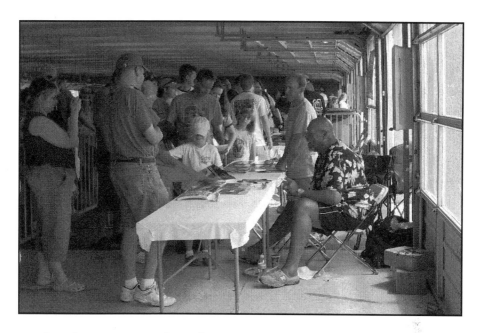

We loved seeing Don Pedro Colley, above, and Byron Cherry, below, at this DukesFest. (And hi, Wayne Wooten, on the right!)

Will Rodgers, aka "The Voice Man," did some emceeing for the event. He's shown above at the watermelon eating contest.

There was lots of fun in downtown Covington in the days leading up to the 2008 DukesFest. Take the two young gentlemen on the opposite page, for instance, all gussied up as those Hazzard County lawmen we adored even though we didn't want to, Rosco and Enos — or was it Rosco and Cletus?! They came in from New Jersey in a modern Hazzard County Sheriff's car that they said was actually pulled over for speeding by the (real) police! The constables warned the guys not to be wearing those uniforms in the vehicle, also. They are rather convincing, ya know?

The sweet, smiling Judy Bruce, who was one of the kids in the orphanage in the pilot episode, "One Armed Bandits," was there in Covington, at the A Touch of Country "Dukes" display, opposite page.

Other "Dukes" Events

BRBTV has been truly blessed to attend many other "Dukes" events over the years besides DukesFest, and it's our fun experiences with those events that is adding so many doggone pages to this book for this edition! Here you'll see a photographic glimpse of the events we've attended (and maybe one or two we didn't but got the photos from someone else) — not every "Dukes" event, for sure, but a lot of 'em! "Dukes of Hazzard" events heated up 'round about 2005 or 2006 then went great guns for a couple years, then slowed down a bit, then seemed to see a resurgence around 2011 with the Hazzard Homecoming. In 2013, for instance, there were "Dukes" events in corners of the country where we'd never seen them before: Texas, Louisiana, Maryland! It's not just Georgia or Tennessee anymore, folks!

But beyond the photos you'll see here, we can honestly tell you that what the "Dukes" events have given us are the best friends over the years! The folks BRB has met in the process of compiling the content for this book are counted among the very best friends she's ever had.

Roads Back to Hazzard Tour
March 4-5, 2006
Holiday Inn, Conyers, Georgia, and the surrounding areas
"Hazzard" historian Jon Holland and his Hazzard County Car Club took fans back to the roots of the show with the Roads Back to Hazzard Tour in Georgia in 2006. It all began on Saturday morning at the Holiday Inn in Conyers, Georgia, where the cast stayed during those early filming days in late 1978. The club collected some great "Dukes" memorabilia to auction, showed some "Dukes" original episodes and audition tapes, and, best of all, led attendees on a tour of the original filming sites along the Conyers, Covington and Oxford countryside. The self-guided tour came with a booklet listing each of the sites, with "then" and "now" photos, and the tour hit a lot of the goodies shown earlier in this Fun & Useless Information chapter. On Sunday, the event continued with a visit to some of the mechanics who worked on the original General Lees for the show, at H&H Body Shop in nearby Norcross, Georgia. The money raised from the tour benefited the Rainbow Covenant Ministries in Covington, which, Jon Holland says, is "about as close to the Hazzard County Orphanage as you can get."

Jon Holland (left), Jeremy Ambler and Grant Moroney (right) of the Hazzard County Car Club, with Ed Czekaj of North Carolina (and his son Chris, center), who won the raffle prize of the day, an autographed General Lee door.

BEHIND THE SCENES

"'Dukes of Hazzard' in 1978 could not have — there's no way that it couldn't have worked, as long as they got the casting right. And I don't mean actors. That sounds like, 'well, we did it!' We didn't do it. We just happened to be people that got along and enjoyed being heroes."

— John Schneider, TNN's special "The Life and Times of the Dukes of Hazzard"

A closer look at that General Lee door, on which Jon Holland meticulously hand-painted the "01." Below, some of the items featured in the event's silent auction.

General Lee Jump at Hardcore Racing
April 29, 2006
Hardcore Racing, Flint, Michigan

Yowza! If there's anything we "Dukes" fans like, it's a General Lee jump. Hardcore Racing, a racing performance specialist in Flint, Michigan, listed their General Lee (built by General Lee Enterprises, by the way) on eBay as an "as is" auction of the car in whatever condition it would survive. Then they jumped it over six parked cars (one of them stacked on the others) on the grounds of their business.

James Smith drove the car, original "Dukes" mechanic Tom Sarmento was there for the jump, and the Discovery Channel was on hand to tape it. Hardcore Racing posted the video of the jump at their website, WeRaceHardcore.com.

Photos in this section courtesy of Hardcore Racing and shot by Mike Yoksich, Colette Lane and Frank Clark.

"Dukes" Display at Motor City Comic Con 2006
May 19-21, 2006 (and many other years, as well!)
Rock Financial Showplace, Novi, Michigan

Paul Harrington and his traveling array of "Dukes" vehicles and collectibles have been a regular fixture at this event and others like it. Based in Ruscom Station, Ontario, Harrington has also been planning a less-mobile, more permanent display at his home. He heads up the Canadian Dukes of Hazzard Fan Club and he's a diehard fan, for sure, even featuring a "Dukes"-style car chase with General Lee and Rosco-like car at his 2000 wedding to his wife, Cheryl! For the 2006 Motor City show, he invited BRB to be a part of his display, so we took copies of the earlier edition of this book to sign and had a great time talking to other "Dukes" fans.

In Harrington's trailer, shown here (in which he hauls his General Lee), he's got props from the original Georgia Boar's Nest, signed photos and much more. You can keep up with Harrington's "Dukes" world at CanadianDukes.com.

How can Rosco possibly catch them Duke boys at the Hazzard Lake if he doesn't have a boat?

Below, there's always a nice assortment of "Dukes" goodies for sale at his display, which this year included both TV and movie versions of Rosco's car.

BEHIND THE SCENES

"I enjoyed making the series, every doggone minute of it, with the exception of going into the pond so often, and crashing up the trees, getting wet, getting hit with pies, and the falls and scrapes and bruises that were always acquired from most of the shows. I especially liked doing the scenes where I got to act the fool with Sorrell Booke."

— *James Best, on JamesBest.com*

Harrington has had every "Dukes" cast or crew member he's ever met (and that's a lot of 'em, believe you-me) sign the trunk of his General Lee, which he purchased in 1991. And at events such as this, he's certainly not above grabbing various celebrities to pose with it. Below, it's David Faustino, Bud Bundy of "Married ... with Children."

"Dukes of Hazzard" Night at Lanier National Speedway
June 10, 2006
Lanier National Speedway, Braselton, Georgia

Donnie Clack, owner of the Lanier National Speedway, assembled a special "Dukes of Hazzard" Night at the track, featuring some General Lees and cop cars from the show in a special chase around the track (see below), plus James "Rosco" Best and other fun. He told BRBTV he would like to make it an annual event. Keep your eye on LanierSpeedway.com!

James Best brought five of his original paintings to the event (see next page), which was held the weekend following CMT DukesFest 2006. Dorothy Collier Best told BRBTV that he'd sold the other 14 of the 19 they originally took at DukesFest!

Unveiling of the Rebuilt Lee 1
November 11, 2006
Historic Town Square, Covington, Georgia

It was much discussed in the "Dukes" fan community for a long time, and then it was officially unveiled in the birthplace of the "Dukes": the rebuilding of the very first General Lee used in the show, recovered years earlier at a yard in rural Georgia.

It was enough to make you cry, seeing the car affectionately dubbed Lee 1 pull up in the historic Square of Covington, Georgia, on that Saturday, with John Schneider — the only "Dukes" star to ever drive the car — behind the wheel. But when Schneider came outta that car (through the window!) wearing his trademark Bo Duke beige-yellowish shirt ... holy cow, this author thinks she did start to cry! With his hair grown out a bit — sooooooo Bo-esque — Schneider climbed out and immediately started meeting and greeting and signing for the massive throng that was crowded around the gated-off and police-guarded alcove of the car, there across the street from Covington's famous courthouse. And he didn't stop. For hours. He kept signing and signing, determined to make the day of every fan who was there. He did make our day, for sure.

Above photo and following four photos by Lee Secrest.

Many fans drove a long way to see the historic Lee 1 unveiling and Schneider (BRBTV's buddy Paul Harrington of the Canadian Dukes of Hazzard Fan Club and his crew — son Lance and buds Mike and Jason — drove all night from those northern regions, then turned right back around

and drove back to get to work on Monday!). Schneider, gracious as always, coupled Friday and Saturday showings of his independent film "Collier and Co." locally with the Lee 1 unveiling.

But the event was, of course, all about the car (just like the "Dukes" was, don't we know!). This was the very first General Lee, the car that made the very first jump for the show, and though its life was short (the pilot episode, then an appearance as the wrecked Petty car a couple episodes later in "Repo Men"), it was given new life now. The owner of the car, Marvin Murphy, who acquired it a couple years earlier, went to great expense to restore the car to the condition it was when it left the ramp at Oxford College on November 11, 1978, 28 years to the day before this grand unveiling.

And indeed, the car looked beyond beautiful, with as many parts still original as possible (though, truth be told, that depends on who you ask!), its familiar orange-red exterior shimmering in the sparse sun of the afternoon (Schneider told fans that it was raining on that day of the 1978 jump, too!). Marvin Murphy told BRBTV that the motor was the same, along with the steering wheel, dash, even some of the grease and grime were still there from its 1978 high-point. A sticker from a California college was still on its windshield, a remnant from Warner Bros' purchase of the vehicle in 1978. Whatever your view on the car and what it truly is, it was a lovely sight that day.

BRBTV didn't have the camera in tow that day, unfortunately, but our friend Lee Secrest had us covered. Anyway, the sight of Schneider standing by the car surrounded by the throngs is burned in our memory, thankfully. Plus, Chad's dad got a shot of this author with Schneider — we're going to get that from him one of these days!

The Rebuilt Lee 1 on Display in Indianapolis
December 28-29, 2006
Indianapolis Auto Show, Indiana Convention Center and RCA Dome, Indianapolis, Indiana

After completely restoring Lee 1 to what he would tell folks was the same condition the car was in when it took that first jump for the show, Marvin Murphy and his wife Joyce took the car to the Indianapolis Auto Show in December 2006. It was the car's first official appearance since its November 11 unveiling in Covington. The show was the event that kicked off the vehicle's two-year tour, leading up to its official 30th anniversary in 2008. As part of the appearance, Murphy invited friends out to a local restaurant in Indianapolis to celebrate what he dubbed the "Lee 1 Family Christmas." BRB attended, along with several others, on December 28.

"Lee 1 has been given a place of distinct honor in this year's Indianapolis Auto Show," Murphy said in a press release sent out at the time. "Never before has the auto show been able to make a special place in their event for such a special automobile. The sponsors of this event are excited to have Lee 1 join them to help showcase the restoration of an American icon."

Marvin Murphy with his pride and joy.

Hair Dare Dukes Days 2007
August 11-12, 2007
Colasanti's Tropical Gardens, Ontario, Canada

They were comin' in from all over the place for this celebration of all things orange 'n' "01" — Ohio, Massachusetts, Tennessee, Kentucky, Michigan, Georgia, even New Zealand! We had the boisterous Byron Cherry, the still-lumbering Don Pedro Colley, the entertaining Paul Casey, and silly little BRB herself. And amid the sea of beautiful, classic cars from the "Dukes of Hazzard" realm, from other corners of the pop-culture world, and from the just-plain-classic-car-world in general, we had all kinds of fun. We had Will Rodgers doing fabbo imitations of all the "Dukes" characters, joined by singer Billy Stephenson on stage, we had Sheriff Little outta control riding a kids' scooter around the grounds, we had a-female-attendee-who-will-remain-nameless grabbing Coy Duke's nicely preserved behind numerous times, and we had Lees, Lees and more Lees. What more can you ask for?!

But this event wasn't just a time to get together and get all crazy about the "Dukes." Paul Harrington of the Canadian Dukes of Hazzard Fan Club raised some good solid cash for the Canadian Cancer Society, shaving his head for the cause — and even inspiring his little girl Sarah to cut her hair short for the very first time! She raised $2,100 just on her own.

And we learned some fun stuff. Do you remember that episode "Comrade Duke," where Coy and Vance meet the defecting Russian gymnast Natasha?

Coy flips for the girl, literally and figuratively, performing an aerial flip during the episode. Cherry told BRBTV that he was into gymnastics, among other sports, in his younger years. When the producers considered hiring a stunt guy to do the flip, to the tune of $1,200, Cherry stepped up and offered to do it. That flip took 28 takes, he says, and one of those takes was right on his head! (He wouldn't do the flip again at the Hair Dare event — we asked!)

While BRBTV was chatting with fellow fans at the Hair Dare Dukes Days, the topic of the Mean Green Machine came up. The tanklike vehicle only appeared in two "Dukes" episodes, during the Coy and Vance season. Whatever happened to that? one fan wondered. And what exactly was it, anyway? At a show like this, where everything from the General Lee to Daisy's Jeep Dixie to the "00" Mustang, the "Carnival of Thrills" car and everything else shows up, you sure don't see a Mean Green Machine pull into position on the lawn, now do ya? Well, BRBTV posed the question to Cherry, who laughed that the Mean Green Machine was essentially "some plywood over a chassis." It was a car engine with a steering wheel sticking up, he said, and just a plywood casing that was painted the green color. Where did this contraption ever disappear to? Cherry had no idea. *Hmmm* ....

Andrew Watts of New Zealand, on the left, whom Byron Cherry nicknamed "Zealand" during this event, traveled all the way from home to meet the actor, here also with Kevin Bertram of Michigan. Below, worlds collide with the local 501st Legion "Star Wars" chapter.

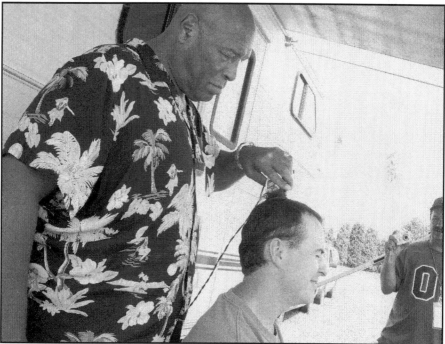

Don Pedro Colley cuts the hair of John Staton of Ontario.

Hillbilly Woodstick 2 Dukes of Hazzard Cruise
October 2007
Covington, Georgia

Wayne Wooten and his wife, Donna, put together an enjoyable, free, safe, fun and peaceful event for not only "Dukes of Hazzard" fans but for Wayne's Dodge Charger Registry members, as well. There were beautiful Chargers of various years and colors on display at the antiques mall on Elm Street in Covington on Saturday. They came from all over: Indiana, Michigan, Tennessee — even Australia — to do the cruise, which began on October 5, 2007, in North Carolina and ended in Georgia, in the birthplace of the "Dukes."

The event had several special guests: Byron Cherry, James Best, Don Schisler, Tom Sarmento and Tony Kelley. (Jerry Rushing, the man who started it all for the "Dukes," joined up with the group in North Carolina but was unfortunately unable to travel to the Georgia leg of the event.)

The mayor of Covington, Sam Ramsey, below, stopped by the Super 8 Motel around lunchtime on the Friday of the event with a special welcome for all of the event's guests and attendees. He asked everyone in the motel's conference room to introduce themselves and tell where they were from, to see how many states were represented.

After this, guests and attendees reconvened upstairs in the hotel's meeting room for a special time of stories and questions for the cast and crew. It was standing-room-only as the crowd packed into the meeting room of the Super 8 Motel in Covington, to hear stories from the event's guests.

Judy Bruce, shown here with her daughter, Brooke, on Saturday, has her own "Dukes" claim to fame. She was one of the children of the orphanage featured in the show's pilot episode. She was that cute little girl who climbed into the back of Boss Hogg's Cadillac and fiddled with his hat. Judy was still living in Metro Atlanta as of the time of this event.

This blazin'-orange-beauty-in-progress belonged at the time to Billy Stephenson, who also attended the Hair Dare Dukes Days in Canada a couple months earlier. Billy told us that he bought this Charger from a friend who'd gotten it on eBay, and he drove 12 hours nonstop with a

trailer to pick it up. "I put a fuel pump in it, and it's been runnin' ever since," he said. But it wasn't a General Lee back then. "I hand-painted everything on it." Billy said he drove it to all the shows he did. "I never trailer it." He has since sold the car to another hard-core "Dukes" fan.

Dodge Chargers from all over the place went along on the cruise (we were rather partial to the red-and-black beauty there on the right). This was part of the display on Saturday at the antiques mall on Elm Street in Covington, before we all relocated to the Lions' BBQ cookoff in Covington, eventually ending up on the Square later on in the afternoon.

All roads lead to the Square, don't they, now? They sure do, when you're talkin' Covington! On Saturday afternoon and evening, General Lees and other Chargers were wound all around the Square, with lots of folks checkin' out the scene.

"This hobby is for us," Wayne Wooten told fellow "Dukes" fans in the crowd at the event's close near the monument on the Square. Wayne also had a raffle drawing for a snazzy General Lee model car, signed by all the event's special guests, as well as some other cool prizes.

Wayne said he planned to continue the event. "It'll always be free of charge," he told the attendees at the close of the event. "It'll always be this kind of event."

"Dukes" Display at Motor City Comic Con 2008
May 16-18, 2008
Rock Financial Showplace, Novi, Michigan

Paul Harrington and his wife, Cheryl, brought even more stuff this year than in previous years at the Motor City show.

As mentioned earlier, Paul was on the set of the 2005 "Dukes of Hazzard" movie. His collection of props from the film includes production signs and a rear bumper from a jumpin' General Lee. He also has a collection of props from the TV series, shown below.

Paul has some items from the original Boar's Nest in Georgia, utilized in the first five episodes of the show.

Felix Silla, also appearing at this year's Motor City show, stopped by our table to chat. Below, Will ("The Voice Man") Rodgers joined the "Dukes" display area.

Hazzard in the Hills
August 16, 2008
Helen, Georgia

It was a very nice time at this Saturday event, Hazzard in the Hills hosted by avid "Dukes of Hazzard" fan Chad Fullerton of northern Georgia (shown at the mike in the first photo below). Set in the lovely "Alpine Village" of Helen, Georgia, the one-day event featured special guest Sonny Shroyer signing autographs for fans and taking an honored seat in the parade down the main street of town. Also meeting and greeting were Tom Sarmento of the Hazzard County Stunt Team, authors Jon Holland and that silly redhead chick, BRB, as well as Don Schisler, transportation director for the series and a man who was instrumental in the choice of that fabulous Dodge Charger as the General Lee.

Don Schisler, at right on the opposite page, was on hand to chat with fans. He was a kind and friendly fellow, and he *looooovvvved* talking the "Dukes." Also at the Hazzard in the Hills event was his lifelong friend, Don Toth, shown on the left with him. Both worked on a variety of Hollywood projects. Schisler even told BRBTV how he worked on five episodes of

"Dallas." He couldn't recall the season or year, but he remembered meeting Larry Hagman. "He was so nice," Schisler said (echoing the sentiment of virtually everyone BRB spoke to in the production of the "Destination: Dallas" reference guide!). Schisler's job on "Dallas" was working the camera car, or insert car, as it's often referred to on the call sheet. He was towing vehicles that were holding actors in conversation for a scene.

Schisler's friend Don Toth, meanwhile, was working for Channel 2 in Atlanta, and worked for them for a number of years, ever since he helped them out technically in covering the Oklahoma City bombing in the mid-'90s. Toth also worked on movies such as "Robocop" and the Jack Nicholson flicks "Terms of Endearment" and "The Witches of Eastwick." He remembered Nicholson being a "sweetheart," a genuinely nice celebrity when not every celebrity is. "He's such a personable fellow," Toth told BRBTV.

Toth was living in Metro Atlanta, as was Schisler and his wife at the time. The two friends grew up together in Dearborn, Michigan, where Schisler worked for the Ford Motor Co. for more than two decades. It was more than appropriate, BRB told him on this day, that he was wearing a shirt depicting cars — because this is a man who made cars his life! And his contribution to the beautiful blazin' orange TV icon, the General Lee, will forever be appreciated! Schisler passed in 2009. Look for more on him later in the book.

Hair Dare Dukes Days 2008
August 23-24, 2008
Leamington, Ontario, Canada

This annual Hair Dare Dukes Days fundraising event in Leamington, Ontario, Canada, celebrated the "Dukes" and raised scholarship cash for a student surviving cancer. Byron Cherry, Don Pedro Colley and Felix Silla were special guests at this year's event again.

The show was subtitled a "car show and swap meet." And yes, the interesting show cars were in abundance. Now, we've all seen General Lees before, and there were certainly some General Lees at this event, but we're going to go with the diversity angle this time, highlighting another one of the other cars we beheld ... on the opposite page ...

How's that for interesting? The owner of this little cutie had an blazin' orange "01" van at the previous year's Hair Dare show. He told BRBTV the van had been scrapped, but his fabulous "Dukes" memorabilia now lined the inside of this "Baby General Lee." It's an impressive assortment, and we were mighty impressed by the raised lettering on the doors ...

Above, the three "Dukes" cast guests chill in the hotel lobby.

Natalie Brock of Buffalo, New York, at right, was at the show with her "Starsky and Hutch" Gran Torino. Here she chats with Don Pedro Colley.

Above, our buddy Will ("The Voice Man") Rodgers of Chattanooga does some announcin' for the event.

Traditionally, the show had raised money for the work of the Canadian Cancer Society. This year, the funds zeroed in on a scholarship fund for a student surviving cancer. Some folks took pledges to make their own "hair dare." Every year, show organizer Paul Harrington vowed to shave his head to raise funds, and his friend Glenn Call of Massachusetts generally followed suit, as he did again this year.

Above, Cuz' Don Covell of Lawton, Michigan (whose police cruiser is also featured in this book) was kind enough to give BRB a lift from the hotel to the Leamington Fairgrounds in his General. Now, BRB doesn't own her own General, you understand, so it's always a thrill.

Is there something ironic about having Cousin Itt of "The Addams Family" cut your hair? We won't say that Silla didn't seem to enjoy it!

Chip Foose Braselton Bash
September 20-21, 2008
Year One, Braselton, Georgia

This September 2008 weekend saw the Chip Foose Braselton Bash presented by Year One at its Braselton, Georgia, headquarters. The event, named for automotive design guru and TV star Chip Foose, benefited the Progeria Research Foundation, an organization dedicated to discovering the cure for Progeria, a fatal, "rapid aging" disease that afflicts children, causing death of heart disease at an average age of 13. BRBTV was there on Saturday, as a guest of Mr. Marvin Murphy, the Florida resident who completely restored the car so affectionately dubbed Lee 1. The car was on display at the event.

"It is for sale," Marvin told BRBTV at the time. "I bought it and fixed it up with the intention of selling it for the show's 30th anniversary. It will sell for seven figures. I wouldn't be at all surprised if it sells to someone out of the country."

Murphy, below left, also had as his guest Don Schisler, right, original transportation director for the "Dukes."

Hillbilly Woodstick 3 Dukes of Hazzard Cruise
October 2008
Trenton and Covington, Georgia

Weeeeeellllllllll .... we could've shown you Byron Cherry, up there on stage at Jenkins Park in Covington performing two Elvis Presley hits — complete with gyrations. We could've shown you Don Pedro Colley, actually driving a Chickasaw County Sheriff's car for the very first time since the show's filming (yes, that's what he said). We could've even run a nice photo of Wayne Wooten's slightly mangled 2005 movie (screen-used) General Lee, there on display. And on top of that — we might have even shown you the cool in-car simulation at the Hazzard County Stunt Team's display that made you feel like you're really jumpin' that General.

Yea. We could have shown you all that and more — if we would have had a working camera! Rats! But we can still tell you! And you can just picture it all in your mind, right? *Right!*

Anyway ... The Hillbilly Woodstick 3 Dukes of Hazzard Cruise kicked off in Trenton, Georgia, over the weekend of October 18 with lots of fun moments. The cruise continued through parts of northern Georgia, some of South Carolina and North Carolina that following week, making the journey to Hickory, North Carolina.

BEHIND THE SCENES

> "Anytime we showed up on that set, it was a lot of fun. It was hard to not have fun."
>
> — Ben Jones, to BRBTV

Professional Stuntman Invitational
June 27-28, 2009
Concord Motorsports Park, near Charlotte, North Carolina

Did you ever see — live and in person — the "A-Team" van leaping through the air, some racing and wrecking, a couple Confederate generals, Boss Hogg proposing marriage, and the rig from "B.J. and the Bear" doing laps? Well, you did if you were at 2009's Professional Stuntman Invitational in North Carolina. The Hazzard County Stunt Team, Mr. Wayne Wooten, and a crew of dedicated professionals sure put on a good show.

The event celebrated the work of seasoned stuntmen from shows and movies like "Die Hard," "Rush Hour 3," "Twilight," "The Fall Guy," "Knight Rider," "Sliders" and, of course, "The Dukes of Hazzard." Buzz Bundy, Tom Sarmento, Ted Barba, James Smith, Lee Smith, Russell Solberg ... some of the biggest names in the stunt industry put on the thrills and chills for fans at the Invitational, which ran all day Saturday and Sunday in some rather-brutal heat that soared through the 90s. The stuntmen also signed autographs, and they were joined at the event by Greg Evigan of "B.J. and the Bear," Sonny Shroyer, Don Pedro  Colley, Byron Cherry and Rick Hurst, along with Jerry Rushing, the man who of course inspired "The Dukes of Hazzard."

Emceed by Will ("The Voice Man") Rodgers, the two days at the track featured racing, vending, rides in star cars, a fabulous stunt show (our favorite part, truth be told!) and a display of collectible autos with everything from the General Lee to Herbie the Love Bug and the notorious Christine. And, just to assure that the event would be remembered, avid Boss Hogg fan Rusty Cash of Chattanooga, clad in his lily white suit, proposed to his girlfriend Dana there in front of the crowd. The

box holding the diamond ring was passed along by the various celebs until Rusty finally laid claim to it, then gingerly laid down a white towel so he could descend to one knee. "I was so nervous," he said later that night. "I don't even remember what I said." Well, we were sure glad that white suit wasn't flannel like Sorrell Booke really wore on the "Dukes"!

On the opposite page, BRB poses with Richie Allgood and his lovely Lee, the trunk lid of which she'd just signed. Below that, yes, it's the Family Truckster of National Lampoon's "Vacation." Or a very nice replica of it. Right down to the luggage and the ... er, family member ... on the roof (not a *real* family

member, of course! and take heart — there was no dog on the leash in the back!). Gary Schneider, known so well in the "Dukes of Hazzard" community for his General Lee story, brought this attention-getter to the show. He told BRBTV at the time that he'd owned the car for about a year, and he had just completed it a month earlier. He'd taken it to a couple other car shows around his local Chicago area, but this was the first bigger show for the Truckster, which also made some laps around the track at the Concord Motorsports Park on Saturday. And this beauty didn't get trailered here like some of the other unique autos — it made the drive itself, all the way from Chicago.

Designed by George Barris, the Wagon Queen Family Truckster was a fictional car created for the 1983 movie and based on a Ford LTD Country Squire station wagon. Schneider's is actually a 1986 model, which he says is the same body style as 1983. Don Schisler also served as the process car driver in "Vacation" and inspired Gary to build the car. Schisler provided him with a rarity — the only known remaining crown emblem from the cars.

"Dukes" Display at Motor City Comic Con 2010
May 14-16, 2010
Rock Financial Showplace, Novi, Michigan

Paul Harrington and his traveling array of "Dukes" vehicles and collectibles did it again, in 2010, at the Motor City show. That year, Don Pedro Colley and Byron Cherry joined Paul at the "Dukes" display, along with BRB again and Will ("The Voice Man") Rodgers. And this particular year, the event organizers set up a panel discussion for the "Dukes," and it was great fun.

In the panel, Colley told the story of his spin on the classic show "Daktari" that eventually led to his role on the "Dukes," through the Leonard Kaufman connection. He described his strong, stern audition as Sheriff Little, when he could barely be convinced to read from a script, he was so in character:

"Sheriff Little is being told this big lie about Boss Hogg," he said to set the audition scene, "and he has a shotgun, and he cocks his shotgun as emphasis to the lie. Well, you don't have a shotgun in the producer's office. You can't very well walk around ... So I said, if you focus the sound of 'cow chips' just right, it can sound like you're cocking a shotgun. Cow-chips! Cow-chips! So I came up on the line, and I went, 'Cow-chips!' Paul Picard came right up out of his chair about that far. Boom! And he looked at me, and right after that, he's stumbling and fumbling and says, 'Well, thank-you, thank-you for the audition. That'll be enough.' I said, 'Oh, thank-you, Mr. Picard!' I took off my hat. I shook his hand. ...

"I left the office, and I no sooner got outside of his office than the telephone rang for the secretary. She says, 'It's Mr. Leonard. He wants you to come over and talk to him.' So I went over and said thank-you and so

forth. And while I'm in Leonard's office, the phone rings again, and they said, 'Be ready to go to work tomorrow morning. The script is on your way. And later this afternoon you'll get a costume, and you'll pick up your costume,' and so forth. And the rest is 'the rest of the story.'"

Cherry, meanwhile, shared the story of his original audition for the "Dukes" (which was for the part of Bo, at the very beginning of the series' production) and how he later nabbed the role of Coy Duke.

Hair Dare Dukes Days 2010
September 18-19, 2010
Comber, Ontario, Canada
In two cool, cool days in Comber, Ontario (yes, they thought BRB was crazy for wearin' her Dazzey Duks!) this eighth annual benefit event from Canadian Dukes of Hazzard Fan Club president Paul Harrington served up cars and stars in the name of "The Dukes of Hazzard." It also raised scholarship funds for a student surviving cancer. Don Pedro Colley was featured again that year, as was BRB. We took some great video, so check it out at the BRBTV YouTube channel.

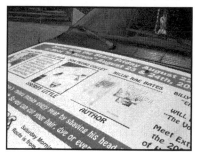

Above left, Doug McQuillin of Ontario brought his "Mad Max" car as well as a replica of the red pickup truck from the "Twilight" movies. Edmund Call of Massachusetts brought the beautiful blue "00" Mustang.

Hazzard Homecoming 2011
August 13-14, 2011
Thorton Hill Hounds Raceway, Sperryville, Virginia

Well, Ben and Miss Alma went and threw a little "Dukes" shindig, and a few people done showed up. OK, more than a few. Make that thousands. "Dukes of Hazzard" fans from all over the country and even other countries (that's you, Paul and Zealand!) made it out to Virginia for the first Hazzard Homecoming. Guess us fans were just craving a big "Dukes" event — it had been a while. And rain? Yea, there was a little rain. In fact, it lightly rained for a half-hour or so. Did anybody notice? Maybe. Did anybody stop what they were doing? Not even a little.

The spacious, hilly grounds off Highway 522, with the beautiful Blue Ridge mountains rising up in the distance, provided the perfect setting for Hazzard's fans to come "home" to this city where the very first DukesFest occurred back in 2001. Everything from General Lees to Hazzard County sheriff's cars to Boss' big long white convertible to Cooter's tow trucks and more covered the landscape. Stella Parton took to the stage in the afternoon, even doing a little church with "This Little Light of Mine." And Cooter's Garage Band performed later on.

Much of the original "Dukes" cast was there: Sonny Shroyer, Catherine Bach, John Schneider, host Ben Jones, James Best and Rick Hurst. Stella Parton signed autographs as well as her new book, "Tell It Sister, Tell It: Memories, Music and Miracles," just released a couple months before with proceeds supporting domestic violence shelters.

Lines were *loooooong* — one lady told us she waited in Bach's line for five and a half hours! It was nice and warm with a strong, cooling breeze a-blowin'. And BRBTV got to chat with a lot of good folks we only see every so often, like Miss Jo McLaney, above, who traveled all the way from our beloved Covington, Georgia, to say hello to her "Dukes" pals like Sonny Shroyer.

Above, when John Schneider took off his overshirt on stage to reveal this tank top underneath, the ladies in the crowd went wild — hear it on one of the videos from our coverage of the event, on the BRBTV YouTube Channel!

BRB hams it up, so to speak, with that ole Boss — aka Rusty Cash.

Hazzard Homecoming 2012
August 11-12, 2012
Ben Venue Racecourse, Washington, Virginia

The second Hazzard Homecoming, moving its location from last year's venue a few miles down the road, boasted a rousing success, as thousands of fans flowed in from all over, waiting in *loooooonnnng* lines for items signed by the cast members, listening to good ole country music on the stage, eating a funnel cake or two, beholding a bunch of General Lees and other beautiful cars, and just all-around taking in the awesome sights.

The event, again hosted by Ben Jones and Alma Viator, was a grand reunion of the core cast, with the first half of the weekend punctuated in the evening by their appearance on-stage, performing (you guessed it) the "Dukes of Hazzard" theme song and other faves.

Clarissa and Kevin, above, traveled from Oak Ridge, Tennessee, for the event.

Above is a real money shot of the cast posing for some photos behind the stage after performing on Sunday evening (they were still looking for Sonny Shroyer, though).

Dukes of Hazzard Georgia Reunion
March 8-10, 2013
Old Middle Georgia Speedway, Byron, Georgia

Chris Jennings of Gray, Georgia, held his own "Dukes" event, featuring the core surviving cast and even coverage by the "Today" show. John Schneider, Catherine Bach, Ben Jones, Rick Hurst and James Best did an interview on the show grounds early on Saturday before the show opened; check out the fuller video of what they said on the BRBTV YouTube channel.

Beyond that, it was a rip-roarin' good time with a great turnout.

We got some great video of Rusty Cash talking about his experiences as a Boss Hogg impersonator. Below, a Boss Hogg-mobile! Gotta love that!

Meet Some Lees

Some would say, when examining "The Dukes of Hazzard" and its powerful lore in the past couple decades, that it's all about the car. There are an overwhelming number of male fans of the show, after all — male fans who love the car, look for the car, build the car, show the car, maybe even jump the car. This blazin' orange 1969 Dodge Charger has been quite an inspiration.

Take a look at these beauties, for instance, from the CMT DukesFest 2006 display, as we get started on a sort of mini-General-Lee-tour ...

BEHIND THE SCENES

"I've been doing this for a long time. I've been doing show business for 35 years ... We want to thank y'all for keeping our show alive."

— Ben Jones, from the stage at CMT DukesFest 2006

Screen-Used Gem

It's not every day you get to meet a Lee that was actually used in the filming of "The Dukes of Hazzard." John and Jaci Jablonski and Rick and Paula Jablonski, two brothers and their wives, all of Ohio, jointly own this lovely Lee. BRBTV got a chance to chat with Paula Jablonski at DukesFest 2006 about the car, which is one of the treasured 17 Lees recovered from Warner Bros. by Wayne Wooten and his Dodge Charger Registry of Grafton, Virginia, a few years after the show left the airwaves. Only the transmission has been replaced on this car; everything else is original, Jablonski said, even the tires.

And this Lee makes the rounds, for sure. "We're here every year," Jablonski said, "and then usually every weekend we're somewhere with it."

This Lee, a stunt car, was used in the episode "Goodbye, General Lee" (and possibly others, though "Goodbye, General Lee" is the one that's documented for it). It's done jumps and wheel stands and the like for Bo and Luke. Jablonski tastefully declines revealing the price she paid for it — or what it's worth. But hey, in Hazzard County, everything's priceless ...

It's All About the Details

Donnie Clack, owner of Lanier National Speedway in Braselton, Georgia, added some nice little stars-and-bars centerpieces to the wheels on his Lee. Clack lives in Loganville, where the original Jesse Duke farm was located. Ironically, when the show filmed in Georgia in 1978, he told BRBTV, he lived right in Conyers and could hear the stunts and car chases up and down the road!

Right Where it All Began

There's something downright poetic about seeing the General parked in front of the Holiday Inn in Conyers, Georgia, where the cast and crew of the show originally stayed during filming in 1978. This one is owned by Jeff Cockrell of the East Coast General Lees and was in Conyers for the Roads Back to Hazzard Tour in March 2006. You can check out Jeff's club at EastCoastGeneralLees.com.

Shinin' in the Sun

This fabulous fiery beauty below belongs to Jeff ("Jett") Yaskow of Buffalo, N.Y. He was working on the car in 2006, dressing up the interior all in tan, among other things, and his Lee made its way around the track at CMT DukesFest 2006. Jeff proudly admits to BRBTV that his life "revolves around the Dukes." He's part of the Confederate General Lee Fan Club, at cglfc.com.

These two photos courtesy of Jeff ("Jett") Yaskow of Buffalo, N.Y.

A Duke that Loves the "Dukes"

Ronnie Duke (yes, Duke), owner of Hardcore Racing in Flint, Michigan, has owned seven General Lees over the years, including this one from General Lee Enterprises that was jumped in April 2006 (see the story in the section on "Dukes" events). In fact, Ronnie had a General Lee within a couple weeks of the show's original airdate! Just a kid back then, Ronnie already owned a '69 Dodge Charger. When the show premiered, Ronnie's uncle, who owned a body shop, made a certain suggestion: "He was looking out the window at my car," Ronnie told BRBTV, "and he said, 'Can I paint your car like that?'" Ronnie drove his first Lee for years afterward, and "got about a million tickets in it," he said.

For his work at Hardcore Racing, this particular Duke worked on automobile projects for the likes of Kid Rock, who owns two Lees, himself. It's obviously a passion!

Editor's note: We first profiled Ronnie Duke for the previous edition of "Them Dukes! Them Dukes!", then news broke in 2013 of his arrest. Out of respect for anyone involved, we won't go into the details of that here, but we did feel it best to leave in the profile and the info about Hardcore Racing and the fun jump they hosted in Flint, as it still is noteworthy to us "Dukes" fans!

Photo above and photo on previous page courtesy of Hardcore Racing.

And What About the Originals?

This Meet Some Lees section wouldn't be complete without mentioning a very special group of Lees — original Lees used in the filming of the series — that were acquired in a very special way from Warner Bros. It's a story that must be told, especially in a day and age when corporate greed seems to rule. And the February 1993 issue of the Mopar Collector's Guide told it well ...

About the time that "The Dukes of Hazzard" went off the air, a guy by the name of Wayne Wooten, who'd loved and admired the Dodge Charger since he was a little tyke and who watched the show faithfully, established the Dodge Charger Registry in Virginia. He got the idea to contact Warner Bros. and just see if maybe ... perhaps ... there might be some information on those beautiful blazin'-orange Lees that he could add to his registry. Well, Warner Bros. checked him out a little bit, and, satisfied that he was a legitimate lover of the car and not some scammer, they invited him to Burbank. There, they showed him a lot of Lee spare parts, which they were offering to give him, and a lot of Lees. They treated him like royalty, evidently sensing his enthusiasm and sincerity, taking him on a tour of the "Dukes" filming sites there in California. And when it all shook out, they offered him the Lees themselves — 17 of them. Wooten himself received a fine, close-up car from the show's filming.

"Warner Bros.' plan was to place the leftover General Lees in the hands of people who genuinely wanted them — not fly-by-night investors who viewed them only as commodities to be bought and sold," the Mopar Collector's Guide story says. A nonprofit organization was set up as a broker to send the Lees off to good homes. The only stipulation Warner Bros. included is that the car owners never charge for displaying the vehicles in shows.

If you want to hear more about how these original General Lees came into private hands from Warner Bros., there was a nice chronicle (with cool photos of the transport) at Lee owner Keith Winfree's website, pages.prodigy.net/tcwinfk (down as of presstime for this edition).

That, of course, covers the General Lees used in the California filming of the show, but what about the original Georgia Lees? Well, there are some interesting tidbits of information about those, too. Chad Fullerton, longtime "Dukes" fan and historian who lives in Georgia himself, not far from where the original filming took place, offers BRBTV some enlightenment ...

"Back in 1978, when filming wrapped for the first five episodes in Georgia," Chad says, "all of the wrecked vehicles used in the series were hauled to a salvage yard in Dawsonville, Georgia. The owner of the salvage yard was a guy named Cliff Shaw. Shaw was into the transmission business and didn't want the cars for any of their exterior parts. He only wanted the transmissions. Most of the cars were stripped of their transmissions and were usually crushed shortly after the transmissions were removed.

"Three 'Dukes' cars, however, weren't crushed and actually sat there in the junkyard until they were purchased and removed in late 2000-early 2001. The 'survivor' cars consisted of 'Lee 1' (the very first General Lee utilized), a Hazzard County patrol car labeled as 'Police 1' and another Hazzard County patrol car labeled as 'Police 2.' When I say 'labeled,' I literally mean labeled. All the first cars built for use here in Georgia were labeled with a small label-gun. The labels were then placed to the left of the car's VIN number located on the dash. When these three 'survivors' were found, all three cars were still wearing the original labels. ... Since then, all three vehicles have been sold, and Lee 1 is being restored.

"After Lee 1 was jumped at Oxford College on November 11, 1978," Chad continues, "the car was pretty much totaled. Then, the script for the

BEHIND THE SCENES

> "Whether or not the show matched the personal taste of network executives and self-styled elitists on both coasts, 'The Dukes of Hazzard' was one of those shows that managed to put together all the right elements that appeal to a large part of America."
>
> — *James Best,*
> *"Best in Hollywood: The Good, the Bad, and the Beautiful"*

episode 'Repo Men' called for a car to be used as a wrecked race car supposedly driven by NASCAR great Richard Petty in a tire commercial. Needing a wrecked stock car, Lee 1 was the obvious choice. The car was repainted a greenish-blue and had a '71' on each door and its roof. After the car was repainted, the guys ran cinder blocks down each side of the car to scuff the paint and make it look as if the car had been wrecked severely. When Lee 1 was found, the driver's side door was missing and the car's 'General Lee' orange paint was still exposed in the door jamb.

"In the original draft of the 'One Armed Bandits' script, the General Lee is briefly described as being gray in color. It was decided just before production began that the color needed to be a brighter color. Gray just didn't show up well on film. Therefore, it was decided that a nice shade of orange would be 'the' color for the car. Instead of using an actual color (Hemi Orange) that a 1969 could have been ordered with, a Chevrolet color (Corvette Flame Red, aka Corvette Orange Flame) was actually used as 'the' color for the General Lee. While the Hemi Orange looked great in person and was actually a Chrysler color, it was deemed 'too red' on film. Therefore, the Flame Red / Orange Flame was called on as it looked great not only in person, but also on film. The actual color of the General Lee is another subject of great debate. The information provided here was actually given to me by Don Schisler. Mr. Schisler was the transportation director during the time that 'The Dukes of Hazzard' was filmed here in Georgia. Basically, he was in charge of overseeing the builds and repairs of all of the vehicles used in the first five episodes."

Chad, by the way, has been working on the Covington, Georgia, Dukes of Hazzard Fan Club.

Chad Fullerton got to meet his first Lee at an early age, around 1980-81, in the photo at right. You can see his dad, Jim Fullerton, an avid "Dukes" fan himself, taking this shot. "He surprised me one day after school," Chad says. "He kept saying that he had a 'surprise' for me. We drove over an hour just to see this replica. Looking back, it wasn't that great of a replica. The graphics were wrong and the wheels were off. Also, the car wasn't even a '69. It was a '70. At least the owners called it 'General Lee II.' Back then, on that particular day, I didn't care. I loved it. If you look closely, you can see a huge smile on my face! ... That picture really brings back a lot good memories from my childhood, and 'The Dukes of Hazzard' was a big part of that."

Photo by Jim Fullerton.

Some Like the Sheriff's Car, Too

Don Covell Jr. of Lawton, Michigan, who goes by "Cousin Don" on the dusty country roads of the Internet, has been a hard-core "Dukes" fan himself. But he didn't start out as a Lee collector — his forte was the vehicle that chased the General Lee around the back roads of Hazzard County: the sheriff's car. He's not alone; there are quite a few car collectors out there who fix up a 1975-1978 Dodge Monaco or Plymouth Fury (or maybe an older Dodge, Plymouth or even AMC) to resemble the car Sheriff Rosco P. Coltrane or Deputy Enos Strate used in "hot pursuit."

You can learn more about Don's journey from the first photo (December 2004) to the second photo (November 2005) at his website, where he has very detailed photo albums: TVAndMovieCars.com.

When Don first got this car, he says, "it had rust holes big enough to fit my fist through."

Photos courtesy of Don Covell Jr.

Don branched out a few years ago, though. He bought himself a General, too. It's shown at right in July 2009 at the Cruise In at the Red Barns in Hickory Corners, Michigan. "This was two years and one day after my Lee arrived at my house," Covell says. "This week I added door locks, painted the rims, painted part of the dash, added a dash cap, fixed the door panels, installed driver's arm rest, and passenger's side window crank. Happy Birthday, MY General Lee!"

Photo courtesy of Don Covell Jr.

Meet the Chick Lee

Andrea Melchiori of Portage, Michigan, an avid "Dukes" fan, found her own General over the Internet in the first week of June 2007, and she brought it to the 2007 Hair Dare Dukes Days. "I have been looking for a couple years for a car, and I've found total junk heaps that I myself wouldn't know how to work on," she told BRBTV at the event. "The scenario with this car was perfect."

A friend of Andrea's who lived just an hour away from the car's location, in Kentucky, Derrick Perkins, picked up the car for her and took it to his place. Then Andrea, along with friend Don Covell Jr., traveled with a U-Haul trailer from Michigan to Kentucky to spend some time working on the car.

Photo courtesy of Andrea Melchiori / Don Covell Jr.

The car was already orange, and it already had the horn and vectors. It did not have the decals, however. "Everything was factory on it," Andrea said. Nothing had to be done with the engine, she noted. "It was in excellent driving condition."

She said, "We did entire restoration photos and everything. We worked for like 14 hours a day on the car, scrubbing and sanding. We did a heck of a lot."

Derrick shared his own photo album from the car's restoration with BRBTV. "Shows how bad her car really was, but we only had a few days and I did what I could in that short time and her very limited funds. Starts from when I pick up the car in Frankfort, then when she and Don came down, we busted tail almost around the clock."

Photos courtesy of Derrick Perkins.

Andrea had already received the broadcast sheet and the actual warranty sheet from the car, which is rare to have. Andrea was still in contact with the car's most recent (second) owner, Chris, who was still in contact with the original owner, who still had the original title for the car. "We're working on getting that. Chris had gone to the hall of records and searched around."

Andrea was actually putting together a scrapbook of the history of her treasured possession, which was to include the broadcast sheet, warranty sheet, title, restoration photos and more. But there was still some work to be done, she said, beyond what folks saw on the lawn at the Hair Dare Dukes Days.

"When I brought the car to Paul's show, it still needed wet-sanding. I still have that to do. In turn, I didn't put any of the trim on the car for Paul's

BRB's bud Andrea Melchiori of Portage, Michigan, ventured to Hot-lanta for the first time with her "Chick Lee" to attend DukesFest.

show. But that's it. Down the road I want to give the engine more power. Put a 383 in it."

A labor of love for this "Dukes" fan? You betcha! "I watched the show when it was brand-new every Friday night, and got into John Schneider's fan club, and have been a fan of his ever since," she said. "When I first saw the show, I fell in love with the car and had to find out the history of what kind of car it is. I loved it, I loved the style and the body, and everything about it."

Andrea also brought the car to Georgia for the 2008 DukesFest, and she and this author had a blast riding around the "Dukes" filming sites and shooting photos with the Chick Lee. You can see Andrea in two parts on the limited-edition official DVD coverage of the 2008 DukesFest — talking about how Rosco is her favorite "Dukes" character and mentioning the episode "10 Million Dollar Sheriff."

What a fun journey it was, no doubt. Andrea has since sold the car, however. And do you know who she sold it to????? Well, if ya don't, maybe we shouldn't tell ... And it's been sold again by him! Wow, those Lees sure are hot commodities.

He's Got His Own Lee 1 — and Lee 2!

For Derrick Perkins, who lives just south of Lexington, Kentucky, there are a couple things that are special about his Lee. For one thing ... well, it's not just one thing — it's two! Derrick actually has two General Lees, which he calls "Lee 1" and "Lee 2." Shown below with Derrick is his Lee 1, and these shots were taken in a theater parking lot on a very hot day in Lexington in August 2007, while Lee 2 was at home (hopefully where it was cooler!). Derrick had both of his Lees at the Hair Dare Dukes Days in Ontario a couple weeks earlier, and he was offering folks rides in them. He also had the cars' trunk lids signed by Byron Cherry and Don Pedro Colley at the event, to add to the many other cast autographs he has.

The other special thing about this Lee owner? Well, you're lookin' at it! (That is, if you're lookin' at the photo below!) Derrick has installed a video camera in his Lee 1 to capture some great "motion pictures," so to speak. The camera was rolling at Hair Dare. Derrick filmed some great stuff with Cousin Don at the event.

Another Duke That Loves the "Dukes" — and He's a Lee, Too!!!!

Photo courtesy of Lee Duke.

What about across the pond? It's nice to see who else out there, around the world, is a "Dukes" fan! But hold onto your Cooter-cap, 'cuz not only is the last name of this Lee owner in the U.K. really "Duke," but his first name is actually Lee! Holy "01"! There's just something so poetic about that. Mr. Lee Duke — who could also be called the Duke of Duke, our buddy Chad notes — got some help from Year One over here in the States with this blazin' orange beauty, to make, as he puts it, his "childhood dream come true."

A Paint Job Fit for Any ... Vehicle?

And what about the inspiration a General Lee provides for other ... *ahem*, vehicles? We've seen motorcycles, tractor trailers, trucks, Volkswagen Bugs and all kinds of stuff painted up with the orange and the '01. But how about ... a General Lee sled? The particular Lee at right is located at the Custom Sled Shop of Ontario.

Below that is a Lee on two wheels! It's a pocket bike, decaled by Paul Harrington of the Canadian Dukes of Hazzard Fan Club. Cute, isn't it?

Photo directly above courtesy of Paul Harrington.

The '01 cutie at right was snapped at Hazzard Homecoming 2011, and the motorcycle and Jeep below were captured at Hazzard Homecoming 2012.

Art Imitates Life, at Least the Life We'd all Love to Live in Hazzard County

Jim Wilson of London, Ontario, had dreams like any other kid growing up in the 1970s who watched "The Dukes of Hazzard" when it originally aired. He wanted to meet the Dukes, he wanted to see the Duke farm, and Hazzard Square, and any of the other sites featured on the show. He wanted to see a General Lee.

"Well, I did watch 'The Dukes' every Friday night when it was new, when I was a kid," Jim tells BRBTV. "Looked forward to it, and my mom would always pop some popcorn on the stove for me; back then we did not own a microwave, LOL."

Jim made his dreams come true. He did grow up to meet the cast members, even see John Schneider and Tom Wopat in concert, and he visited Hazzard Square and the Duke farm. And he's seen a few General Lees over the years,

both at DukesFest and elsewhere, even though he lives in the Great White North where it would seem you wouldn't see such a sight!

"You would be surprised, there are a few General Lees around my area," he says. "I always seem to find somebody who enjoys the show. My good friend Jason Darling, who lives near Kingston, Ontario, is building two Generals right now, a dirt tracker and a nice street car."

But while all of that is mighty fine, that's not the reason we're featuring Jim Wilson here. You see, he's the kind of fan that is so inspired by the "Dukes" that it touches off his artistic creativity. More specifically, it sets him to painting.

All images in this segment courtesy of Jim Wilson.

"As for inspiration for the paintings, I like to capture the feel of the late '70s, early '80s," Jim tells us. "Hard to explain, my childhood seemed to last forever back then, always wondering when will I grow up and be a big person like Bo and Luke. I have always drawn things, have a

gift I guess. I had a special art teacher who would come in once a week to expand what I had done. Taught me perspective, stuff like that. But basically I just draw or paint or weld what is in my mind."

And what a talent and imagination it is. We especially like his interpretation of the recovery of Lee 1, the very first General ever jumped on "The Dukes of Hazzard." Now, there's an interesting thing to paint, especially for what that moment, and the ensuing years of the car's change in ownership and its restoration, have meant in the "Dukes" fan community, both positive and not so much.

Jim is sure capturing a certain feeling in his work. And it's clear that comes from his own love of the show and of all that surrounds it these days.

"I love going to events in the South," he says. "Last year at the Hazzard Homecoming I finally met Tom Wopat, so now I have met everybody, even Honest John Ledbetter, who until his death lived in Canada. I had a nice talk with him about the 'Dukes.' I can see why Cooter lives in the Blue Ridge mountains. I fell in love with 'em, too. Any reason to go back there, I would. Beautiful.

"My favorite 'Dukes' character I would have to say is Uncle Jesse," says Jim, who had the above moment at the site of the original Duke farm in Georgia captured for all time. "I don't own a General Lee yet. That pic of me you saw was just luck that somebody was at the farm with one; he let me pose in front of it. I'd like to mention that the gas pumps were Jason's idea and the

Hoggoco oil cans were mine. He lives and breathes the 'Dukes' like me."

And does it seem unusual that such a fervent "Dukes" fan would be Canadian born and bred? Not to us, as we used to attend the Hair Dare Dukes Days in Ontario and see the love of the show there in the North.

"I don't think the Canadian perception is any different from the American on the show," Jim says. "We both know you can't fly a car without damage, LOL. For some reason there are a lot of Confederate flags flying up here. Everybody wants to be a rebel, I guess, and American flags, after 9-11, the stars and stripes were everywhere in Canada in support."

And the "Dukes" isn't the only classic TV show he loves.

"As for what I watch on TV today, not much. I did enjoy the new 'Battlestar Galactica' series. I also like 'The Big Bang Theory.' Everything else I buy on DVD. Love the 'Waltons.' I went to Waltons' Mountain museum last year after the Homecoming as it was two hours away from there. Makes you

wish you grew up on Waltons' Mountain. I also enjoy the series 'Rat Patrol' from the '60s. 'Magnum P.I.,' I adore that show. 'The Fall Guy,' 'McHale's Navy,' 'Beverly Hillbillies,' 'Petticoat Junction,' aughhh, so many!"

When he's not painting, Jim's day job is at St. Thomas Rent-all in St. Thomas, Ontario. He also enjoys making welding sculptures out of scrap material from work, model railroading. "In my younger years I was a dirt biker. I miss my motorcycle. ;("

But his No. 01 hobby, as he puts it, is searching for 'Dukes' stuff! He does admit it's harder to find in the Great White North.

"Back in the '80s, Canada had Kmart (not anymore), and I got my first 'Dukes' toy, an ERTL General Lee. I was so excited. The '90s were a real dry spell for 'Dukes' stuff. I remember hearing about the first reunion movie, but we didn't have cable. I missed out on it, then when the DVDs starting coming out, I was in heaven. It's like every show is brand new again, and that's when I found out about DukesFest. I HAD TO GO!! My first was 2005

in Bristol, my first real trip South as an adult. Terrible drive there. Long story short, we got there late at night on a back road, thunderstorm, we stayed at a crappy hotel. I woke early next day, it was humid, dark, grey sky, and in the mist, I see my very first General Lee sitting on a trailer. I was so excited, I MADE IT, it was a dream come true, 50,000 people like me in the same town!! And I have been going ever since, pic of that General in the mist included. ;)"

He says traveling to Atlanta was another dream come true. "When I went inside the Duke farm, stood in front of the Boar's Nest, drove around Hazzard Square in my Cadillac at the time. Never thought in a million years I'd ever see this stuff. What HISTORY!"

He continues, "Then a couple years back, I put an ad on Kijiji looking for '69 Charger parts. Well, this guy named Jason Darling answers. He had a trunk lid for me. I met him in Toronto, as it's kinda halfway for both of us. I walked up to him, and I felt like I had known him my whole life. Well, thanks to him, I have a trunk lid and a door, one piece at a time like Johnny Cash. The door blew me away. I met him in Niagara Falls last April for the John and Tom concert. I was thinking I was getting an old rusty dented door; he pulls out of his truck a freshly painted 01 orange door signed by Bo and Luke. I started to well up. I was floored. He is now one of my best friends. I consider him my brother; we text every day, no less, always comparing 'Dukes' stuff. Amazing who you meet through the 'Dukes.'"

Yup! Don't we know it! Many thanks to Jim for sharing his story.

"Dukes" History Also Inspires the Art of this Avid Fan

Consider this "part 2" of the previous segment … We showed you the talent of Canadian artist Jim Wilson, who paints up very nice "Dukes of Hazzard"-themed scenes. Now we take a look at another talented artist out of Ontario. His medium is quite a bit more three-dimensional than the painted canvas. He's put together a beautiful diorama that chronicles an important event in "Dukes" history — the recovery of the very first General Lee used for a jump in the TV series, from a yard in Georgia many years after its 1979 debut. What's more, this artist, Jason Darling, is friends with Jim Wilson, and it's really their artistic collaboration that you see in the first photo below, with Jim's painting in the background.

This famous Dodge Charger, of course, was found still wearing its blue, roughed-up "71" paint job from the fourth episode of the show, "Repo Men," when it doubled as a Richard Petty car. It changed hands a few times after the recovery and has most recently been fully restored to the way it appeared as blazin'-orange, jumpin' "Lee 1" in the pilot episode.

Three photos in this segment courtesy of Jason Darling.

"The idea for the diorama came when Jim and I were talking about it and he had started painting again," Jason says. "I, of course, had many spare Charger model kits so I started my project! I have always followed the 71 story and I was present when it was unveiled at Oxford College (near Covington, Georgia) at the 25th anniversary event by Mr. Bell and helped push it on and off the trailer."

He continues, "I have about 13-14 hours in building the model and have researched it for years. The gentleman who bought it from Travis even contacted me for facts about it before its restoration. I am strongly against 71 ever being restored; I think that was an atrocity."

He says, "Jim Wilson and I pride ourselves in recreating 'Dukes' facts and pieces for each other's collections such as our Hoggoco oil cans and my and Jim's gas pumps, to name a couple. If Jim and I put our collections together, we would have a very nice 'Dukes of Hazzard' museum."

As with a lot of "Dukes" fans out there, the show made a big impression on this creative fan that goes way beyond art. "My favorite character on the 'Dukes' while it aired will always be Bo Duke, and then Uncle Jesse. I live my life with Bo Duke in my back pocket, with Uncle Jesse's values."

He says, "My favorite episode is a tie with 'Happy Birthday, General Lee' and 'The Ghost of General Lee.' I loved the history behind the birthday episode and the emotion behind the ghost episode.

"Jim and I go every day finding new 'Dukes' things and keeping the show alive and honest; we are 'Dukes' cousins for sure," Jason says. "We have helped one another with our collections, and I've even gotten Jim started on some General Lee parts! LOL."

Jason, of course, has his own General. "I'm in the process of building my own second-unit version General Lee, going on five years now, but I'm proud of it. I have been extremely fortunate to attend many 'Dukes' events, and I've gotten to meet every living cast member, something I never would have thought I'd ever get to do four years ago, being that I live down in Canada. The cast of the show are amazing and friendly people."

Jason continues, "I met Jim through an ad on Kijiji looking for General Lee parts — now we're best friends. Funny how 'Dukes' fans find each other."

Thanks to Jason for sharing his story and his fabulous art!

AND NOW A WORD FROM ...

Straight from the stars themselves!

John Schneider:
The end — and return — of Jonathan Kent

This author got the chance to interview John Schneider at the 2011 MegaCon event in Orlando, Florida, where he was meeting and greeting fans along with other celebs. This interview was for the "Comics Continuum" TV show based in Detroit, and it touched on Schneider's work on "Smallville," which at the time was about to end in fine fashion, bringing back the deceased Jonathan Kent for one last spin. The question was, what was Jonathan doing in those final scenes, teased so provocatively in the TV spots? BRB tried to pry it out of him ...

Tell us about the final episodes of "Smallville" and Jonathan Kent's part in them.
"This is an Earth 2 existence."

It's an alternate world.
"It's an alternate world that I'm part of. And I'm not a very happy

camper." (Laughs.) "But it's really terrific. I think the writing on 'Smallville,' as great as it started out, I think the writing on 'Smallville' in this final season, because they wanted it to go out really well — not like 'The Sopranos'; you know, they wanted it to go out really well — I think it's some of the finest writing of the entire 10 years. So it's really good. And then after that there's a two-part season finale, and I'm in both of those."

These two images courtesy of Comics Continuum.

And can you give us anything from that?
"Nothing. And I know it all."

You don't die again, do you?
(Laughs.) "No, do I die again? No. A thousand deaths!"

It looks like Jonathan is about to kill poor Clark in that one scene in the TV promo.
"He's just angry, that's all. It was good. Tom and I worked so well together. We worked together a lot. So it was different not being a loving and comforting father. So I enjoyed that. But again, the writing in it is so good, there's some wonderful twists and turns, even in that, that I think will really delight the people who are watching."

Did you ever expect the show to last as long as it has?
"So few shows ever last 10 years. Hourlong shows, 10 years? Sci-fi hourlong shows, 10 years? It's kind of unheard-of."

How many seasons were you on as Pa Kent?
"I was in five. All of them, for five."

Almost as long as on "The Dukes of Hazzard."
"Yea, seven. Seven years on 'Dukes.' But yea, and mentioned a lot, in the

years that I wasn't there (on 'Smallville'). I was mentioned a lot. So there in spirit."

Do you keep up with Tom Welling off-screen?
"Yea. We play golf."

You play golf!
"We're golf buddies, yep. He started me with that nasty habit.

So looking back now, after playing Bo Duke, and being known so much as Bo Duke over the years, I think there probably are some similarities between Bo Duke and Pa Kent, even putting the age difference aside. (He was really thinking hard, squinting his face as this was being asked!!!! Hedging ..) You know, kinda the ... values?
"The values, yea, I think Jonathan ... maybe Jonathan is a grown-up Bo Duke. That could be. I guess you could argue that. Bo is a look-before-you-leap sort of a guy, and Jonathan's not that, so I guess you could argue. They both check their mail at a mailbox at the end of a dirt road. And they live on a farm. So yea, I could see the similarities. Yea."

(Thanks, John, for saving us on that one!)

When did you shoot your last episode of "Smallville"?
"Thursday. Two days ago. ... I had done my last episode supposedly several times before. So this time, knowing it was true, was sad. It's bittersweet. But again, you can't really — 10 years is such a, such a good run, that you can't be sorry. You can't think, omigosh, we were cut down in our prime. No. So it was good. It was fun. It was good to see everybody again."

Ben Jones:
He ain't crazy OR dumb

BRBTV had the pleasure of chatting with Ben Jones a couple-a days before Christmas 2005 about the "Dukes" and what it has meant to him over the years. Here are the highlights ...

Photo courtesy of Ben Jones.

What is your favorite "Dukes" episode, and why?
"There were a couple of them. One of them was called 'Repo Men.' We shot five episodes of the show in Georgia. 'Repo Men' was the third show we did, and all of a sudden, it seemed to come together. The show had a nice flow to it. People still talk about that episode. It had great action. ... The show went right to the top; once we came on the air in January 1979, within weeks we were a top 10 show, and I think (this episode) captured people's fancy. It holds up very well. Also 'Cooter's Girl.' He meets his daughter, and he's trying to make an impression on her. It was a really, really, good story. It was a real warmhearted story."

Who was the most fun to work with on the set?
"All of them! It's an overused phrase, perhaps, but what we had on that show was tremendous chemistry. We were like family. We were like kids playing in the backyard. When you're a kid, you go in the backyard and you play cowboys and Indians or Superman — and we were getting paid for it! I loved all those people, and still do. I was close to a lot of the folks on the show. I think we've become closer over the years. It's a classic show; those are the things that get better as time goes on. These relationships are still going on. We do a lot of things together now. We have a DukesFest every year. Other members of the cast come to our Cooter's Place stores. I was really close to Sorrell Booke, who played Boss Hogg. He had an interest in politics. Denver Pyle, who played Uncle Jesse, was a good friend of mine. We had a bunch of 'best friends' there."

What are the similarities between Cooter and Ben Jones?
"I've played, in my career, hundreds of different characters, but with a show like that, I was basically creating a character, making artistic choices and creative choices that established that character. It was basically part of my persona. When the show first started, the character was much more

exaggerated. He looked like he had been raised by wolves. As the show progressed, the character evolved and changed and became much more dimensional. Really, for me now, Cooter has become a permanent nickname. All I have to do is put on a ballcap and roll up my sleeves, and I'm Cooter. I wanted to make Cooter someone I could look up to, someone who would always stick his neck out for you and give you the shirt off his back — the old shade-tree mechanic who keeps America rolling."

How many public appearances do you make a year?
"A hundred and fifty, two hundred, something like that. Sometimes twice a day. Every time I'm at Cooter's Place, that's an appearance. That's a special thing, to be able to do; that's an honor."

Have you ever considered going back into television?
"These days, I really don't have the time. Always, if you're a professional entertainer, you also entertain ideas. In the past few years, I've done some films and TV shows. I've got a band, Cooter's Garage Band. And I have Cooter's Place. If the right project came along, and they were interested in using me, then sure. Actors never retire. ... I have pitched to Warner Bros. a project called 'Dukes of Hazzard: The Next Generation.' Having a new generation of kids, with a new car and new dreams."

"Dukes" fans know your feelings about the 2005 motion picture. Were any of the cast members approached about doing a cameo in the film?
"I don't know. No one I talked to was approached to do a role. I was in Los Angeles, and I went by and called them and said I'd like to be involved in the project. They had me come by the casting office and then sort of blew me off. The casting director never spoke to me. They just were not interested in having us involved in the thing that we created.

"I don't know what they were thinking (with the movie). They totally missed the whole point of the show. Our show was sort of like a Western, a 1940s Western. The old B Westerns, the Roy Rogers ones, they weren't realistic; they were fantasies; you could fall off a cliff and not hurt yourself. There were values and a good sense of right and wrong. There was always a lot of slapstick comedy. We used those old-Western ingredients for another generation of Americans. The reason people watched this show and encouraged their kids to watch it is it's a good old-fashioned American show. These Duke boys are heroes; they risk their lives to do the right thing. If I hear it once, I hear it a thousand times a day, 'Thank-you for making a show that our kids can watch.' You don't take that audience and that show and do what they did to it.

"Uncle Jesse was a paragon of virtue. He raised these orphans and taught them a sense of right and wrong. Uncle Jesse Duke is the last character I remember seeing on television saying grace before supper.

"The show is also like a Western in that the look of it does not age. It looks like it could've been made two weeks ago. If you're in rural America, you're still wearing boots and jeans and still driving trucks on back roads. There was very little topical reference in our show. It hasn't aged. WE'VE aged." (Laughs.) "Except John Schneider."

A view of DukesFest 2006.

Christopher Mayer:
Below the radar just wasn't as fun

In the "Dukes of Hazzard" world, where he portrayed Vance Duke — one of the "replacement" Dukes when John Schneider and Tom Wopat temporarily left the show — he was a bit of a Holy Grail. He was the missing signature on the trunk lid of just about every General Lee out there, the only surviving cast member who had not thoroughly embraced the many events of "Dukes" culture over the years. But that changed in 2011, shortly before his untimely death. Christopher Mayer floated up on the radar once again, beginning to make appearances with his "Dukes" cousin Byron Cherry. BRBTV is so thankful to have talked to Christopher Mayer via phone in June 2011, just a month before his death, where he expressed his own thankfulness, certainly, for the chance to meet and greet the fans, which he found very fulfilling.

Photo courtesy of Christopher Mayer.

What was the audition like for "The Dukes of Hazzard"?
"It was insane. There were producer meetings in the studio, and you'd go back there, and there'd be like four blond guys, and four dark-haired guys. I just do the audition and I split. You get a call the next week, and you go back, and there'd be like eight other blond guys and eight other dark-haired guys. They finally got down to the final four guys they wanted for each role. ... They would take you to the airport, and you get out there, and Cathy Bach was waiting for us there. ... You do exteriors out in Valencia, out at Magic Mountain, where they had Hazzard set up. .. Cathy Bach is in a pair of Daisy Duke shorts, and we got to the audition scene. It was kinda bizarre, because the other guys who are going for your role are standing there watching you. ... You just snap the ball through it. But it was acting, you know. Nothing remotely realistic. ... I guess about four or five days later, I was sitting in my apartment, and my first wife was pregnant with my first daughter, Ashley, and my agent says, 'Are you sitting down? Well, you got it!'"

Were you a fan of "The Dukes of Hazzard" before getting the role of Vance?

"I was not really fully aware of it. I was not really a TV watcher. I grew up one of seven kids, back in New Jersey, and New York. I graduated from Colgate University. I was in New York. A girl told me, 'You should be an actor.' I went to New York, and for four months, you could never even find a cab. I had all these headshots taken. And every day at noon, I would hang up my suit in the men's room. I would run all over Manhattan dropping off pictures. For four months. And I would get back and put my suit back on, and do my job, and sweat would be dripping off my nose!

"At that point, I got connected to the Jay Michael Bloom Agency. I end up getting about 35-40 national commercials for him a year. I ended up doing like Esquire and other stuff. ... They read 3,000 men, 3,000 women in this open session, where you read for a play, you read for a series ... They were going to choose two guys and two girls to fly out; this was in 1979, pilot season. They shoot pilots during the day. Now it's all changed. They flew me out from New York, I got a pilot called 'Stunts Unlimited,' with CIA guys, idiotic, but at the time it was a major deal. I got the role, so it was like winning the Lotto. Then I went out there to do a couple other things. ... I did another show called 'Our Family Business' with David Morse. Ted Danson from 'Cheers' was my older brother. It was supposed to be like an organized crime thing. We were a Mafia family. It was great, though, working with Burt Miles. The show didn't sell, but the pilot was still very successful. Right after that was when I was working with the 'Dukes.'

"It was funny, because I was represented by Jay Michael Bloom, who also represented Tom Wopat. I met a man named Ron Samuels, whose wife was Lynda Carter. ... He hounded me for like a week.

"I finally figured it was a career move, I had a pregnant wife. William Morris for representation. It was sort of a bad departure from Jay Michael Bloom, but I felt it was something I had to do.

"It was an around-the-world audition thing. They beefed up the PR around the world. I told my friends about it, and they were like, oh, dude, don't do it.

"I did a guest shot on 'Dance Fever' with Deney Terrio, where one of the girls was Janet Jones, who's now Wayne Gretzky's wife. I'm a fairly good dancer. I love dancing. They offered me the show, and I turned it down. They offered me like $500,000 to do the show. So I turned it down! I crapped the silly string for months! Adrian Zmed of 'T.J. Hooker' took the job."

What's your favorite "Dukes" episode?
"The thing about the show that's interesting ... I like the show because I did shows before and I did shows after. Byron played Coy on the show ... I don't know if people realized it or not at the time, but it was becoming a sort of cultural phenomenon like 'Bonanza.' I had a great time on the show. I did personal appearances every weekend. I was on the set until 9 o'clock every night during the week. Obviously it was of wonderful financial benefit.

"You had to have absolutely split-down-the-middle driving time — half the time Byron would drive, and half the time I would drive." *(Because as Byron has commented, the one who drove got the most fan mail!)*

"Television is the opiate of the masses, but at the same time, the way it touches people, it's such a great thing. The average person aspires to that. You can go and meet people and shake hands, and I love going out and making people smile, look them in the eye, shake their hands.

"I'm 57 years old now. I want to be a part of it. I'm not MIA. I've been in the Dukes of Hazzard Witness Protection Program." (Laughs.)

Who was the best to work with on the show?
"Ah, they were all good. ... They were all very pleasant and everything else. You did have the thing that you were a replacement; you weren't the original guy. I liked working with Ben Jones. Sorrell Booke was amazing. He showed me like these little nuances. Sorrell was the most impressive, because he showed me how to mark the script. A really gentle person. 'All you have to do is look them in the eyes, tell them the truth.'

"Cathy is beautiful. Denver and Sorrell Booke and Ben were the best, because they had been around. They were accomplished and knew the nuances. And they helped me in my role."

In retrospect now, years later, how do you feel like you were treated on the set by the other cast members, besides Byron?
"Byron was like a younger brother. I had been in the business long enough to do like 30 commercials, I had done two TV pilots. With Byron, I was very protective of him. ... In the beginning, people didn't know what to do. Now, the cast is on Facebook talking about playing golf together. But 30 years ago, it felt like two girls with the same dress on at the prom. We kept the show flowing. As a result of that, the numbers did drop a little bit."

Do you have any keepsakes or mementos from the set of "The Dukes"?
"Yea. I have my dressing room nameplate, with the Confederate flag and 'Chris Mayer.' I have pictures."

What are the similarities between Vance Duke and Chris Mayer?
"My brothers would break my balls about it some back in New Jersey. My given name is George Charles Mayer III. My nickname was Chip Mayer, oldest of seven kids. So when I took the name Chris, I figured Christopher Mayer would be a great name. I would go back home after they saw the show, and my brothers would be like, 'Hey, Chris!'" (sarcastic) "I'm not from the South; I'm from New Jersey. That was a challenge. I took some lessons, tried to take on a Southern accent.

"Vance was about family, he was about kids, he was about being respectful to women and not treating them like objects. And if you want a fight — hell ya, right now!"

What do you remember about doing your voicework for the animated "Dukes" series?
"When I was down there, the guy who was the director for Hanna-Barbera was Gordon Hunt. He was their animation director. We would go over there to the studio and lay down the tracks to do our work. He would have his little blond daughter running around the sound stage. It was Helen Hunt. I think she was really the one who inspired me to be an actor. Just kidding!

"We did the show at the Hanna-Barbera cartoon studio. That's where we did the voiceovers for the show."

Did you and Byron tape your lines together in the studio?
"Yea, we were together. They had this thing called Favored Nation, where you get people unilaterally involved ... Some of those actors were making

four times what I was making at the time. ... In this thing called Favored Nation, we shot all episodes. One hundred is the magic number to get into syndication. You can then sell it into syndication and make buku money.

"We sat together, right next to each other and just read the script. They had little gels to show what the characters looked like. It wasn't like we were doing the 'Brothers Karamazov.' It was a lot of laughter, fun stuff.

"I was also very friendly with the girls in the comptroller's office, and one time before Thanksgiving the girls were like, 'You've got some overtime coming up.' I said was I really getting overtime? I got an overtime check for like 14,000 dollars."

Have your daughters seen the animated "Dukes"?
"Yea, they did. I never had the opportunity to record it myself. I had a fan who sent me copies. When they were younger, yea, they did watch it. And they cracked up about it.

"When we first did the show, a lot of people thought I should be doing serious acting, not bright colors and notes like it was then. Now in hindsight, it's become something that's very sweet and a cultural icon. Even though we were in a replacement role. It gave me an opportunity to bring my first daughter into the world in something other than a cold apartment.

"I'm not a computer guy or a Facebook guy or all that Twitter or Skype stuff. When I first set up a Facebook page, I felt like I was walking around with my zipper down. Because I'm super private. That's not me. I've really been off for so long. But now I'm going to try to be more on. It's a great way to make people smile. It's fun to be a part of something that still has an intense devotion.

"You go down south or to western Pennsylvania, and they're just crazy about it (the show)."

What do you imagine Vance Duke's life looks like these days, if they were to do a "Dukes" next generation approach like TNT is doing right now with "Dallas"? Would he be married? Have kids? What career would he have?
"If they did it, they would do it with John and Tom. They wouldn't do it with us. ... Even though we were part of the show and came into it as ingénues with no ego and just wanted to do it, there was still a feeling that we were

not there permanently. I was looking at it as a way to have fun and get exposure and make some money.

"Vance would have a lot of kids. And I'd be married to a really pretty girl that looked like Cathy Bach. I'd be in fairly good shape, but maybe have a little more on my waistline. I would be somebody who would be involved in the community, maybe something with kids. I would be involved in Hazzard County and helping the community.

"Kids and women are it, man. They're the hinge on which the gate swings."

What do you think is the most important thing you took away from the whole "Dukes" experience?
"Some of the stuff about being a cause célèbre, if you will ... We were on the show in a secondary role, but with the personal appearances, which I did a lot of that year, it was amazing how the fans would walk up and not blink an eye. They didn't need a DNA test or anything. They were just thrilled to be there and get a picture with me. They would laugh and there would be kids with wheelchairs and all that. That would rock my world.

"Patton said victory is fleeting. It's amazing and it's good to get that ability ... It's like a girl winning the beauty contest, to be chosen the winner after competing. I grew up an athlete. Francis Ford Coppola said an actor is an athlete of the heart. So I came away from it with an engendered heart."

Let's talk about your time on "Santa Barbara." What's your most vivid memory of working on that daytime soap?
"I think it was just the amount of dialogue, because normally you do a film or a TV show, and it's an hourlong show, and we would take a week to do that. We would do interiors, with a blue screen behind us with the General Lee and all that ... But on a soap, it's a 3-10 deal. ... You go in there, and everybody's working like they're hung over. And you do a dry run through different scenes. There was a lot of dialogue, and a lot of choreography. You might have to move to another area and sit down. And if you miss that, you feel like a big screw-up. I wouldn't look at my lines until the day of the shot. There were days I had like 30 pages of dialogue. The amount of dialogue you had to learn day to day is one of the most challenging things about doing a soap."

What was Judith McConnell like to work with?
"She was fun. She was … fun." (Laughs.) "Yea. Just accessible and stuff. She was open to working on things. The cougar. That carried on and off the set. Just kidding."

I believe you got to work with Robin Wright as Kelly, then Kimberly McArthur, then Carrington Garland! Was that a little discombobulating?
"Robin was a hoot. She ended up telling me at one point, I had gotten to be a bit of a maniac then because my first marriage had broken up … She looked at me and she said, 'You're too crazy. I'll tell you what I am going to do.' This was right at that time the movie 'Casualties of War' was being shot with Sean Penn and Michael J. Fox in Thailand. She said, 'I'm going to go over to Thailand, and I'm going to meet Sean Penn and I'm going to marry him.' She prophesied that. She's cool, really cool. It just cracked me up. Only such a beautiful woman could go like, 'I'm going to go over and meet the president of France and I'm going to … '"

Now, we know why T.J. was interested in Sophia, for her money, but do you think perhaps he was actually in love with Kelly, or was he just interested in her Capwell cash, too?
"I usually go with my own instincts. Everybody looked at it like, you were supposed to be the Chippendale dancer, the gigolo. But it's all about the girl. You can find money anywhere."

T.J. was a pretty evil guy, but it must have felt like a juicy role. Were there things you would've changed about the character, if you could have?
"Like that movie 'The Butterfly,' if you change one thing, it will have a ripple effect. To be a gigolo was a character they needed to even out or overall texturize the character list. It was fun to do it, because to be an opportunist, you have to have that personality to live in L.A. So it was like I was subliminally culturally acclimating myself. And there's more texture to that than just playing romance. So no, I wouldn't have changed anything.

"I did a pilot with Henry Winkler called 'Morning Glory,' and it was supposed to be a morning talk show. I played a Geraldo Rivera-type guy, an arrogant, vain, morning TV host.

"Things changed for me after that. I got married for the first time. I had two beautiful daughters. I was still doing film, like 'Apollo 13.' Then I got into construction and did that for about 15 years. The whole lay of the land started to change. Whatever inertia I had for the first 15 years of my life … I wanted my girls to have stuff. So I changed venues and did that. It was a wonderful, wonderful 20 years. But as I got older and had the responsibilities of being a father, I was looking for something a little more steady."

Do you have any desire to return to acting?
"Yea. I've actually got something in the works. A friend of mine who does faux finish work wants to do a reality show called 'Faux-Get About It.' They have guys who do this in L.A. … HGN is working on it. We shot a pilot. … They're trying to shop it."

You are a believer in Christ. I imagine it's difficult to be an ambassador for the Lord in Hollywood.
"You can't hide your light under a basket. You are children of light, and it's a crooked and perverse generation. With Jesus Christ, the fear of death is gone, and I have a hierarchy of behavior that affects how I see my life. … Hollywood can be somewhat heady. You can lose your way easily. I was raised with a dad who was very much like that, even though my mom and I and my siblings were very much lucky."

What would you mainly like to speak about, to others?
"Neither Greek nor Jew, male nor female. All are one in Christ."

Byron Cherry:
The show must go on!

As we've seen Byron Cherry at "Dukes" events over the years, BRBTV has mentioned several descriptors that the casual observer could associate with this great guy ... fun-loving, boisterous, always smiling, the life of the party. Well, after the October 2007 Hillbilly Woodstick 2 Dukes of Hazzard Cruise, we had one more to add to the list: trooper!

If you were anywhere near the cruise's display at the Lions' BBQ cookoff in Covington on that Saturday, you saw our lovable Coy Duke hauling around boxes and setting up tables and canopies as if he were part of the backstage crew instead of the honored guest. You saw him traipse up on stage to talk about the "Dukes," then go up again a little while later to put on a pig's snout and oink! You saw him turn in an interview for a local radio station, strike a pose with Miss Hazzard County, then follow the crowd to the Square in Covington, having already been all over the place, including the antiques mall on Elm Street, earlier that day. You saw him pose with

"Dukes" museum curator Jo McLaney and sign items at the A Touch of Country shop, and you saw him sign, sign, sign and turn a smile and a good-natured attitude toward everyone who approached him. You saw him do all of this, after having spent a week on the road with the cruise, making other appearances, and (very importantly) you saw him do all this on Saturday after he spent the first part of the day very seriously sick to his stomach from food poisoning that struck a number of people in the area! If that's not being a trooper, we're just not sure what is!

All of those appropriate lauds aside, however, Cherry also took part in the "Dukes" reminiscing of the event and offered some fun stuff as he spoke to the standing-room-only crowd in the meeting room of the Super 8 Motel in Covington on the Friday of the event.

As he took the floor, he first thanked Wayne and Donna Wooten for organizing the show, as well as the fans. "Without you guys, the show would be nothing," he said.

"I used to come to Covington to hunt and fish," the Atlanta native pointed out. Cherry still has family in Atlanta.

Then he told about how he first came to be associated with "The Dukes of Hazzard."

"I'd see John (Schneider) all over Atlanta. I knew him. We go way back. We were doing little commercials here and there, enough to get by, nothing big. As an actor, you try to stay positive, but you do 10, 20 auditions and nobody hires you, you think you're in the wrong business. I was up originally for (the part of) Bo, but I missed the audition. A few years later, the same agent calls me and says, 'Hey, Byron, you ever hear of a show called "The Dukes of Hazzard"?' I said, 'Yea, I watch it every Friday night!'" Cherry laughed.

"I went over there, and they gave me a three-page scene. Stratton was playing Daisy, and I was trying to play the Coy Duke character. He was talking like a woman, and I just started laughing. This was in Atlanta, Georgia. I hadn't been to L.A. yet. I got through the scene, and mostly it was just laughing. They overnighted it to Warner Bros."

Byron Cherry with Miss Jo McLaney at A Touch of Country in Covington during the Hillbilly Woodstick event.

When Cherry got the news that he'd made the cut, though, he had trouble believing it! While he was out on a family dinner at TGIFridays (for his mom's birthday), the bartender approached the table to tell Cherry he had a phone call. It was Jimmy, his roommate. "He said, 'Byron, you're going to Hollywood, man! They called you.'"

Cherry thought it was a joke and hung up! At the third call, he finally believed. "I think the next day I was on a plane to do a screen test," he said. "I get out there, and they give me prep. I said, 'Who am I going to read with?' and they said Daisy Mae, and I said, 'No, really?' The real Daisy Mae! That audition was supposed to last two days, and it was almost a month for me, because they'd bring in people from all over the place. I didn't know I really had the job. I was the only blond-haired, blue-eyed guy there!" Again, Cherry laughed.

"Finally, the producers called me in after reading hundreds of people. I walked in there and they had a big ole bottle of champagne."

Cherry also learned that it was his workout buddy, Chris Mayer, who got the role of the other Duke cousin. The two remained good friends until Mayer's untimely death.

(Don Schisler, by the way, threw in a comment during this talk: He said that Byron Cherry was being modest, because he himself saw the casting call for this Coy Duke role, and there were thousands of people there.)

Well ... We'd have to say that Warner Bros. made a fine choice.

Don Pedro Colley:
Sheriff Little speaks ....

OK, so ... what do you do when you see the imposing, stern, lumbering Sheriff Little of "The Dukes of Hazzard" riding around on a kids' motor scooter, his legs hanging out all over the place? You laugh and take photos, that's what! And that's exactly what he was doing — and we were doing — at the fifth annual Hair Dare Dukes Days event in Ontario, Canada, in August 2007! Don Pedro Colley, who at the time was 69, set up shop at the table next to BRB at the event and told all kinds of great "Dukes" stories, and other stories about the many roles he's had in Hollywood. But did you know that he also wrote an episode of "Little House on the Prairie"? *Yessireee*, he called the episode "The Celebration," and in it a young girl gets lost and is helped by Dr. Tain, the physician to the Indians, who is discriminated against because he is black. It's the only television Colley has written. "I got an inspiration," he said.

Colley spoke well about his "Dukes" days and his costars. Denver Pyle, for instance, was the first actor that he ever met when he began his career in 1966. Colley called Pyle a wonderful human being. He also shared some tidbits about the making of the show. Sheriff Little is remembered so well for yanking the doors off cars or kicking off the fenders. Colley explained how this was done, by taking off the nuts and bolts, then reattaching with piano wire. Someone off screen would be waiting for the cue to yank the fender off when Colley kicked. Fun!

Colley also told about a time when his Sheriff Little persona came in handy in real life. His home in Oregon was broken into by some neighborhood thugs that had been hitting a lot of houses. The police considered them longtime criminals and were trying to catch them. Colley took matters into his own hand, a la Sheriff Little. He actually got a double-barrel 12-gauge shotgun and went over to the thieves' house. "Sheriff Little went to work," he says with a smile. He asked them who their fence was. A bit of a shootout ensued. "I didn't shoot at anyone," Colley clarifies. "I did it to scare them. They were avoiding being brought out of the shadows."

Opposite page: Don't mess with Sheriff Little! Colley gets some new wheels, and collars the Hair Dare show's organizer, Paul Harrington.

Colley also talked about the creation of the Sheriff Little character on the show. "The producers said the reason they were developing Sheriff Little was as the antithesis of Boss Hogg," he says. The kind of sheriff who has a presence without saying a word, he adds. "That's the kind of presence that I tried to project into the character."

He says he sure had a lot of fun with the lumbering lawman. "Sheriff Little is based on a lot of people I've seen in my life. This head is like a card file — I've got all kinds of stuff I can pull out if I need it."

The local TV news station interviewed Colley as he signed autographs at Hair Dare. In the midst of all his other roles on movies such as "THX 1138" and "Beneath the Planet of the Apes," Colley sure didn't mind reminiscing to the TV audience, or the myriad fans at the event, about his co-starring role as the stern sheriff of Chickasaw County, Georgia. "You don't mess with him. He's a good guy, but he's a cop. ... He's a real person. I try to bring that into him."

In August 2008, at the same event — Hair Dare Dukes Days — BRBTV got another chance to hear Colley's thoughts and reminisces (we see him at a lot of these events!). This time we found out more about how that whole Sheriff Little thing came about.

It was a 1967 episode of "Daktari" — his very first screen credit — that laid the groundwork. In the episode, "Killer Tribe," Colley was guest-starring as tribesman Mtola in "chest-high weeds." In one action-packed scene, he says, "I slide down the embankment, roll over, and the camera turns and sees what's chasing me." Things didn't go quite as planned, though, but the classically trained Colley improvised with the logistics and saved the scene.

Years later, he got a call from the show's producer, Leonard Kaufman. "I really didn't have an agent at the time," Colley says. Kaufman began to describe for Colley a part on this one particular little show, "The Dukes of Hazzard," a part that at the time was called Sheriff Lucas. "I never have forgotten what you did for me," Kaufman told him.

During his audition, Colley burst into the room strongly and took an "ice-cold" Sheriff Little stance. He didn't have the attention of the show's bigwigs, at first, though. They were still looking down at their papers. He waited. He wasn't going anywhere, after all. When one, executive producer

Paul Picard, finally looked up and met his "gaze" (to put it politely), "the pen slipped out of his hand, the piece of paper fell on the floor," Colley laughs.

"After the interview was over, I took off my hat, shook his hand," Colley says. "The interview was over — I was out of character now."

That regular gig put Colley's career into a more comfy position, but this is a man with a wealth of experience. He also reminisced about the two-hour episode of "Starsky and Hutch" that he did in 1977, "Starsky and Hutch on Playboy Island," featuring someone else we know, Joan Collins. And later, as our group had dinner, Colley regaled us with stories of Jack Palance and others from his earlier days in stage productions. Fun, indeed.

BEHIND THE SCENES

> "I just thought it was kinda exciting, that they were making a TV show about my life. I was a bit of an outlaw back then."
>
> — *Jerry Rushing, with a smile, to BRBTV at CMT DukesFest 2006*

Felix Silla:
Reminiscing about his "Strange Visit"

Perhaps best-known as Cousin Itt of "The Addams Family," as well as Twiki on "Buck Rogers in the 25th Century," Felix Silla also starred in an episode of "The Dukes": He was the alien in "Strange Visitor to Hazzard." BRBTV got a chance to chat with Silla a bit over the weekend of the Hair Dare event in Canada in August 2008, at the next table over in the fairgrounds building.

Born in Rome, Silla lives in Las Vegas these days, he told us. He's had quite an amazing career, portraying everything from a Talosian on the classic "Star Trek" episode "The Cage" to a child gorilla on "Planet of the Apes" and Baby New Year on an episode of the classic "Night Gallery." Did you know he was the polka-dotted horse in "H.R. Pufnstuf"?

Silla's table display included his original call sheet (in the photo below) from his episode of the "Dukes" at the tail-end of the show's run. Silla said it took four days to shoot the episode, and it was a chilly December. The date on the call sheet is December 7, 1984. The episode aired on January 25, 1985. Silla reminisced with us about that tannish alien getup he had to wear, which included some careful matching makeup around his eyes.

You've gotta love a call sheet that lists Flash as playing ... Flash! Rawfff!!!!!!!)

BRBTV asked if he's still got a lot of these kind of call sheets from "The Addams Family." No, actually, he doesn't, though he does have quite a few from "Star Wars: Return of the Jedi," where he was an Ewok.

Silla remains in contact with his "Addams Family" co-stars. "There are only four of us left," he pointed out, himself, John Astin, "and the two kids," Lisa Loring and Ken Weatherwax.

You can learn more about Silla, and even purchase his photos, at his official website, FelixSilla.com.

Don Schisler:
It all started with a phone call

Don Schisler worked as the transportation director for "The Dukes of Hazzard," and he sadly passed on in 2009. BRBTV had the pleasure of talking with him at Wayne Wooten's 2007 Hillbilly Woodstick 2 Dukes of Hazzard Cruise, in Covington, Georgia. We also saw him at a couple other Georgia events. Below is our BRBTV News Blog coverage of Schisler's talk at the 2007 event.

"This all started with a phone call," Don Schisler said as he took the floor at the Super 8 Motel during the weekend to relate his experiences with the hit TV show "The Dukes of Hazzard."

"The film commissioner of the State of Georgia had recommended me to do the picture cars. I'd done picture cars for years on commercials and other features. The phone rang and it was John Marenda, and he said, 'Can you meet at the Holiday Inn tomorrow morning?' This was about six weeks before the first day of principal photography."

So did Schisler bite? You betcha. This Dearborn, Michigan, native, who attended Wayne State University in Detroit and even worked for Ford Motor Co. for a time, became the transportation director for our beloved show. "I'm sort of a Georgia redneck version of a casting director for cars. The General hadn't even been chosen as a Dodge Charger. The art director and the director have the big say-so. For the General, I put up three cars: I put a Firebird, a Mustang and a Charger as a he-man sort of thing. The

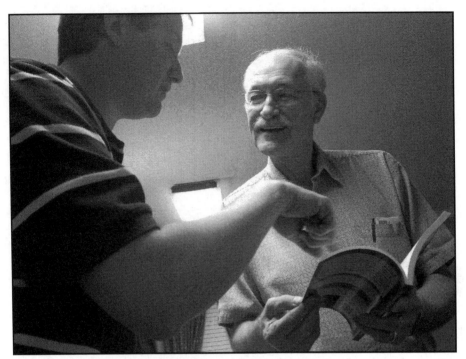

Don Schisler looks over Jon Holland's "Dukes" book, "The Roads to Early Hazzard," at the 2007 Hillbilly Woodstick 2 Dukes of Hazzard Cruise.

Charger was the best choice because it was a little bigger and it's about as macho as they come. In retrospect, they don't come any better."

Schisler told the group gathered in the meeting room of the motel in Covington that Friday that his wife read the script for "The Dukes of Hazzard" back then and said it would never reach the screen. "She said, 'There's no story here. There's no meat here.' It was very vanilla. But when you put the whole thing together — the right people, the right location — everything went together magically, to end up being something that went to No. 1 on the charts."

And Schisler's own role was so crucial, since this was to be a show that was as much about a car as it was about people. But for the action to start, models of that "he-man" 1969 Dodge Charger had to be secured. "These were cars that had been flailed for all those years. The first thing we had to do was get them to the shop. And it was safety, safety, safety. ... It changed my whole life when Rodney Mitchell was killed." (Just a day away from leaving the set for another production, Mitchell died on June 18, 1980, when a camera car rolled over as it hit a soft side of the shoulder of the road in Lake Sherwood, California.)

"The cars arrived here to the Holiday Inn," Schisler continued. "I don't think any of them was a good start. They had to have new batteries. One of the worst things we had to do was get the rear brakes to work. So the first thing we did is we went to the parts store ... I went down to the drag race shop and bought all the line locks, and I put the line locks in the circuit going to the front wheels. They were originally hydraulic locks for wreckers. My dad was service manager for Hudson in Pittsburgh, Pennsylvania, and all the Hudson's would buy line locks. I had a liberal education when I was 12 years old with line locks in Pittsburgh. The Baxleys were hitting me over the head, why couldn't you make these rear brakes lock up? So that worked out. I carried one of those in my camera car."

Appropriately enough, Schisler's work sped by as fast as the General on one of them back roads!

"The whole thing went through in a flash. In retrospect, it was like one week. I think it was actually a month and a half. It was just pandemonium, 24-7. ... The body shop had it even worse." (Yea, they did! See the next section!)

But it's par for the course, Schisler said. "Episodic TV always suffers from major problems. A lot of crazy unplanned things. There's some real wild stuff that goes on."

Sounds like Schisler, who still lived in Metro Atlanta at the time, loved every minute of his work on the "Dukes."

"It's been a great ride," he said. "I never thought it would do what it's done today. The magnitude."

Tom Sarmento:
Keeping the motor running

We got the chance to chat a bit with the show's lead mechanic Tom Sarmento at the 2007 Hillbilly Woodstick 2 Dukes of Hazzard Cruise in Covington, Georgia . And there was frankly just one thing we had to know the answer to ….

On which dad-gum episode were the barrels of molasses?????????????????

It was a bit of an inside joke, you see, springing from the event's Friday autograph session with the star guests, and we're more than happy to let you in on it. BRB got Tom a-talkin', askin' him which "Dukes" episode he remembered the most, or which one he had a funny reminiscing for. He began to tell us about an episode where everything seemed to go wrong, though he couldn't remember the title of that episode! All he remembered is that it was probably either right before or right after the Coy and Vance time (but not during) and that it involved some wayward barrels of molasses.

"You knew that was going to be a bad episode right away," he mused. A truck of molasses was brought in the night before filming and parked at what was thought to be a good place. But, he said, the truck moved from its position during the night and the molasses spilled all over the place.

Then the cows came from the nearby hillside.

"And where there's cows, there's cow pies!" he laughed. He said the mess destroyed a couple million bucks worth of equipment, including two Panavision cameras. An expensive episode, to say the least.

But the question remains ... just which episode was it? What was the scenario for which this sticky prop was used? A typical cop chase, mayhaps? We racked our brains. "Dukes" fans, we're relying on you. Meanwhile ....

"This brings back memories," Sarmento said as he paged through "Them Dukes! Them Dukes!" Sarmento turned in seven good years on the "Dukes," making sure things went as smoothly as possible with the show's vehicles.

"We did a lot of stuff," he told the group gathered for the Friday afternoon talk at the Super 8 Motel in Covington. "We did a lot of changes, etc. We had like 317 of those Chargers; we had over a thousand of those police cars."

He continued, "All these guys that we had on the show — they're all directors, production coordinators now." Stunt guru Paul Baxley, father of stunt coordinator Craig Baxley and uncle of fellow stunt coordinator, Gary Baxley, was instrumental in that, he said. "The man made people's careers. A lot of people didn't like Paul, but he made the show what it came to be."

Sarmento represented the Hazzard County Stunt Team at this event. You've seen these guys and their daring deeds at DukesFest and other events. When Sarmento settled into the antiques mall on Friday with the Stunt Team's display, he showed BRB the particular General Lee he had with him — the General Lee used in the reunion jump in Covington a couple years ago (photo below).

He says that after the jump the car needed a whole new front end, but the rest pretty much stayed the same. In addition to this blazin' orange beauty, the Stunt Team's display included lots of Hazzard County goodies: T-shirts, decals, lanyards, hats and beautiful 8-by-10 color photos of various "Dukes" jumps.

Tony Kelley:
Keeping the motor running, too!

Tony Kelley was just a young-un when he began his role in the "Dukes of Hazzard" world. As a tender 18-year-old working at H&H Body Shop in Metro Atlanta, he was called into service to keep a small fleet of blazin' orange 1969 Dodge Chargers in fine running (and filming) form for the first five episodes of the show. BRBTV got to hear more about it at the 2007 Hillbilly Woodstick 2 Dukes of Hazzard Cruise in Georgia.

"When our first General Lee hit the yard, we'd been waiting on it for a week," Kelley told the standing-room only crowd at the meeting room of the Super 8 Motel in Covington. "That was the first jump car. We thought, who in the world would paint a car orange, put a flag on it and call it General Lee? It's just unbelievable how it took off and was done."

Kelley's job was to take a wrecked car and overnight turn it into a gleaming car ready for filming the next day. "There was only three of us in the body shop. People would come by in the afternoon just to see what kind of wreck was coming into the body shop. They'd be hanging out, and then the stunt man comes in because he left his stunt gear in the Charger one time. He said, 'I'm glad to see there's more than three of you'all, because we wreck 'em just as fast as we need 'em.'"

Indeed. We know just how often we saw that General Lee in the air! And every time you saw a General Lee in the air, show creator Gy Waldron has said, that was another General Lee wrecked. In the case of the very first General Lee ever jumped, however, the path to film-readiness was a bit different. The car that's affectionately labeled Lee 1 may have arrived at the shop as a wrecked orange Lee, but it was put back into commission as the even-more-wrecked blue Petty car for the episode "Repo Men." Kelley, who assisted in the search for the car that ended at a rural Georgia yard a few years back, reminisced with BRBTV just before the meeting-room talk. He said that he and the guys at H&H Body Shop had a little fun with putting the shop's name on the car before it was sent back for filming. Alas and alack ... the production team removed the name before shooting!

Back then, in late 1978, Kelley didn't get to see the results of his work. "All the stuff we did was prior to the TV series ever starting," he said. "When

they got out to California, it had aired and the General Lee had actually been seen by then."

Kelley shared a funny story with BRBTV, then later with the group during the talk, about a case of "mistaken identity" during the transport of one of the Hazzard County Sheriff's cars for filming.

"We were taking a police car back to Conyers, on the back roads," he said. "We started out on Norcross, got onto Beaver Ruin Road, and these police detectives came. They followed us for a little while, and we got to this cutoff road. And pretty soon here comes this police car behind us, and a helicopter above us, and they pulled us over."

In the Hazzard County car was Kelley, camera man Doug Smith and fellow mechanic Henry Holman. *(Yikes! Where's Rosco when you need him?)*

"They had Henry and Doug get out, and I couldn't get out of the back seat. They kept hollering at us, 'Get out! Get out!' And I couldn't get out." *(Dad-gum safety mechanisms!)*

"Doug had all of the paperwork in the front seat in a briefcase, and as soon as he had his hand on the handle to get it, they had their guns pulled and said, 'Don't make another move!'"

It took an hour and a half, including calls to the Holiday Inn in Conyers where the cast and crew had been staying, to sort the mess out and convince the local constables that these kind young fellows were no threat. What really was happening, Kelley told BRBTV, was that someone had been driving around Metro Atlanta with a fake police car, pulling over women.

And that wasn't even the only ... er, hazard ... that Kelley encountered in his line of work for the "Dukes." Remember, a large portion of the work involved fresh paint.

"The dark blue and the red took a long time to dry," he said of the (in)famous Confederate flag on the roof of the General Lee. "Sometimes they would be wet the next morning when they'd come to get the car. I had to run between three of them. Henry, he did most of the paint work, and Danny (Hobbs) did the body work, and I'd stay there and help Danny until we got it ready to prime. At times, both of them would go."

Sound exhausting? Listen on ...

"It'd get to be that I'd sleep in the corner every now and then, or find a car to sleep in. One of the worst things was Boss Hogg's Cadillac. It was actually a gold car. We had to paint it white. I stayed in Boss Hogg's Cadillac, and the next thing you know, I was outside at the side of the building wondering where I was at! We were bad about wearing masks."

Thankfully, Tony Kelley lived to tell the tales. And he doesn't mind being part of a phenomenon that lives on so strongly.

"It's unbelievable that an orange car can be as popular as it is."

Anthony De Longis:
Dealing up action and adventure

Anthony De Longis is a man who's had an incredibly action-packed career — both in front of the camera and behind the scenes. A master at the sword, dagger, knife, all manner of gun, and much more, De Longis has enjoyed decades of not only scene-chewing acting but training other actors for action, as well. He's been a fight director, a swordmaster, a stunt coordinator, a professional weapons instructor. He's well-known as the man who gave Michelle Pfeiffer her whip moves as Catwoman in 1992's "Batman Returns." He choreographed Anjelica Houston in 1995's "Buffalo Girls." He also did a couple episodes of the "Dukes"! In September 2008, BRBTV had the pleasure of chatting with De Longis via phone from his ranch on the West Coast, where he offers anyone who asks the adventure of a lifetime!

You were in two episodes of "The Dukes of Hazzard": "Enos and Daisy's Wedding" in 1985 and "The Hazzardgate Tape" in 1982. What was that like? What do you remember best from those times?
"One of them was with the 'other' Duke cousins, because the main two were out on a contract dispute. These two were nice guys and were just glad to be working. Basically I referred to my role as fist-fodder. I was hired to come in and get beat up. I got that a lot. In 'Enos and Daisy's Wedding,' it seems to me ... I did a thing called 'She's the Sheriff' with Suzanne Somers ... The guy playing Enos was very nice. He was a lot of fun. We were stealing money from him and making him look bad. A couple of car chases, and I did some stuff with a knife. Whenever I could find something physical that was different ... a flip knife, for instance. I did some fancy stuff with that until other people started doing it."

Anything else you remember from the "Dukes"?
"A combination of the backlot at the studio, which was a lot of fun, and being out on location and around one of the ranches where I now live." ... (He talked about 'The Battle of the Dark Knights,' filmed at Petra.) "It's the project that got me started keeping journals. The movie itself was so terrible. ... We were at Ashlan Castle, and then we were at Petra, and then we were at Jerash. I had this memory of taking the horses back and the only light filtering through this labyrinth of narrow passages. I went, 'I'm going to remember the good things and not the bad!' So I have this whole collection of journals."

You definitely have a lot of action / adventure roles, and even a little sci-fi, in your background.
"There's quite a bit of sci-fi. There's the 'Highlander' series. I was on Season 3, and they were very pleased with what I'd done. And I said, 'How do I get back?' and they said, 'You're too distinctive.' I came up with an idea they liked for my character's back story. ... It was a role they wrote for me, then I brought in a style of fighting that they liked. ... I got to go off to Paris and shoot Season 5 of 'Highlander.' I did 'Battlestar Galactica' with Fred Astaire. I was on 'Babylon 5,' 'Star Trek: Voyager.'"

What is your favorite genre to work in as far as acting?
"Not sure that I have one, in that I just love the challenge that comes, no matter what you're doing. One of the things I really like about acting is that it demands your best, and usually under really horrible conditions. It's never what you think it's going to be. It's never what they say it's going to be. ... You're in very difficult conditions physically. For instance, in 'Highlander,' it's raining, practically blinding rain. We've chosen the location because the Eiffel Tower is in the distance, and you couldn't see it. The surface is wet, and we're working with daggers. The ground was very, very slippery. We actually fell down a couple times. It was like fencing on a skating rink. It was a million-dollar production, but it was miserable to work in. It only is that effective because we were able to utilize it and capitalize on it. I love the work because it demands your very best, and often under very impossible conditions. Failure is not an option. So to answer your question, I just like to work! 'Who am I this week? I can do that!'"

How did you get into stunt work?
"I've always considered myself an actor first. My action always tells a story. I have a tremendous amount of respect for the stunt community, and I have felt accepted by them. ... I come in as a weapons and fight specialist, but to me if action doesn't drive character, you're not taking advantage of the opportunity. It's been an outgrowth of my adding to my skills as an actor. I started out with swords. I keep adding to my skill set, and along the way I ended up doing a lot of choreography. That's how I met Lane Davies. I had played Tybalt in 'Romeo and Juliet' at the Old Globe Theatre in San Diego, and then I started to choreograph. A few years later, they did another production of 'Romeo and Juliet,' and Lane was in it, and I ended up choreographing him, and that's the first time we worked together. ... It comes down to, how do we make the scene richer and more evocative for the audience? I have tremendous admiration for people who are very

gymnastic. I like real skills for real time, for example Michelle Pfeiffer in 'Batman Returns.' We wanted something that was going to be hypnotic. I was giving her the tools to help her tell a more amazing story. I also lowered her center of gravity so she was able to work in those five-inch heels. ... I'm basically always telling a story. I grew up on Westerns and Erroll Flynn and Tyrone Power. Doug Fairbanks Sr. Stuff like that. I always thought, this is amazingly stimulating, very visceral. I'm not real interested in eye candy. The computer-generated images, unless it's the 'Matrix' where you're supposed to be defying the laws of physics as we know them. Harrison Ford is a really effective action star, I think, because he looks like an ordinary man in extraordinary circumstances and manages to rise to the occasion. I'd like to think that I, too, could overcome the odds. That's what makes for good drama."

What's coming up in the next six months for you?
"Couple film projects. I've got the History Channel coming up to shoot me for 'Extreme Marksman.'

"I train people professionally here at the ranch." (Rancho Indalo — delongis.com/indalo) "We afford people the opportunity to come in from around the world, really, and stay at the ranch. We have opened this up to the general public, people who've had a dream and never had a chance. If you want to be pampered, go to a hotel, but if you want an action-adventure, come and see us. We're four miles from the freeway; we're an hour from anywhere in L.A. I have an on-site gun range. I shoot guns off my driveway!

"The Indalo is the symbol of Almeria, Spain. When I was doing the 'Queen of Swords,' we were shooting where they did all the spaghetti Westerns and stuff ... it's a genie holding a rainbow, bringing good luck and good weather. A few years later, we moved out of Hollywood and found this place. If you don't like the view, wait a half an hour, and the light will paint you a different one. ... It's even better, because it's a work in progress. We're constantly adding to it and making it better."

De Longis mentioned 2003's "Secondhand Lions," in which he served as a swordmaster: "It's a lovely story, and you've got a top-notch cast. It's a movie you can watch in all companies. I did all the flashback sword action. There's an actor named Christian Kane. ... He just called me up a couple weeks ago. He has a new series called 'Leverage.' There's a big fight

Photo of Anthony De Longis courtesy of John Leonetti.

sequence for introducing his character. So he said, 'I want to get Anthony in here for this.' So he brought me in. ... We put together this incredible fight in the kitchen that gives him all the credibility he could want, and we put it together in about a half an hour. We shoot the whole thing as a master. We did it start to finish every time we did it. ... It was a very nice little piece that we threw it together. I believe they start airing in December."

Do you ever get told you look like James Read?
"I don't know who James Read is. I get a lot of William Smith. He did 'Red Dawn' and a bunch of other stuff. He used to play a lot of bikers and Russians and stuff like that."

Universes colliding! It's a touch of "Star Wars" with some cosplayers and the Canadian Dukes of Hazzard Fan Club's General Lee at the Motor City Comic Con in Novi, Michigan.

BIRTHDAYS

Whose day is when. But not why.

Rick Hurst	January 1, 1946
Sorrell Booke	January 4, 1930
	(died February 11, 1994)
Richard Moll	January 13, 1943
Arte Johnson	January 20, 1929
Catherine Bach	March 1, 1954
Peggy Rea	March 31, 1921
	(died February 5, 2011)
John Schneider	April 8, 1960
Loretta Lynn	April 14, 1935
Byron Cherry	April 17, 1958
Dick Sargent	April 19, 1930
	(died July 8, 1994)
Christopher Mayer	April 21, 1955
	(died July 23, 2011)
Stella Parton	May 4, 1949
Denver Pyle	May 11, 1920
	(died December 25, 1997)
Gary Graham	June 6, 1960

Waylon Jennings	June 15, 1937
	(died February 13, 2002)
Nedra Volz	June 18, 1908
	(died January 20, 2003)
Paul R. Picard	July 17, 1930
	(died October 3, 1994)
Audrey Landers	July 18, 1959
Lydia Cornell	July 23, 1962
James Best	July 26, 1926
Parley Baer	August 5, 1914
	(died November 22, 2002)
Mel Tillis	August 8, 1932
Jeff Altman	August 13, 1951
Jonathan Frakes	August 19, 1952
Sam Melville	August 20, 1936
	(died March 9, 1989)
Sonny Shroyer	August 28, 1935
Don Pedro Colley	August 30, 1938
Ben Jones	August 31, 1941
Tom Wopat	September 9, 1951
Morgan Woodward	September 16, 1925
Paul Baxley	September 24, 1923
	(died March 4, 2011)
Craig R. Baxley	October 20, 1949
Tracy Scoggins	November 13, 1959
Rod Amateau	December 20, 1923
	(died June 29, 2003)

Waylon Jennings is buried in Mesa Cemetery in Mesa, Arizona. Photo by Brian Lombard.

If you have never visited Denver Pyle's grave, you haven't missed much. It's just a marker between these two graves at Forreston Cemetery in Ellis County, Texas. Below, Parley Baer, good ole Doc Appleby, is buried in Forest Lawn Memorial Park in Los Angeles. Photos by Brian Lombard.

Sam Melville had three different roles on the "Dukes," including that of Russel "Snake" Harmon. He died not long after the show went off the air and is buried at Forest Lawn Memorial Park in Los Angeles. Photo by Brian Lombard.

WEBSITES

Where the mailboxes sit in cyberspace — as of presstime, at least!

John Schneider
JohnSchneider.tv, JohnSchneiderOnline.com
Schneider's site offers some photos of his "Dukes" days, as well as pages devoted to "Smallville" and his music, which he continues to do. He also offers a webstore with some nice "Dukes" photos and other merchandise for sale.

Tom Wopat
TomWopat.com
Order "Dukes" episode DVDs, get the latest news on Wopat's Broadway career, participate in a message board and more through this official site.

Catherine Bach
CatherineBach.com
Bach's official site, which came along in late 2005, features her biography, filmography and an online shop that includes her "Dukes" photos. She also offers tips on breaking into Hollywood.

Ben Jones
CootersPlace.com
Fun! It's Cooter in the modern age, selling some "Dukes" wares from Gatlinburg, Tennessee. He's got a good collection of stuff, and he also keeps you updated on "Dukes" appearances and events.

Sonny Shroyer
SonnyShroyer.com
This official site has evolved from just one storefront page with a black-and-white photo and very little information to photos, "Dukes" sounds, autographed shots to purchase, and more.

James Best
JamesBest.com
An online store that includes Best's own original art highlights a site that has a lot of design elements. Best has his own "Dukes" info pages, with a personal tribute note. Plus, you can buy a CD of Best singing the song "Me and Flash" and even submit your own "Silly Pet Pics."

Don Pedro Colley
DonPedroColley.com
Colley's official site features a filmography right on the home page, along with pages of photos, links and more.

Stella Parton
StellaParton.com
The country-music songstress has a biography, filmography, photo gallery, and you can get on her mailing list, too.

Felix Silla
FelixSilla.com
Hazzard County's "Strange Visitor" offers a gallery of photos of his TV and movie work, his resume, and a chance to purchase signed photos.

MERCHANDISE

There's a whole lotta "Dukes" stuff out there.

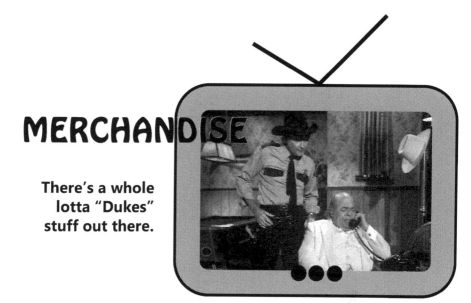

The merchandise celebrating the love of "The Dukes of Hazzard" is plentiful and diverse. Many items, you'll find from the list below, were released around 1981, when the show was really hitting its popularity. The manufacturer and date are listed where known, and this list tends to stick to more "official" merchandise, as opposed to knock-offs. This is not all-inclusive, but if you're a collector, it might tell ya something ya don't have ...

Toys

- Dolls by Mego, 8" high, 1980-82:
  - Bo Duke, wearing a light-colored button-up shirt, jeans, belt and boots.
  - Luke Duke, wearing a light-blue denim button-up shirt, jeans, belt and boots.
  - Daisy Duke, initially in green short-sleeved shirt, denim short-shorts and white flat ankle-strap sandals, later in blue short-sleeved shirt, white short-shorts and white flat ankle-strap sandals.
  - Boss Hogg, wearing his trademark white flannel suit, hat.

They're real dolls: The Mego line, 1980-82. Images courtesy of MegoMuseum.com.

- Coy Duke, packaged on Bo Duke's card though with a slightly different head mold and with light-colored button-up shirt, jeans, belt and boots.
- Vance Duke, packaged on Luke Duke's card though with a slightly different head mold and light-blue denim button-up shirt, jeans, belt and boots.

- Action figures by Mego, 3.75" high, 1981: Bo Duke, Luke Duke, Boss Hogg, Coy Duke (packaged on the Bo Duke card, but unlike the 8" Mego doll, a "Coy" sticker was placed over Bo's name on the card), Vance Duke (packaged on the Luke Duke card, but a "Vance" sticker was placed over Luke's name on the card).
- Dolls by Exclusive Toy Products, 8.5" high, 1997, in limited-edition numbered runs of 12,000: Bo Duke, Luke Duke, Daisy Duke.
- Action figures by Figures Toy Co., announced in 2013, with photos released, planned for 8" and 12" varieties. First wave: Bo and Luke, Boss Hogg, Rosco.
- Die-cast cars by Racing Champions, 1/64 scale, 2002: General Lee, Enos' police car, Rosco's police car, Cooter's 1970 Chevy Camaro, Hazzard County Department of Sewers van.
- Die-cast cars by Racing Champions, 1/144 scale, 1998 and 2002: General Lee, Rosco's police car, Daisy's Jeep.
- Die-cast cars by ERTL, 1/64 scale, 1980 and 1981: General Lee, Boss Hogg's Cadillac, Daisy Duke's Jeep, Hazzard County sheriff's car, Cooter's pickup truck.

Megolike: The set of three dolls from Exclusive Toy Products.

Below, prototypes of the 12-inchers from Figures Toy Co., announced in 2013. Photo courtesy of Figures Toy Co.

Vroom, vroom: The cars at left surfaced on toy-store shelves in 2002. Below that, ERTL came out with this new movie version of the General in 2005. Below, a 1/25 scale die-cast kit by ERTL in 2000.

- "Three-Vehicle Action Chase Set" of die-cast cars by ERTL, 1/64 scale, 1997: General Lee, Rosco's police cruiser, Boss Hogg's Cadillac.
- Three-vehicle "Hot Pursuit Set" of die-cast cars by ERTL Joyride, 1/64 scale: General Lee, Rosco's police cruiser, Daisy's yellow Road Runner.
- Three-vehicle set of die-cast cars by ERTL Joyride, 1/64 scale, 2005: General Lee, Daisy's Jeep, Boss Hogg's Cadillac.
- Orange vinyl plastic car carrying case by ERTL, holds 24 cars of 1/64 scale, 1981.
- Electric slot car racing set by Ideal, 1981.
- Slam Shifter car racing set, 1981.
- General Lee 1/18 scale car by ERTL, steel, 1982.
- General Lee 1/18 scale car by ERTL, "Gold Chase" steel edition, 2002.
- 1968 Mustang GT 1/18 scale car and 1/64 scale car in one set by ERTL.
- General Lee by Idea / TCR, 1981.
- General Lee by Corgi, 1/36, with metal figures of Bo and Luke.
- General Lee 1/18 scale car by ERTL, 2005, new movie version.
- General Lee 1/18 scale car by ERTL, chrome version, 2005, new movie version.
- Finger racer cars by Knickerbocker: General Lee (1981) and white sheriff's car.
- General Lee wrist racer car by Knickerbocker, 1979.
- Remote-controlled General Lee, #503, 1/24 scale, by Procision, 1980.
- Remote-controlled General Lee, 1/18 scale, 2005.

Above, View-Master reels. Below, a set of 12 marbles from Marbles Co. of Chicago, from their Television Legends series.

From Michigan "Dukes" fan Andrea Melchiori's collection: Two copies of the same "Dukes" jigsaw puzzle, but one is signed by John Schneider's mom.

At least four "Dukes" watch styles were produced in the 1980s. This one was found in a comics / pop-culture shop in Royal Oak, Michigan, in 2000.

- Model kits by AMT / ERTL, 1/25 scale, #8597 General Lee in 2000, Daisy's Jeep in 1999.
- Model kits by AMT / ERTL, 1/25 scale, Daisy's Jeep, 2005 movie version.
- Die-cast model kit by ERTL, 1/64 scale, General Lee.
- Model kits by MPC, Cooter's tow truck, Boss Hogg's hauler, "Dukes' Digger."
- Plastic-car playsets with mini figures: Bo and Luke with the General Lee, Boss Hogg with his white convertible, Daisy with Dixie, 1981.
- "Speed Jumper" action stunt set with motorized General Lee.
- County road map playset, nontoxic poly, by ERTL.
- General Lee play dashboard with steering wheel, 1981.
- Board game by Ideal, 1981.
- Plastic tabletop pinball game, 1981.
- Rub-down transfer games by Presto Magix, 1981: "Scrap Metal," "Derby."
- Card game by International Games Inc., 1981.
- UNO card game and UNO score sheets, 1981.
- View-Master reels, 1982 and 1983.
- Colorforms playset, 1981.
- Etch-a-Sketch, 1981.
- Painting sets, 1981.
- Jigsaw puzzle by Warner Bros. Inc., 1981.
- Jigsaw puzzle, 200 pieces, 1981 (different image).
- Jigsaw puzzles, set of three by American Publishing Corp., 200 pieces and 11" by 17" completed, 1982.
- Dashboard driving toy, battery-operated, by Illco, 1981.
- Playset of toy General Lee, Boss Hogg's white hat, CB, 1981.
- Playset of cowboy hat, handcuffs, belt, Rebel flag, keys and gun holster.
- CB walkie-talkie set by Gordy International, 1981.
- Record player in folding case, 1980.
- Plastic guitar by Emenee Ind. Inc., at least two varieties, 1981.
- Set of 12 marbles from Marbles Co. of Chicago.
- Yo-yos, 1981: General Lee, Sheriff Rosco.

Opposite page: Some more-modern goodies spotted at a toy show in Kalamazoo, Michigan, in November 2013.

Accessories

- LCD quartz watch with black rubber watchband, 1981, packaged on card.
- LCD quartz watch with stainless-steel flexible watchband, 1981, Unisonic (there are at least two other variations on those styles of watches).
- Wallet, 1982.
- Handbag (see photo below).
- Lighter, windproof, handmade, by Zippo, 2005.
- Yellow stretch belt with General Lee logo buckle, 1980.
- Shoelaces, 1981.
- Iron-on transfer showing Bo and Luke and the General Lee.
- White pajama set with logo on front, 1981.

Found on eBay: This cute little handbag, 9" by 7" by 4" wide, with silk lining, zipper pockets inside and a zipper closure.

One of several TV trays, above. At left, T-shirt designs. For the 2005 movie, Zippo released this handmade, collectible, windproof lighter below.

Above, a lunchbox spotted at the toy show in Kalamazoo: We love how this scene is so typical "Dukes," with Bo climbing in the General through the window and Luke sliding across the hood. The 1980 thermos below will keep what's hot hot and what's cool cool. The calculator was snagged at a comics/pop-culture shop in Royal Oak, Michigan, in 2000. For the 2005 movie, a 22-ounce cup, below.

BILLIE RAE BATES

Books

- Coloring and activity books including "The Chase" by James Sherman and "Behind Bars," 1981.
- "The Dukes of Hazzard Annual" publication with stories, photos and puzzles, 1979.
- "The Dukes of Hazzard Scrapbook" by Roger Elwood, Weekly Reader Books, 1981 and 1983.
- "The Dukes of Hazzard Punch-Out Fun" by James Razzi, Random House Books for Young Readers, 32 pages, November 1982.
- "The Dukes of Hazzard: Gone Racin'," a rare paperback novel by Eric Alter, Warner Books, 1982 (first printing: 1983).

Bo and Luke meet a famous racecar driver who's impressed with their driving. Jesse, meanwhile, learns that he owes 10 years in back taxes on the farm — to the tune of $10,000 — but it's Boss Hogg behind that, of course. To pay the taxes, the boys hatch the idea to head down to Florida with a finely tuned General to try to win the big one: the Daytona 500. Boss gets wind of it and he, Rosco and Cletus follow them down there to mess things up the best they can. The

There were only two editions of this scrapbook, 1981 and 1983.

Below, a coloring book from 1981.

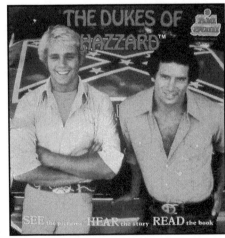

Tell me a story: A 1983 Kid Stuff Talking Story Book, 7" by 7" size.

There were lots of these kinds of TV show novelizations done in the '70s and '80s (we have books on "Happy Days," "Dallas" and "The Partridge Family," for instance) but only one done on the "Dukes." This one is not easy to find, but we got lucky, spotting it at a comic and pop-culture shop in Metro Detroit in summer 2013. The price? Are you ready? $1.95.

timing for this novelization — part of a trend of TV show novels at the time but apparently the only one done on the "Dukes" — is interesting. The book does not feature Enos, but it does throw in Coy and Vance at the end (and the two other cousins are pictured on the back cover). Flash is a boy in this, by the way! The book takes the perspective of the balladeer, narrating as with the TV show. There's an inset in the book that features black-and-white promo photos of the cast, including Coy and Vance in a couple, and even Enos in one.

- "The Dukes of Hazzard: The Unofficial Companion" by David Hofstede, St. Martin's Griffin, 1998, updated 2005.
- "Trespass in Hazzard County: My Life As an Insider on the Dukes of Hazzard" by Richard D. Jensen, iUniverse, June 2003.
- "The Roads Back to Early Hazzard," by Jon Holland, Booksurge, 2007.

- "The Real Duke of Hazzard: The Jerry Rushing Story," by Jerry Rushing and Michael D. Barnes, Creation House, August 2005.
  BRBTV enjoyed Rushing's autobiography, because it's quite real and honest, and it's a testament to Rushing's salvation. Read our review of the book on Amazon.
- "My Hero is a Duke … of Hazzard" by Cheryl Lockett Alexander, PublishAmerica, September 2012.
- "Best in Hollywood: The Good, the Bad, and the Beautiful," by James Best, BearManor Media, 2009.
  This author has to admit that, after seeing James Best at "Dukes" events for years, she found herself having new respect for him after reading his autobiography. A rags-to-riches story is always appealing, and here Best chronicles his humble beginnings in being adopted from Kentucky into an Indiana family then joining the military, where he first was exposed to the acting world. I greatly appreciated the credit Best gives to God for his many blessings over the years. And there's a lot of rich color here, in his life, through his experiences with the military police, his arrest and time on a work gang, his story of calling Charlton Heston a son of a b-tch (to his face), hanging with Jerry Lewis and Burt Reynolds, and more. The things that Best says about what Hollywood has become make perfect sense. Bathroom humor nowadays, substituting for creative writing. *Yep*, that sums it up. And as you read through his many years in the profession, you see his knowledge of the trade and technique coming through (and he did teach it, after all, with some pretty famous students).
- "Redneck Boy in the Promised Land: The Confessions of 'Crazy Cooter,'" by Ben Jones, Harmony Books, 2008.
  As with James Best's book, Ben Jones' personal account of his "Dukes" years and beyond is fascinating. It's always good to hear a person's own point of view. Jones shares some insight on Hollywood and also his faith, similar to Best. But for Jones, his life story is colored by not only the "Dukes" but also his years of alcoholism and recovery, as well as his political career. How he got himself up out of the pit of despair of his drinking is compelling. His section on the "Dukes" shares the same sentiment as Best of ruing the day that filming relocated to California. Jones gives the sweet anecdote of, since he was living in Georgia at the time, actually driving by the original Georgia Boar's Nest on his way to the airport, then landing in California a few hours later to arrive on the set and see the West Coast Boar's Nest. It well-illustrates his culture shock — and which culture he preferred. From this author's

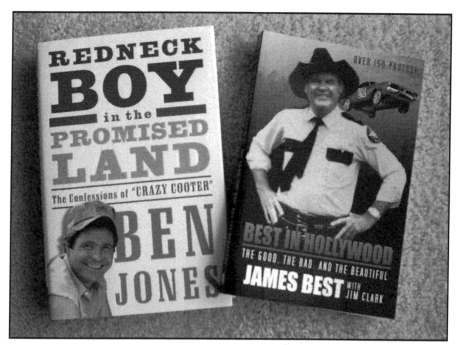

BRBTV bought these two at the first Hazzard Homecoming in Virginia, the one on the right signed by that ole Rosco.

For the hard-core: The bid for this General Lee replica was nearly $17,000 — with the reserve not yet met — on eBay in October 2005.

perspective, having attended lots of "Dukes" events over the years, the fact that I could buy a bottle of water at Hazzard Homecoming for only a buck is really what I need to know about Ben Jones. Plus, when I was first researching this book years ago and trying to contact all of the "Dukes" surviving cast, he was the one who was kind enough to do an interview. As actors go, he's very real.

Miscellaneous

- Photo button depicting Bo and Luke Duke by Leisure Craft, 2".
- Bubble-gum cards wax pack, 1980.
- Boss Hogg's bubble-gum cigars, 1981.
- Trading cards by Donruss, set of 66, 1981.
- Trading cards by Donruss, set of 44, 1983.
- Whistle / flashlight by Gordy International, 1981.
- General Lee aluminum license plates, black version and orange version with "01" on each.
- Notebooks for school, various photos, 1980.
- Drawing pad, 80 sheets, by WriteRight, at least four designs.
- Pillow case and sheet set, Warner Bros., 1982.
- Sleeping bag, 1980.
- Halloween costumes, 1980: Bo Duke, Boss Hogg.
- Guitar picks, set of 10 depicting "Dukes" characters.
- Wall clock, 8.5".
- Wall clock featuring Jessica Simpson as Daisy Duke, 7", 2005.
- Digital stick-on car clock by Unisonic, 1982.
- White plastic tumbler cup, 4.75" high, 1981.
- White plastic bowl.
- White plastic mug by Deka, 1981.
- White ceramic mug with movie image, 2005.
- White plastic fast-food cups, 1980: Bo Duke, Luke Duke, Boss Hogg, Daisy Duke, Rosco, Uncle Jesse.
- Plastic cups from McDonald's, 1982: Boss Hogg, Daisy Duke, Rosco and Flash, Uncle Jesse.

You can sleep on that one: BRB's one-time-fiancé saved this beauty of a sleeping bag from an attic or trunk or something. Whatever. It's coooool!

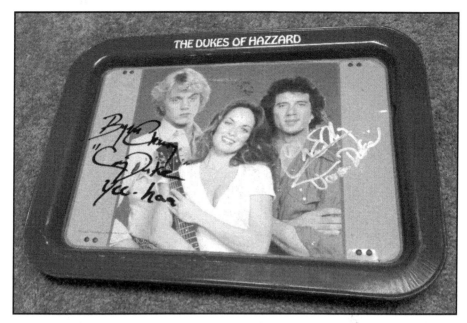

This TV tray is signed by Byron Cherry and Christopher Mayer and was nabbed by Michigan "Dukes" fan Andrea Melchiori from Cherry himself.

- Plastic bright-orange "01" 22-ounce cup, 2005.
- TV tray, metal, 17.25" by 12.5", at least three designs, 1981.
- Metal lunchbox and thermos bottle by Aladdin, 1980.
- Metal lunchbox and thermos bottle featuring Coy and Vance Duke by Aladdin, 1983.
- Calculators by Unisonic, at least three styles, including with gold Confederate flag embossed on black sleeve, 1981.
- Paint-by-number suncatcher by Crafthouse, 1982.
- Acrylic paint-by-number set by Warner Bros., 1982.
- Windshield decal, 36" long.
- Personalized door-hangers.
- Radio in orange-red plastic with General Lee shape, 1981.
- Hazzard County Sheriff's Department patch, 4" in diameter.
- Tricycle by Coleco, plastic with decals, 22" long.
- Bobbleheads, hand-painted resin, 7-8" tall: Bo Duke, Daisy Duke, Luke Duke.

Music

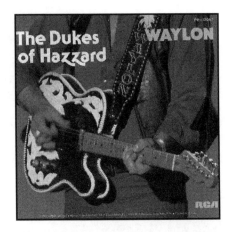

- LP, 1982, with side one featuring "Good Ol' Boys," "The General Lee," Laughing All the Way to the Bank," "Up on Cripple Creek," "Cover Girl Eyes," "In the Driver's Seat"; side two featuring "Flash," "Down Home American Girl," "Duelin' Dukes," "Keep Between Them Ditches," "Ballad of the General Lee."
- Record and read-along book set by Kid Stuff, with color cover and black-and-white interior, 7" by 7", three different varieties, 1983.

- "The Dukes of Hazzard" TV soundtrack on CD and album by Scotti Bros., 1981.
- "The Dukes of Hazzard" theme song on a 45 record by Waylon Jennings, RCA, 1980.
- "The Dukes of Hazzard — Music From The Motion Picture (Soundtrack)," Sony, July 19, 2005.
- John Schneider's albums:
  - "Now or Never," 1981
  - "Too Good to Stop Now," 1984
  - "Trying to Outrun the Wind," 1985
  - "A Memory Like You," 1985
  - "You Ain't Seen the Last of Me!", 1987
  - "Take the Long Way Home"
  - "Worth the Wait"
  - "John Schneider — Greatest Hits," 1990
  - "White Christmas," 1991
  - "An Acoustic Christmas," 2004
  - "Hell This Ain't Heaven" (featuring a duet with Johnny Cash)

- Tom Wopat's albums:
  - "Tom Wopat," 1983
  - "Don't Look Back," 1990

- "Learning to Love," 1992
- "A Little Bit Closer," 1992
- "The Still of the Night," 2000
- "Annie Get Your Gun" Broadway cast recording, 1999
- "Red, White and Boots," celebrating the early American West, with many other celebrities
- "Tom Wopat Sings Harold Arlen: Dissertation on the State of Bliss," 2005
- "Consider It Swung," 2011
- "I've Got Your Number," 2013

Interactive Games

- "The Dukes of Hazzard" by ColecoVision.
- "The Dukes of Hazzard" released in 2000 by South Peak Interactive; PC.
- "The Dukes of Hazzard II: Daisy Dukes it Out," released November 6, 2000 by South Peak Interactive; PlayStation.
- "The Dukes of Hazzard: Racing for Home," released November 21, 1999 by South Peak Interactive; PC, PlayStation, Nintendo GameBoy.
- "The Dukes of Hazzard: Return of the General Lee," released September 29, 2004 by UBI Soft; PlayStation 2, Xbox.

Video / DVDs

- Episode videos by Family TV Classics and Columbia House.
- "The Dukes of Hazzard: Reunion!" on VHS by Columbia House.
- VHS tapes of the episodes released by Warner Studios in January 1998: "Officer Daisy Duke," "Deputy Dukes," "The Big Heist," "Mason Dixon's Girls," "High Octane," "Road Pirates."
- "The Dukes of Hazzard Pilot TV Episode," DVD released in 2005 by Warner Bros.
- "The Dukes of Hazzard — Volume 1" Region 2 (European) DVD, including the episodes "Treasure of Hazzard," "Officer Daisy Duke" and "Mason Dixon's Girls."

- "The Dukes of Hazzard — Volume 2" Region 2 (European) DVD, including the episodes "Double Sting," "The Duke of Duke" and "Follow That Still."
- "The Dukes of Hazzard — The Complete First Season (1979)," released June 1, 2004 by Warner Home Video.
- "The Dukes of Hazzard — The Complete Second Season (1980)," released January 25, 2005 by Warner Home Video.
- "The Dukes of Hazzard — The Complete Third Season (1981)," released May 31, 2005 by Warner Home Video.
- "The Dukes of Hazzard — The Complete Fourth Season (1982)," released August 2, 2005 by Warner Home Video.
- "The Dukes of Hazzard — The Complete Fifth Season (1983)," released December 13, 2005 by Warner Home Video.
- "The Dukes of Hazzard — The Complete Sixth Season (1984)," released May 30, 2006 by Warner Home Video.
- "The Dukes of Hazzard — The Complete Seventh Season (1985)," released December 5, 2006 by Warner Home Video.
- "Hog-Wild Edition" DVD set with the unrated versions of the 2005 "Dukes of Hazzard" theatrical release and the "The Dukes of Hazzard: The Beginning" 2007 release.

The best place to pick up the more-obscure "Dukes of Hazzard" goods listed in this chapter may very well be on eBay. You can go to the eBay home page and do a search on the title of the show. Newer "Dukes" videos, DVDs, music and apparel are available on Amazon.com.

From Don Covell Jr.'s "Dukes" collection: a cool General Lee bike! Too bad it's kid-sized!

It's not official (or unofficial) "Dukes" merchandise ... but it is the famous music release that made Daisy's cutoffs a new pop-culture phenom: Rap star Duice's 1992 "Dazzey Duks."

Some "Dukes" goodies on display, above and below, at Geppi's Entertainment Museum in Baltimore, Maryland, part of the collection of Steve Geppi.

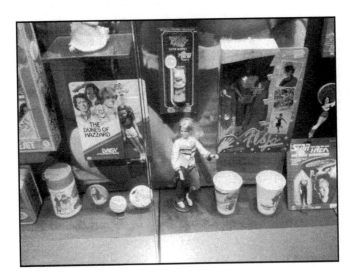

Acknowledgments

Special thanks to the following for their kind assistance and permissions with this book:

- Andrea Melchiori
- Andrew ("Zealand") Watts
- Anthony De Longis
- Atalie Anderson and Strang Communications / Creation House
- Audrey Landers
- Ben Jones and Alma Viator
- Bill Jennings
- Billy Stephenson
- Brian Heiler of the Mego Museum
- Brian Lombard
- Byron Cherry
- Catherine Bach, Steve Rohr and Century Public Relations
- Cecil and Anne Etheredge of Conyers, Georgia
- Chad Fullerton of the Covington, Georgia Dukes of Hazzard Fan Club, as well as his parents, Jim and Jackie Fullerton of Georgia
- Christopher Mayer, now with the Lord
- ComicsContinuum.com
- Dale Etheredge of Covington, Georgia
- Derrick Perkins
- Don Covell Jr. of TVAndMovieCars.com
- Don Pedro Colley
- Don Schisler, rest in peace
- Donnie Clack of Lanier National Speedway in Braselton, Georgia
- Doug McQuillin of Ontario
- Ernie Hudson
- Felix Silla
- Figures Toy Co.
- Frank Clark and the crew at Hardcore Racing of Flint, Michigan
- Glenn Call, rest in peace, plus Edmund Call and their mom :)
- Hot Rod Movie Posters and www.sd455.com

- Jack Price of the online Hazzard County Directory
- James Best and Dorothy Collier Best
- James Hampton
- James R. Green Jr.
- Jason Darling
- Jeff Cockrell of the East Coast General Lees club
- Jeff ("Jett") Yaskow and Natalie Brock of Buffalo, N.Y.
- Jerry Rushing, along with Larry Wolfel of TravelerMovie.com
- Jim Wilson
- Jo McLaney — *we all miss you, dear friend*
- John and Jaci Jablonski and Rick and Paula Jablonski
- John Leonetti
- John Schneider, Chad Collins and JDS
- John Staton
- Jon Holland of the DukesofHazzard01 site and Hazzard County Car Club
- Judy Bruce
- Kevin Bertram
- Lee Duke
- Lee Secrest
- MADman and www.madpalace.nl
- Marvin and Joyce Murphy
- Matt Busch
- Mike Serrico
- Morgan Brittany
- Paul Harrington of the official Jerry Rushing Fan Club and the Canadian "Dukes of Hazzard" Fan Club
- Richie Allgood
- Scott Bates
- Sonny Shroyer and Scott Dickison
- Tom Sarmento
- Tom Wopat, Aki Oduola and Impact Artist Management
- Tony Kelley
- Wayne Wooten
- Will Rodgers, "The Voice of Hazzard County"
- WPY

Spence Beamon, Detroit musician and systems expert, thank-you for the support, both technical and moral!

Bro, thanks for the use of your fabulous, faithful 35 mm camera.

Veronica, I couldn't have set up the camera tripod without your special instruction!

My rockin' former coworkers in the features department at The Detroit News: Ralph, Sandy, Eric, D.Good, Alan, Don and Lisa: thanks for the "Dukes" watch and calculator — I miss you guys all the time!

And my thanks, also, to all the fans out there who emailed me during the early years of the Them Dukes! Them Dukes! website on BRBTV.com. You've inspired me, and like the Dukes, you've shown me that certain qualities in life, like honesty and honor, never die and never really go unappreciated ...

Bibliography of Supplemental Sources

Like the other books in the BRBTV book series, "Them Dukes! Them Dukes!" was compiled and written, first and foremost, from BRB's own viewing and love of the TV series. The episode synopses, for instance, are her own original content, bulked up over the years from further viewings! (And we love those further viewings!) BRB would like to acknowledge, however, the following supplemental sources, often attributed within the text, for extra fun facts and tidbits on the show:

The Internet Movie Database (IMDb)
TV Tome / TV.com
Tim's TV Showcase
Country Music Television
Wikipedia
"The Complete Directory to Prime Time Network and Cable TV Shows" by Tim Brooks and Earle Marsh, Ballantine Books
About.com

Thanks, Mike. There's only an inch or so of it left ....

"*Just the good ol' boys*
Never meanin' no harm ...
"*Yeeeeeeee-haaaaaaaaaa!!!!!!!!!!!!!!!!*"